WINGS OVER MESOPOTAMIA

Air War in Iraq 1914-1918

Mark Lax ~ Mike O'Connor ~ Ray Vann

CROSS & COCKADE INTERNATIONAL
THE FIRST WORLD WAR AVIATION HISTORICAL SOCIETY
in association with
THE AUSTRALIAN SOCIETY OF WORLD WAR ONE AERO HISTORIANS

Published in Great Britain in 2017 by
Cross & Cockade International
© Cross & Cockade International 2017

www.crossandcockade.com

All text, photographs and original artwork remain the copyright of the authors and sources credited.

Design and origination by CCI Prepress.
Printed in England by Warwick Printing Company Limited.

ISBN 978-0-9555734-8-4

All rights reserved. Apart from any fair dealing for the purpose of private study, research, criticism or review, as permitted under the Copyright, Design and Patents Act 1988, no part of this publication may be reproduced or transmitted in any form or by any means, electronic or mechanical, including photocopying, recording or by any information storage and retrieval system, without permission from the publisher in writing.

Copies are available from the Society website
www.crossandcockade.com or from
The Sales Manager, Cross & Cockade International,
'Woodlea', Tattershall Road, Woodhall Spa, LN10 6TP
sales.manager@crossandcockade.com

For subscription information for our two societies contact

Membership Secretary: Andy Kemp, Hamilton House, Church Street, Wadenhoe, Peterborough PE8 5ST, UK
membership.secretary@crossandcockade.com

and

The Australian Society of World War 1 Aero Historians
www.ww1aero.org.au
Membership Secretary: Andrew Smith, 20 Springfield Street, Blacktown NSW 2148, Australia
membership.secretary@ww1aero.org.au

Contents

Abbreviations	iv
Introduction	v
The First Air War in the Cradle of Civilisation	1
Faltering Steps	5
The Australian Half-Flight	7
The RFC Egypt Detachment	13
The Australians Begin Operations	16
The RNAS Contribution	19
The Advance	23
The Move Towards Kut	26
The Mesopotamia Aircraft Park	28
Townshend's Push North	33
The German Air Service Arrives in Theatre	36
Disaster at Kut	40
The End of the Australian Half-Flight	46
Kut – The Aftermath	47
RFC Flying Services Rebuild	48
The Turks Maintain Air Superiority	49
Preparing to Advance	53
On to Baghdad	55
Changes over the Summer	61
RFC Reinforcements Arrive	62
Beyond Baghdad	69
The Last RFC Unit Reaches Mesopotamia	74
The Birth of the RAF	80
German Reinforcements	83
Armistice but No Peace	90
Endnotes	95

Men and Machines of the Mesopotamia Air Campaign

Selected Personnel Biographies	96
POW Survivors up to the Fall of Kut	106
Officers, NCOs and Air Mechanics of 30 Sqn and the Australian Half-Flight made POW, Siege of Kut-al-Amara 1916	106
Australian Half-flight Other Ranks & Reinforcements	107

RFC/RAF Officers, Mesopotamia 1915-1919

RFC Egypt Detachment	108
30 Squadron	109
63 Squadron	113
72 Squadron	115
31 Wing HQ & Aircraft Park	117
RNAS Detachment	119
RNAS/RFC Kite Balloon Personnel	120
Other Ranks and their Work	121
The Importance of Water Transport	123
RFC/RNAS Aircraft Serials, Mesopotamia 1915-1919	127
Bibliography	138

Dedicated to Polly O'Connor

MIKE O'CONNOR
1947-2013

Abbreviations

AASC	Australian Army Service Corps	IF	Independent Force
Adj	Adjutant	IFC	Indian Flying Corps
AIF	Australian Imperial Force	IIFA	Injured in Flying Accident
AFC	Australian Flying Corps; Air Force Cross	Inf	Infantry
AAP	Auxiliary Aircraft Park	Inj	Injured
AMDT	Australian Mounted Divisional Train	Instr	Intructor
AP	Aircraft Park	KIA	Killed in Action
Arr	Arrived	KIFA	Killed in Flying Accident
ASC	Army Service Corps	KRRC	King's Royal Rifle Corps
Asst	Assistant	LAMB	Light Armoured Motor Battery
att	attached	MGC	Machine Gun Corps
b	buried	MIA	Missing in action
Bn	Battalion	MID	Mentioned in dispatches
Brig	Brigade	MSM	Meritorious Service Medal
Commis	Commissioned	MT	Motor Transport
CWGC	Commonwealth War Graves Commission	NKG	No known grave
DCLI	Duke of Cornwall's Light Infantry	NTS	Night Training Squadron
DCM	Distinguished Conduct Medal	O	Observer
Disch	Discharged	P	Pilot
DOI	Died of injuries	Prom	Promoted
DOW	Died of wounds	RAS	Reserve Aeroplane Squadron
DYOL	Duke of York's Own Lancers (Skinner's Horse)	RE	Royal Engineers
EO	Equipment Officer	RFA	Royal Field Artillery
FltCdr	Flight Commander	RGA	Royal Garrison Artillery
FltLt	Flight Lieutenant	RHA	Royal Horse Artillery
FO	Flying Officer	RS	Reserve Squadron
FSL	Flight Sub-lieutenant	RTA	Returned to Australia
FTL	Forced to land	SMA	School of Military Aeronautics
Gaz	London Gazette/gazetted	SNBD	School of Navigation & Bomb Dropping
GL	General List	SR	Special Reserve
HD	Home Defence	TDS	Training Depot Station
HLI	Highland Light Infantry	TS	Training Squadron
IA	Indian Army	TF	Territorial Force
IARO	Indian Army Reserve of Officers	Trg/Trnd	Training/Trained

Introduction

For over forty years the late Mike O'Connor and I (assisted by the late Colin Waugh, whom I originally contacted in the 1960s) had been researching the RFC/RNAS in the 'side-shows', concentrating on the RFC campaign in Mesopotamia.

After being absent from Cross and Cockade International for several years, I re-joined, to discover that Australian member and former President of the Australian Society of World War 1 Aero Historians, Mark Lax, had written a history of the air war in Mesopotamia, published in four parts in that Society's '14-'18 Journal between 2005 and 2013.

Originally Mike and I began our research in the early 1970s, many years before the advent of the Internet; tracking down surviving officers and their families via squadron nominal rolls compiled from The National Archives and using records held at Somerset House.

The results were beyond expectations with families allowing us to copy log books and diaries, plus photo albums that yielded in excess of 1000 photos (with a further 2000 plus images relating to the RFC in other 'side-shows'). Families also contacted RAF records in Gloucester on our behalf, for copies of relatives' service records etc.

When I contacted Mark, he readily agreed to an expansion of his original articles, both in general text, and with the addition of nominal rolls, serial numbers etc, plus many more photos that Mike and I had acquired. Throughout the research, I was Mike's junior assistant, and as for me, I regard this completed history as a fitting tribute to a very much admired friend and fellow researcher who is sorely missed.

Ray Vann

Acknowledgements

Original text by Mark Lax, additional text and appendices by Mike O'Connor and Ray Vann. The majority of photographs are from the Ray Vann/ Mike O'Connor Mespot collection.

Amongst those who helped us with our researches are the following: Rosemary Bayllo, Mr K. Boyd, Mrs J.M. Cliff, Mrs R.T. Colley, Allen Deacon, Mr M. Drummond, Viscount Exmouth, Lt-Col Fielden, Patrica Hallett, Mrs S. Kemp-Welch, Pamela Kimbell, Mr J.H. deV. Leigh, Mrs N. Lloyd, Mrs S.V. MacLean, Mr R. Partridge, Mrs P.J. Perrin, Mr D. Phillips, Mrs D. Pugh, Mr J. Ravnkilde, Mrs M.B. Smith, the late George Sutcliffe RNAS, Lt-Col H.W. Underhill, Mr H.F.M. Watts, Major S.H. Windsor, Mr P.J. Wells, Mrs J. Winterbotham, and Middle East specialist H.V.F. (Victor) Winston.

Thanks also to *The '14-'18 Journal* Editor Peter Chapman and to the CCI Archive, and members David Barnes, the late Jack Bruce, Chris Cole and Gerald Muir; Mick Davis, Barry Gray, Stuart Leslie, Chas Schaedel, Stuart K. Taylor, Jeff Taylor, and Peter Wright.

Other material has come from the Australian War Memorial, Fleet Air Arm Museum, Imperial War Museum, The National Archives, Royal Aero Club Trust, Royal Australian Air Force Museum, and Royal Air Force Museum.

We are very grateful to Ken Farmer GAvA, who kindly painted the front cover picture, and our sincere thanks go to Colin and Barbara Huston (CCI Design and Prepress) who prepared this work for publication.

Mark Lax, Ray Vann

*Front cover: **Aid for Kut: Short Type 827 seaplane, 8044;** by Ken Farmer, GAvA*
*Rear Cover: **Tigris Morning: Caudron G.III and HMS Firefly;** by Ken Farmer. Below: The busy Shatt-al-Arab waterway at Basra. Short 8047 stands on the RNAS slipway, surrounded by shipping of all sizes from the local Arab bellums to ocean-going steamers.*

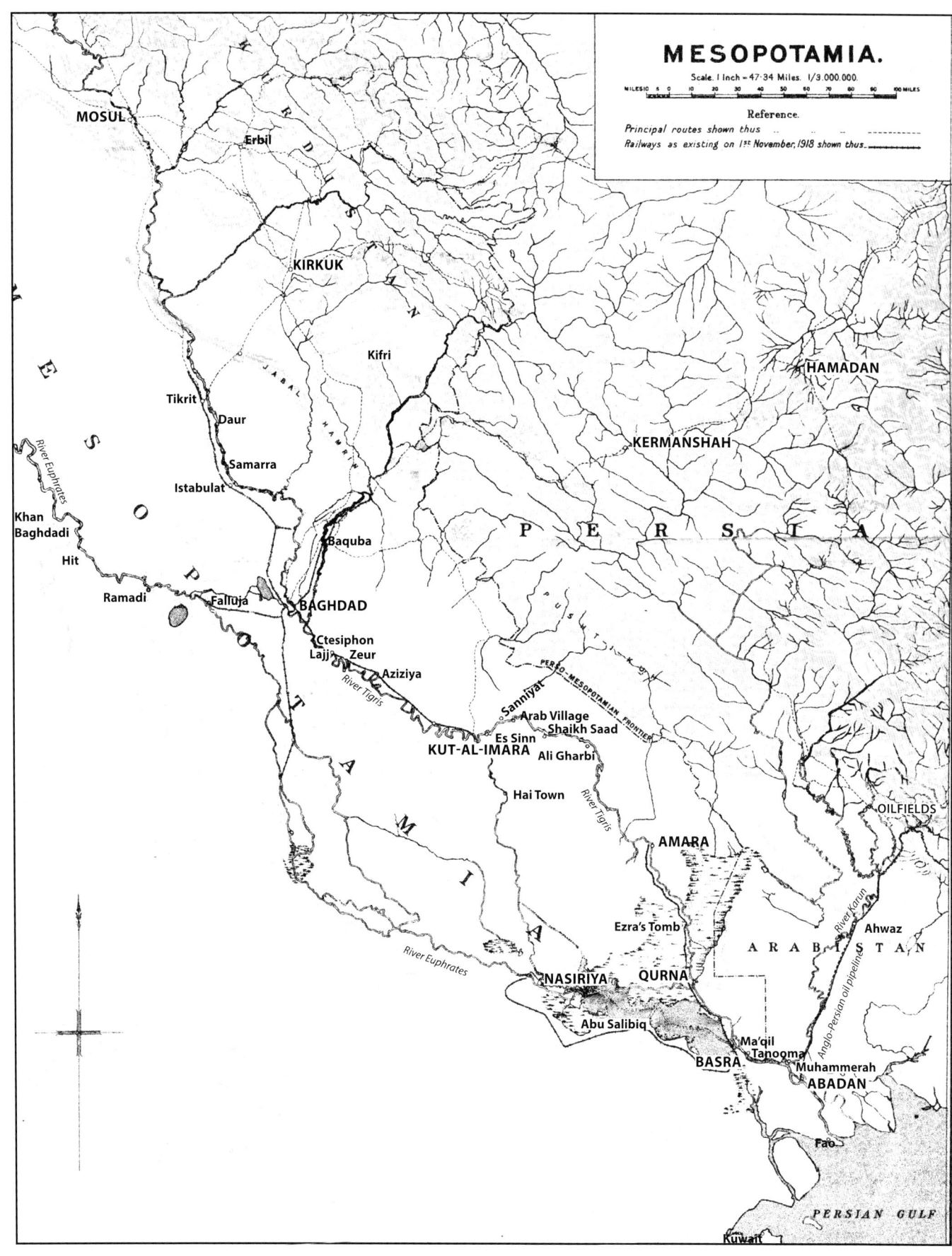

Principal places mentioned in the text. Various spellings/transliterations will be found in maps and documents of the period.

A few examples; Basra/Busrah/Busreh; Ezra's Tomb/Al-'Uzair (modern); Ma'gil/Magil/Margil/Al Ma'qil (modern); Ora/Orah: Qurna/Kurna; Nasiriya/Nasiriyeh; Nisibin/Nusaybin; Sanniyat/Sana-i-Yat. Spellings often appear to be based on how different people understood the names when spoken.

The First Air War in the Cradle of Civilisation

The reason for it all – and a sign of the modern age: the Anglo-Persian Oil Company's port and company town at Abadan on the Shatt-al-Arab at the head of the Persian Gulf. From here, a double pipeline ran 150 miles north-east to the oilfields of Persia.

William Knox D'Arcy (1849-1917) the British-born entrepreneur, who emigrated to Australia in 1866.

In a splendid example of the 'Spirit of the British Empire' an Englishman, William Knox D'Arcy, in expanding British interests, discovered oil in South Persia in 1908. The search and exploration had begun in 1901 when D'Arcy had obtained from His Royal Highness the Shah of Persia, a concession for 'working petroleum in all its forms'. Eventually, after exhausting his own capital, D'Arcy succeeded in interesting other investors, from Burma, India and England, with the result that oilfields of immense size were tapped in Arabistan, within the territories of the Sheikh of Muhammerah, a loyal friend of the British Government.

Unlike today, the discovery of such large oil reserves in 1908 hardly warranted front page news. British industry was still very much reliant on coal and steam for its power, the motor car was still considered to be a 'rich man's toy' and the machinery of the industrial revolution required oil simply for lubrication. The British Navy patrolled the high seas in coal-burning ships, and it would be another year before Louis Blériot crossed the English Channel and made the aeroplane the new wonder of the age.

British interest in the Persian Gulf was centuries old, starting with a trading agreement between the British East India Company and the Shah of Persia. As British influence and interests expanded across the Middle East, so she began to patrol the Gulf waters, stemming the tide of piracy, slave-trading and gun running favoured by the Arabs, who had carried out their 'trade' without hindrance from their Turkish overlords. The Sheikhs of Kuwait and Muhammerah, whose territories lay either side of the Gulf, both welcomed the activities of the British, and quickly became trusted friends as their lawful pearling trade flourished under the Royal Navy's protection.

An aerial view of the Shatt-al-Arab, probably near Basra, from 2,000 feet. The water level appears to be high, with a number of fairly large vessels anchored in the channel and smaller craft closer to the shore.

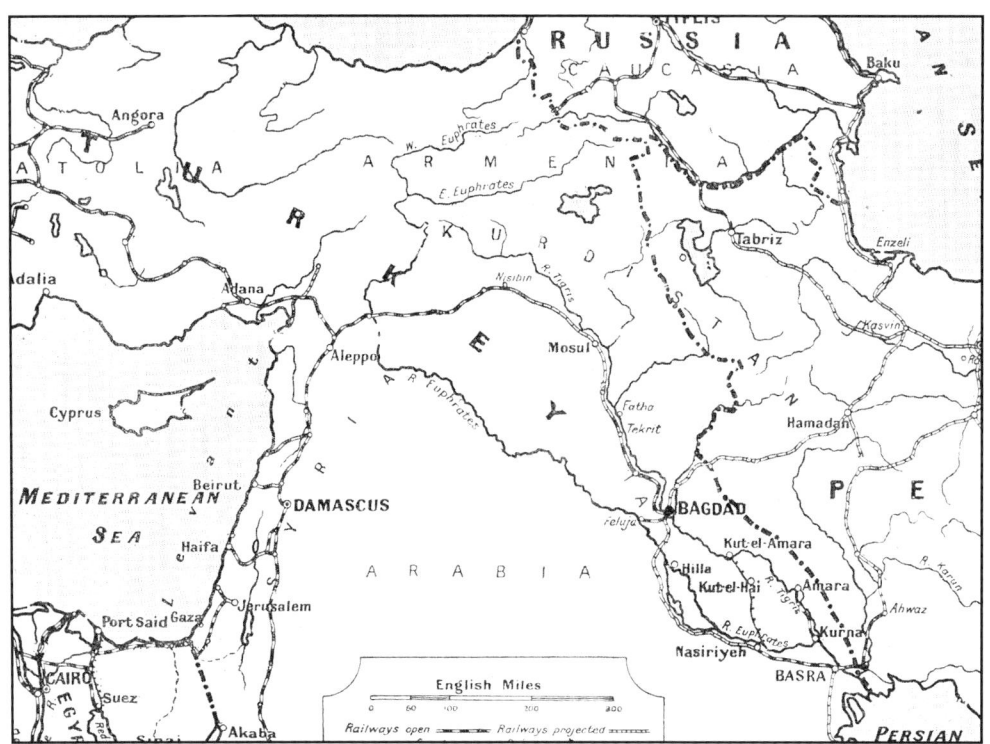

A cause for concern. The Berlin-Baghdad Railway, intended to give Germany the commercial and military advantage of direct access to the Persian Gulf while avoiding the Suez Canal, had not been completed by the outbreak of war. Two extensive and critical gaps in the line were between Nasiriya and Baghdad, and Nisibin (Nusaybin)-Mosul-Tikrit. Though work on the railway continued during the war, the line was not completed until 1940. The movement of troops and supplies by both sides in the conflict always involved either river or road transport at some stage.

To the west of Persia lies 'the land between the rivers', Mesopotamia. Ruled by the Ottoman Empire since 1638 when its capital Baghdad was attacked and the Persian garrison and 30,000 inhabitants are said to have been massacred. Mesopotamia was the land of Adam and Eve, the land of Noah and Father Abraham, the land of Babylonia where Daniel dwelt in captivity and was delivered from the den of lions: a land bristling with biblical references and the cradle of civilisation.

By the beginning of the twentieth century, the Ottoman Empire included all of what is now Turkey; Lebanon, Syria, and Israel, as well as Jordan, Palestine, Saudi Arabia, part of the Sinai Peninsula and Mesopotamia.

Mesopotamia, or Iraq as it was always referred to by its Arab inhabitants, was approximately 620 miles in length by 450 miles wide, its eastern border resting on the Jebel Hamrin range of mountains and the Push-I-Kuh hills, while to the west lay Jordan and Syria.

Two major rivers, the Tigris and Euphrates, bisect the country, snaking in a mainly north to south direction, joining about one hundred miles above the head of the Persian Gulf where they flow to the sea in a mighty waterway, the Shatt-al-Arab. Once, at the very dawn of history, 2000 years before the time of Christ, Mesopotamia possessed huge natural resources, but by the twentieth century, much of the country was a barren desert wasteland with only small pockets of fertile land flanking the rivers, date palm fringed creeks and a huge tract of marsh lands in the southern coastal area.

At the head of the Shatt-al-Arab estuary lies the island of Abadan on which the Anglo-Persian Oil company established its refinery. Abadan was one hundred and fifty miles from the oilfields in Persia, so a double pipeline was laid, and in the years from 1908 to 1912, Abadan developed into one of the greatest oil shipping ports in the world. Totally British controlled and operated, Abadan's importance to Great Britain was further enhanced in August 1914, when the Admiralty began to replace its Fleet with oil-burning instead of coal-burning ships, and bought a controlling interest in the oil company. At the time the Admiralty was highly criticised for its so called 'extravagance', but as the world situation deteriorated, it was perhaps a piece of forward thinking and planning that was to later pay huge dividends.

Britain and its Empire had every reason to be concerned with the growing influence of Germany, not only in Europe but also in the Middle East. In the latter half on the nineteenth century, under Bismarck's direction, the Fatherland had become more and more industrialised. Unlike Britain, it did not have an empire

The immediate area of Basra could look like 'the Venice of Arabia', but conditions further up-river were very different.

'Those of us who had been in the Dardanelles had half expected that this end of Turkey would be much like the other – broken country and sandy scrub, with hills. But here there is only a broad swift river, a strip of vivid green verdure, and beyond, the immense plain stretching to the horizon.'

'Martin Swayne', (Maurice Nicoll)
In Mesopotamia. Hodder & Stoughton, London, 1920.

The confluence of the Tigris and Euphrates at Qurna, some 48 miles by river from Basra. The lush growth of palms and vegetation does not appear to extend far inland from the river, though the map on the inside front cover shows the extensive, but seasonally variable, marshland to both east and west. Photograph taken in 1918.

with which to sell its products and expand its influence. To the east however, lay the vast Ottoman Empire, economically centuries behind Europe, but controlling a huge area rich in natural resources.

From about 1875, the Germans began to 'open up' the Ottoman Empire, providing the materials and expertise to begin projects such as railways, mining and the exploitation of raw materials that the Fatherland badly needed. A direct railway route between Berlin and Constantinople opened in 1888 and by 1902 a scheme for a direct Berlin-Baghdad railway had been formulated – a scheme for which the British had gained a concession in 1851, only to let it lapse.

Hand in glove with the industrialists were the German diplomats who for the next forty years plotted to expand German influence in Constantinople. Agents were soon at work, spreading disquiet about British intents and influence in the Middle East, and encouraging the Turks to believe that Germany would be a better ally. Soon, objections were being raised to long standing arrangements enjoyed by Britons trading in Baghdad, Basra, and along the Tigris River. Distrust was fomented between Britain and Russia over Turkey and between Britain and Turkey over Egypt. British officers training Turkish naval personnel were replaced by Germans, and in every bazaar there was talk of 'Jihad', a holy war directed at the infidel that would sweep eastwards and threaten to cause India's highly volatile North West Frontier to erupt.

When the British Government agreed to the Royal Navy's controlling interest in the Anglo-Persian Oil Company, it placed the protection of its interests within the sphere of command of the Viceroy of India and the Indian Army. This decision was to be the first of many hastily ill-conceived ideas that would jeopardise the eventual military campaign in Mesopotamia and result in one of the biggest disasters ever suffered by the British Army in its history.

In the years prior to the outbreak of the First World War, the British Army in India comprised 80,000 British troops and 140,000 Indian regulars. It had been the subject of a major re-organisation by Lord Kitchener who had taken over command in 1902 after Lord Curzon had been appointed Viceroy. Successive reductions in army budgets had meant that the army in India, committed to mobilise divisions for both Europe and Mesopotamia, barely had enough manpower and equipment to fight the warring tribes on the North West Frontier.

Now it was expected to fight in a global conflict without modern weapons, without machine guns and heavy artillery, and with a medical service totally unprepared to cope with the casualties that might be expected. Soon, they would be facing a Turkish Army which, despite being led by often brutal officers, was nevertheless excellent at defensive fighting and who were equipped with the latest weapons from their German allies.

British war plans called for the Indian Army to act as reserve forces for the Empire in time of war. Consequently, Kitchener had divided the Army into Indian Expeditionary Forces (IEF) labelled 'A' to 'G'. IEF 'A' was to be used on the Western Front, IEF 'B' and 'C' for East Africa. It was IEF 'D' that was required to protect interests in Mesopotamia. The remaining IEFs were to be used in Egypt and Gallipoli.

The Indian Government, represented by the

Viceroy, by now Lord Hardinge, and the Commander-in-chief India, Sir Beauchamp Duff had repeatedly argued with Whitehall over the merits of sending Indian Expeditionary Forces to France, Egypt, Mesopotamia and German East Africa, all despite their previously agreed pre-war commitments.

An Indian Army mountain battery (above) and a large convoy of troops (left) struggle in hot desert conditions that could limit marches to eight miles a day. In addition, the often flat and featureless landscape, combined with heat haze and mirage, made accurate ranging very difficult for artillery (below) – a problem to which air observation offered a solution.

Mesopotamia also produced another extreme: seasonal floods and marshes which, though often shallow, could cover very large areas, again because of the very flat low-lying lands around the great rivers. Here cavalry of the Indian Army are advancing near Basra through flood water that might vary in depth from six inches to three feet: 'Too much water for soldiers, not enough for sailors'.

Faltering Steps

On 2 October 1914, the War Office ordered the Indian Government to embark a brigade of the 6th Poona Division to the Persian Gulf to protect the oil port. Things did not start well and were a portent of the disasters that were to follow. The original ships selected were found to have draughts of more than eighteen feet and would be unable to sail over the sand bar and into the Shatt-al-Arab and so it was not until 16 October that the advanced elements of IEF 'D' could sail under the command of Brig-Gen Sir Walter Sinclair Delamain, to be followed by the main force commanded by Lt-Gen Sir Arthur Barrett.

Unfortunately, Delamain's orders were rather vague. First, he was to occupy Abadan and protect the oil pipeline already threatened by local tribesmen and German agents. The second part of his orders were only possible with a landing which he was not equipped to achieve (he would do so using the ship's life boats and commandeered native boats) plus the occupation of Basra in the event of hostilities.

Bullied and manipulated by Germany, Turkey finally entered the war on 31 October 1914 declaring a 'Jihad' against the allies. However, Barrett's 6th Division quickly seized the Basra area and by December, had advanced up the Euphrates River as far as Qurna – reputedly the site of the Garden of Eden.

By January 1915, faced with a slow and methodical campaign up the Tigris and Euphrates Rivers, Barrett cabled the War Office on the 9th and asked for reinforcements, including aeroplanes. He followed up this request a few weeks later with a hastener and on 7 February, the War Office agreed to send two aircraft, which would have to come from India, but could not supply pilots, observers or mechanics, who would have to be found elsewhere. Meanwhile, Barrett had initially taken Qurna before coming to a halt due to the winter rains and consequent widespread flooding. The conditions forced his retirement back to Basra. The plan to seize and hold just Basra and the surrounding oilfields was about to become a quest to capture Baghdad.

The ease of the campaign to date fought against mainly Arab and Kurdish forces and not the tough Anatolian Turk had lulled the military into a belief that the rest of Mesopotamia would be a pushover. In the New Year, rumours of Turkish reinforcements, Arab unrest and the pending Dardanelles Campaign all conspired to force the Viceroy of India to reinforce Barrett to guarantee the oil supply, a plan Barrett had been asking for all along. In early April, the 12th Division under Maj-Gen George Gorringe[1] arrived, but in reality it was a hollow force of three infantry Brigades and some artillery.

With its arrival, the Indian Government chose to form the Second Indian Army Corps and placed the over-confident General Sir John Nixon[2] in command. At the same time, in 1915, Maj-Gen Sir Charles Townshend[3], Nixon's nominee, relieved the now ill Barrett, who returned to India. Here the Mesopotamian Campaign plan took a new turn.

Before leaving India, Sir Beauchamp Duff had

Lord Hardinge, Viceroy of India

Brig-Gen Sir Walter Delamain

Lt-Gen Sir Arthur Barrett

Maj-Gen George Gorringe

General Sir John Nixon

Maj-Gen Sir C. Townshend

given new instructions to Nixon which included a possible advance on Baghdad. The plan was unknown to the British Government or Lord Hardinge, although a copy was mailed to London, but it did not arrive until May. By now Nixon, still convinced that the oil wells and pumping stations in Ahwaz in north Persia were not secure, demanded more reinforcements. On 22 April 1915, 9,000 troops under Gorringe's command set off and marched north east along the Karun River. In comparatively cool weather the Turks were pushed back after some heavy fighting, and the pumping stations and pipeline were secured, repairs carried out, and pumping resumed some weeks later. The pipeline was never to be seriously threatened again.

Disaster in the Dardanelles and failed offensives on the Western Front now led the War Cabinet to look elsewhere for a success that would boost morale and restore British pride. But problems still remained – a faltering medical service; troops decimated by the weather conditions and illness; and a port at Basra, barely able to cope with three ocean-going vessels a month pre-war, that was now expected to cope with a huge influx of men and materials. Finally there was a total lack of river transport which was the only realistic means of traversing the hot, dry and unforgiving country. It had been calculated that at any one time there would have to be five ships going up river, three coming down, four loading and twelve unloading, without leaving time for repairs. Basra to Ali Gharbi and back took ten days. While Amara to Kut in a straight line over the desert was 90 miles, by river it was at least triple the distance. Desperate calls to India and the UK finally led to half a dozen Thames steamers, forty flat bottom boats, six motor lighters plus numerous barges eventually arriving in the Persian Gulf under their own steam. Forty more river steamers were sent from India.

Now a series of letters, telegrams and cables travelled between London, India, Lord Hardinge and the GOC Nixon. On 23 May, Hardinge sent a telegram to Lord Crewe, outlining Nixon's plan to advance up the Tigris River to Amara, an important administrative and commercial centre covering the main route to Persian Arabistan. Approval was given, but Nixon was instructed to go no further until ordered, but the mirage on the horizon that was the prize of Baghdad was irresistible.

Meanwhile, General Townshend planned to move out of the Shatt-al-Arab coastal area as soon as the rains ceased. Every yard advanced up the Tigris River system would stretch the supply lines and make him vulnerable to Turkish cut-off. However, he was determined to move out as soon as possible but operations could only resume in April and for these, air reconnaissance would be a distinct advantage. As no airmen were available and none would be forthcoming from the RFC, the Viceroy of India sent an urgent request to the other British colonies on 8 February 1915. 'Could you provide any trained aviators for service in the Tigris Valley?' The request also sought mechanics, flying machines and motor transport.

At the beginning of the War, the Indian Flying Corps consisted of just three machines with a further four on order. The Government of India had formed the Indian Flying School at Sitapur on 1 February 1913, and it was staffed by officers from the Indian Army who had learned to fly at their own expense while on leave in England. At the outbreak, plans for training pilots in India were shelved due to the high and immediate demand for both aircraft and pilots to meet the war effort elsewhere. The few pilots and machines in India were immediately offered up to the War Office and were accepted, the aircraft and crews being sent to Egypt. So when the call came from Barrett for aeroplanes for Mesopotamia, only two serviceable aircraft (Shorthorns) were available.

Fortunately, Australia replied that they could furnish officers, men and transport, but no machines – the aircraft would have to be provisioned locally – and although the match was not ideal, it would initially suffice. Given that Australia only had seven qualified pilots, the offer of four was extremely generous, and so the Australian Half-Flight was spawned.

Despite the superiority of the rivers to the roads, travel by water in Mesopotamia presented many difficulties to a military campaign. Only vessels of shallow draught could even cross the major sandbar to enter the Shatt-al-Arab or provide reliable transport on the Tigris and Euphrates. The side-wheeler below, serving as a troop transport on the Tigris, may, like many other craft suitable for shallow waters, have come out from the UK under her own steam to assist in the campaign. An Inland Waterways Construction organisation was later formed to build barges and other vessels locally, and the Flying Services would rely heavily on such craft.

The Australian Half-Flight

*Half-Flight Officers: Standing l-r; Lt E.J. Fulton; Capt F.C.C. Yeats-Brown; Lt W.R. Wills.
Seated; Capt T.W. White; Capt H.A. Petre; Capt P.W.L. Broke-Smith; Capt H.L. Reilly; Lt W.H. Treloar.*

While awaiting the dispatch of the Australians, on 25 March 1915 the Government of India re-organised their flying service and appointed Capt Phllip Broke-Smith[4] of the Indian Army as Deputy Assistant Director of the Aviation Organisation and allocated one flight of aeroplanes and established depots at Basra and Bombay. On 9 April, Broke-Smith arrived in Basra on the staff of GOC Indian Expeditionary Force 'D' to organise the aviation service and a depot (at Ma'gil just north of the town) while they awaited the Half-Flight's arrival. He would be followed by a New Zealander, Capt Hugh Lambert Reilly, and Lt (Later Capt) Wilfred Ridout Wills, an Indian Public Works Department engineer now with the rank of Lieutenant Indian Army Reserve of Officers.

So who were the Half-Flight? Officially, they formed on 1 April 1915 at CFS, Laverton.[5] According to Fred Cutlack, author of the *Australian Official History* volume VIII, covering the AFC, the officers were four in number. They comprised Capt Henry Petre (pronounced 'Peter' and known as 'Peter the Monk'), Capt Thomas White, and Lt George Merz all from the Central Flying School, and Lt Harry Treloar. Treloar was an Australian who had earned his pilot's licence in England and had recently returned to Australia to enlist. The remainder were 41 Other Ranks, including 18 mechanics. Cutlack gave their origin thus:[6]

The Sergeant-Major (Alex Shorland), Staff-Sergeant (Cyril Heath), and another sergeant were from CFS; the Quartermaster-Sergeant (Septimus Garling) and the Farrier-Sergeant (John Neenan) were from permanent artillery units in NSW and the corporals, drivers and mechanics were from the AIF Training Camp at Broadmeadows in Victoria.

While most had not seen an aeroplane let alone worked

The Indian Flying Corps' contribution of aircraft: IFC2 Longhorn, IFC3 Caudron, IFC1 Shorthorn.

The Half-Flight in camp at Point Cook, March 1915.

Known members of the Half-Flight
1: Murray 4: Brown 5: Passmore 6: Laidlaw (on CSF Staff, but did not go with the Half-Flight) 8: Menzies 11: Gower 12: Abdy 15: Bell 16: Niskanen 17: W. Lord 20: Lewis 22: Frazer 23: H. Lord 24: Chapple 25: Shorland 26: Merz (with cat) 17: White 28: Heath 29: Cowper 31: Munday 32: Edwards 34: Hudson 35: Clayton

Transformation scene: the Half-Flight, now properly kitted out, photographed at Bombay in May 1915, with Capt White and Lt Treloar seated in the middle of the front row.

The Half-Flight camp at Ma'gil, about three miles from Tanooma, with the Shatt-al-Arab in the background. A closer view below.

MF Shorthorn IFC1 and Caudron G.III IFC3 were transported up the Tigris to Ma'gil by RFC steamer T3 and its barge.

on one, the mechanics selected all had experience in motor-engineering shops and were soon brought up to the mark before embarkation. The 41 were later joined by a further 10 mechanics in August and much later in May 1916, a transport reinforcement of seven drivers arrived to complete the Australian contribution. The Australian Government had also suggested a Mule team and two workshop lorries should be included, and this was agreed.

The men were assembled and issued rudimentary kit — .303 rifles and bandoliers, water bottles, haversacks and tropical clothing including khaki breeches and leggings. The only distinguishing feature was the Australian Flying Corps patches on their shoulders. As to their progress, the unnamed author of a note now preserved in the Australian War Memorial attested:[7]

We embarked on 21st April 1915 at Melbourne on Mail boat P&O 'Morea'. We had a good time going over calling at Adelaide, Perth, Colombo and arrived Bombay on or about 18 May 1915. We trans-shipped at Colombo and travelled to Bombay on a different steamer.

...At Bombay, we were put up in an Indian Barracks called 'Kalabar' [i.e. Colaba]. We were there for about three days, when we received orders that the whole of the mule transport was to remain behind and we were to embark for Basrah. We were paid three month's pay in advance at Bombay, and received 30 Rupees (£2) per month extra, above the Australian rates of pay from the Indian Government.

We took no machines whatever; the only things we took were tools, transport spares and everything for carrying on the good work. We bought tools in Melbourne. In the first place we had a leather bag for each mechanic, each outfit costing about £7. We took a travelling workshop made at Newport, which was fitted with a lathe, drilling machine, farrier's instruments, forge, anvil, and drills of every description. It was mounted on a Commer Lorry and was overhead drive power from the motor. Our stores Lorry was a Garford. It was complete in every detail, nothing wanting, also was made in the Newport Workshops. In addition we had two G.S. Wagons and a Villiers 4½ H.P. motor cycle. That was really our motor transport. Then we had mule transport consisting of about half-a-dozen G.S. Wagons and 30 mules from South Australia. These followed us from Australia on the next boat.

The vehicles were given AFC serial numbers AFC1–AFC7, and included a wood-workshop Daimler and a Hupmobile staff car. Upon arrival, the same witness found:

The whole of the place was in a state of turmoil. Passing into the river on the 26th of May 1915 we disembarked and went to a place called 'Tanumah'. This was to be our first aerodrome but it was under water and it needed great efforts to make it suitable. Captain Petre selected the site for the aerodrome which after draining turned out very good. The work of draining etc was done by Arabs.

When the aerodrome was being finished we built workshops and supplies were received from forwarding officer in Bombay. The material came from supplies by the Indian Government as it was an Indian Expeditionary Force. In some cases we had stuff sent to us by the Indian Government which was of no use. Petre so organised our position as to be able to give a rough estimate of material required, which he forwarded to the Indian Government, stating the exact date that it was required. We carried spares in very small quantity. We had a lot of stuff from the Flying School at Cetaphore but it was found to be quite unfit for use. We had in addition to Australian mechanics, four NCOs from the Indian Flying Corps. Had Indian labour, Indian carpenters who were rather slow but the work was good and the fitters and turners we had were always reliable. Here on the drome we installed our workshops, erected our planes and prepared for work of service flying.

The aerodrome had been organised on the old Arab cemetery, the only high ground around, and would remain the aircraft park and major workshops throughout the campaign. While the Half-Flight and later 30 and 63 Squadrons would fly from numerous

The Half-Flight camp at Tanooma, on the opposite bank of the Shatt-al-Arab from Basra, June 1915. The two lorries, converted to mobile workshops by the Newport Railway Works in Australia, were the only mechanical transport in Mesopotamia at the time.

Top: One of the workshop trucks with its equipment and fittings displayed on completion at the Newport Railway Works in Australia.

Middle: Work in progress at the Basra Aircraft Park; and flatbed truck AFC4.

Bottom: In position outside a hangar at Basra, with a Farman just visible behind.

Capt T.W. White (pilot) and Capt W.R. Wills in Maurice Farman Longhorn IFC2 at Basra, about to depart for Kut.

airfields during their stay, usually no more than nine or ten mechanics went forward, with most remaining with the depot. As well as their transport, the Flight had a river steamer, the SS *Bahmashir*, and two barges to support forward operations.

While Capt Petre had sailed ahead, White, Treloar and 37 other ranks sailed for Bombay on 20 April, with Quartermaster Sergeant Garling and the other four troops bringing the Motor Transport two weeks later. A further shipment of horses and mules followed later again and then Merz, who was detained on instructional duties until June. It had been intended that the four Australian pilots and Capt Reilly from Egypt were to be assembled at Bombay,[8] but as Petre and Merz were elsewhere, that plan was waived. Upon arrival in Basra on 26 May 1915, the Australians were met by four other officers with whom they would work closely. These were Broke-Smith and Reilly, Lt William Burn (another New Zealander who had been born in Australia), and equipment and workshops officer, 2Lt Wills. They had a staff of 16 British and Indian drivers and mechanics. The Half-Flight were then Gazetted into the Indian Army (for command and discipline purposes) but always kept their Australian identity.

Now that Broke-Smith was assigned to GHQ staff in Basra, Petre remained in command and White was put in charge of the Aircraft Park at Ma'gil.[9] Fortunately, the expedition arrived in theatre in time to take part in Townshend's summer offensive up the Tigris Valley, but to their dismay, they found their equipment was no better than the training aircraft they had left in Australia.

All modern machines had been dispatched to France; reserves went to Egypt, and Mesopotamia got what was left – in this case two Maurice Farmans delivered on 14 May 1915; a Shorthorn (IFC1) and a Longhorn (IFC2), both with under-powered 70hp Renault engines. A week later, two more Shorthorns (IFC7 and IFC10) arrived, but without engines. Thomas White was later to recall the Shorthorns were purchased from funds donated by the Rajah of Gwalior and the Longhorn had 'seen considerable service in Egypt and subsequently spent most of its time in the workshops'.[10] Mesopotamia was definitely a side-show. As to weaponry, Private Brown continued; 'they were not armed, carrying only two carbines with 15 rounds of ammunition for each pilot and observer. Bomb racks to carry four 20lb Hale bombs were fitted. The bombs were made at Kirkee Arsenal in India and proved very 'dud'.[11]

One of the aircraft was very well used having been at the Cetaphore School from shortly before the start of the war and another reputedly had already seen considerable war service.

According to Petre,[12] the Farman's engines only arrived on 24 May and with only one spare, yet test flying began on the 27th when Reilly and Broke-Smith made a 35 minute flight in a Farman recording a speed of 55mph at 4,800 feet. Major Reilly (with Major Broke-Smith) and Capt Petre (with Lt Burn) made the first two operational flights on 31 May from an advanced landing ground at Chitrish, one and a half miles south of Qurna. These were reconnaissance of the enemy positions north of the town.

Their reports led to a successful British advance on the town in what has been referred to as the Battle of Norfolk Hill and the subsequent capture of 2,000 prisoners, 17 guns and the sinking of two gunboats – the most effective form of enemy surface transport. To keep up with the advance, a forward landing ground was established at Abu Rabah with two Farmans, four officers, 13 mechanics and a stores tug, and as it was so successful, this concept of using forward landing grounds was adopted. The effectiveness of aerial reconnaissance convinced Nixon to press for more aircraft and on 12 June, he asked for additional air support. By month's end, the War Office agreed to detail a flight of the RFC from Egypt, but it would be slow in coming.[13]

The following section traces the story of that unit up until its arrival at Basra in December 1915.

The RFC Egypt Detachment

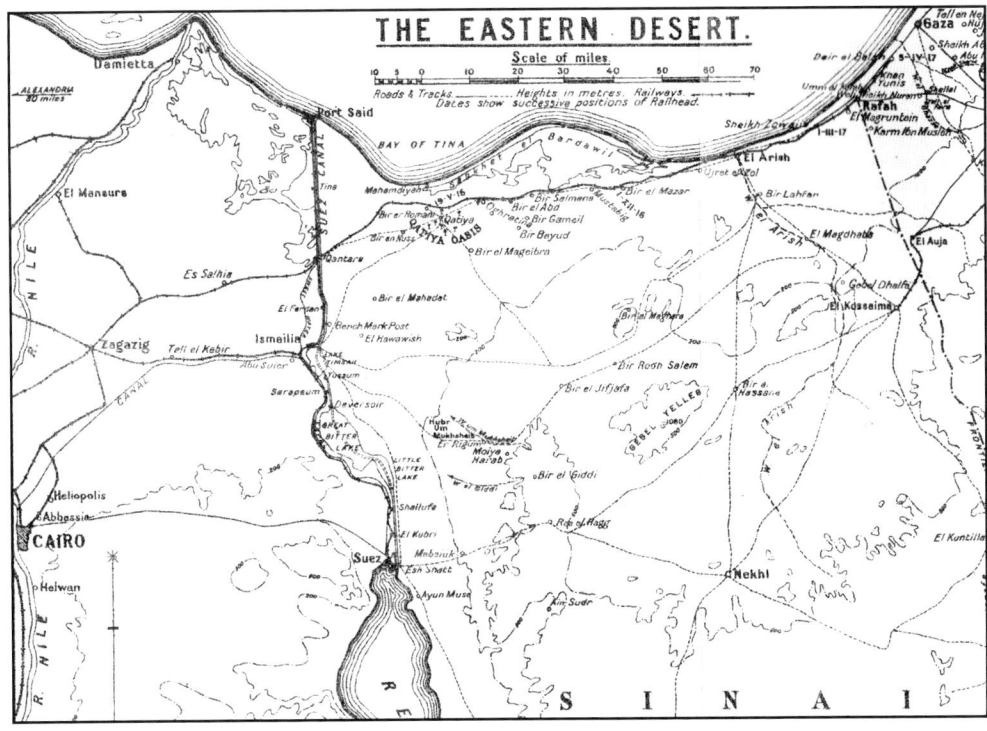

Capt S. Massy

Lt S. Cockerell

The Detachment's original location, almost 4,000 miles by sea from their ultimate destination, and below, the camp at Ismailia, near the Suez Canal.

As early as 1911, Lord Kitchener, then the Consul General of Egypt, had recognized the danger of a Turkish invasion across the Sinai desert to threaten the lifeline that was the Suez Canal. Any invading Army could be far better detected from the air, and on 4 November 1914 the SS *Beethoven* sailed from Avonmouth docks with an RFC detachment on board. In command was Capt Seaton Massy, together with Capt Reilly, Lt Samuel Cockerell, plus one Maurice Farman Shorthorn (1914 type) two Maurice Farman S7 Longhorns (1913 type), Crossley tenders, one Leyland lorry, two RAF pattern hangars and enough stores to last for six months.

The detachment arrived at Alexandria on 17 November, and established themselves at Ismailia approximately half way along the Canal. The hangars were erected, and three sheds at Heliopolis were also moved to this location. Landing grounds were set up at Qantara (also known as Kantara) on the east bank, with another organised at Suez on 2 December. On 27 November, Lt Cockerell with Army observer Capt Barlow flying Shorthorn 369 made the first reconnaissance flight over Bir-el-Gilban and Bir-Abu-Abuk with excellent visibility being reported from 4,000 feet.

On 6 December Maurice Farman 712 was erected, but on the 15th MF 369 was smashed on landing at Suez due to 'bad ground', Lt Cockerell breaking his left arm while his observer, Capt Leopold Royle (Egyptian Coast Guard Administration) was badly bruised.

On 21 December 1914 more equipment arrived in the charge of Lt Sydney Parr, together with three civilian mechanics from the Indian Central Flying School, a BE2a and two Maurice Farman Type 1913 Shorthorns, all without engines. Two NCO pilots (Sgt Cyril Edgar Foggin and Cpl William Boyle Power) plus Capt Gilbert Rickards and two Renault engines also arrived.

Flying during December 1914 was only possible after 08.00 due to early morning ground mist and in the afternoons strong winds and sand storms also prevented flying.

On 6 January 1915 the BE2a was erected, and on the 12th Henry Farman No.1, one of two such machines acquired by Captain Massy from Heliopolis.

The BE2a which was fitted with a larger fuel tank for a long range flight to El Murra by Capt H.L. Reilly and Lt L.V.A. Royle.

On 17 January the RFC made its first contact with the enemy when Capt Reilly with Lt Douglas Royle Tweedie discovered 720 Turkish infantry and 50 cavalry at Bir-el-Abd. Three days later Tweedie, this time acting as observer to Capt Rickards, discovered 1,000 Turkish infantry and 200 cavalry at the same location and bombed them. Further flights during January gave evidence of a major Turkish offensive being planned, and this was launched on 3 February aimed at the central sector of the Canal. On the opening day of the attack the RFC flew five-and-a-half hours of aerial reconnaissance, increasing to 14 hours two days later. The GOC of the Canal Defence Force was constantly updated on movements and enemy strength, despite only four machines being available, and on the 6th, the Turks began to retire.

During March the detachment carried out twenty six recce flights one of which, by Capt Reilly with Lt L.V.A. Royle as observer was to El Murra, a distance of 176 miles. A large petrol tank was fitted to the BE2a for a flight that was to take three hours 28 minutes. On arrival, some 207 tents and 300 infantry were found and bombed despite some heavy and accurate ground fire. On 20 March the unit suffered the loss of Lt Cockerell who died of acute smallpox. Four days later Lt Parr and the four mechanics from India left for Mesopotamia.

During April the two Farmans from India were shipped to Force 'D' in Mesopotamia and on the 30th, unit strength was four officers and 44 other ranks. On 16 April five machines left Ismailia at 05.00 for a raid on El Murra, landing at an advanced landing ground at Qatia to refuel. The distances flown would be in excess of 140 miles but seven out of nine bombs carried were dropped successfully.

Once flying had commenced, the hours soon mounted. In May, 34 reconnaissance flights were completed, with approximately 4,900 miles flown, and over 90 hours spent in the air. Twenty three recce sorties

A very rare bird ... Henry Farman No.1 or 2. Its engine, nacelle, lower wings and undercarriage were Farman components; the upper wing Farman modified with Short seaplane parts, while the tail unit was an original local design.

Maurice Farman 369 at Ismailia. It crashed into the Suez Canal on 26 July 1915.

Capt H.L. Reilly

RFC FLIGHT: MACHINES ON STRENGTH IN EGYPT APRIL 1915

Maurice Farman	369		(1914 Type S.11 Shorthorn) erected 26.11.14
Maurice Farman	712		(1913 Type S.7 Longhorn) from UK, erected 6.12.14
Maurice Farman	713		(1913 Type S.7 Longhorn) from UK, erected 15.12.14
Henry Farman No.1			from Heliopolis December 1914, erected 12.1.15
Henry Farman No.2			from Heliopolis December 1914, erected 20.2.15
Maurice Farman	IFC7		(1913 Type Shorthorn) without engine from India Dec 1914
Maurice Farman	IFC10		(1913 Type Shorthorn) without engine from India Dec 1914
BE2a			from India December 1914
BE2c	1757		Arrived from UK April 1915

were flown in June, and 27 sorties in July including the first photographic flight on the 19th by Sgt Foggin with Capt Owen Mostyn Conran (Royal Lancs Regt & RFC) in Longhorn 712. However, flying was not without its accidents. On the 26th Farman 369, pilot Sgt Power and observer Capt Conran, crashed into the Suez Canal two miles north of El Ferdan with the crew sustaining cuts and bruises and one, a broken rib.

On 31 July, Capt Massy was informed by signal that the Egypt detachment was to become 'C' Flight of 30 Squadron, the order being backdated to 24 March 1915. They would soon move to Mesopotamia and to join up with the other elements already in place, including the Australian Half Flight. Massy was posted to Basra in November, with command of what was left in Egypt going to Capt Rickards. On 26 November 'C' Flight was relieved by 'A' flight of 14 Squadron, RFC who had docked at Alexandria and who together with 17 Squadron, RFC, would soon take over flying duties in Egypt.

On 9 December 1915, 30 Squadron were finally ordered to proceed to Basra. These included Capt Rickards, 2Lt Donald Alistair Leslie Davidson (P), Lt Herbert Prinsep Somers Clogstoun (P), Lt Eric Mackay Murray (P), Lt John Banks Walmsley (P), Lt Lynedoch Wanless-O'Gowan (P) Lt John Ronald McCrindle (P) and Capt John William Thomson-Glover (O) plus a number of other ranks. They arrived on the 27th.

Maurice Farman S.7 Longhorn 712: shipped to Egypt 4.11.1914 in SS Beethoven. Erected in Egypt 6.12.1914. Half Flight Mesopotamia by 21.5.1915. 14 Sqn until 23.7.1916. then to 21 RS Ismailia SOC 9/16.

The Australians Begin Operations

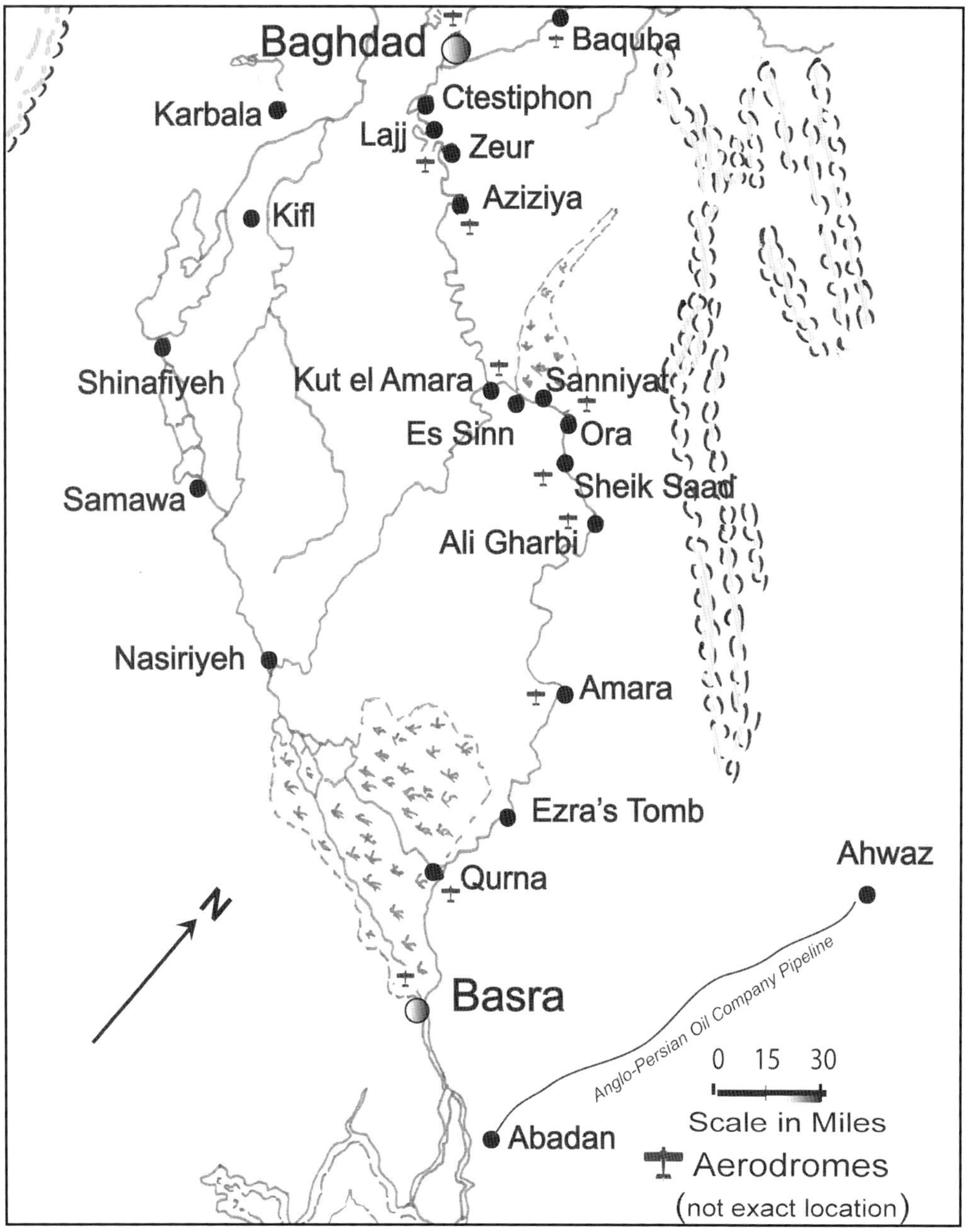

Capt H.A. Petre

An Army officer retrieves a report drropped by streamer from an aircraft.

Advanced airfields were established to meet the Army's need for information that could only be provided by aerial reconnaissance.

On 14 June 1915, Petre sent his first report to the Chief of the General Staff in Victoria Barracks, Melbourne. In it, he stated:[14]

Though for many months no advance beyond Kurna [Qurna] has been possible, from the first day that the aeroplanes were employed the Turkish forces have retreated continuously and the country is now clear of them as far up the River Tigris as Kuwait [Kumeit, about one third of the way from Amara to Kut?]. The cause suggested for this is twofold; as regards the Arabs, they are completely cowed by the very sight of an aeroplane of which they evidently had no previous knowledge. As regards the Turks, they take the use of aircraft as a sign of a completely equipped and organised army and are inclined to give in.

Also on the 14th an aerial reconnaissance of 123 miles was made by Reilly and Burn to locate the enemy's dispositions around Kut. A refuelling point at Ali Gharbi was used, and a sketch map produced which helped Maj-Gen Townshend plan his attack.

On 4 July, two Caudrons were added to the establishment, but they were not up to the hot and sandy conditions. The Caudron G.III was fitted with an 80hp Gnome rotary engine, but had no armament. Usual revs setting was 1200rpm allowing the aircraft to climb and operate at 6,000ft maximum, but the heat, dust and sand meant pilots had to fly lower to observe enemy positions and other features clearly. Eventually, the rotaries gave in to engine failure with disastrous consequences. On a calm day 50mph was possible, but when the *Shamal* wind blew up, the aircraft would sometimes track backwards!

A few weeks later, the Half-Flight began reconnaissance in support of the next army thrust up the Euphrates to Nasiriyeh and as the Official Historian later noted,[15] 'on the 21st [of July] an aeroplane reconnaissance gave General Gorringe for the first time a comprehensive idea of the enemy's disposition and the local topography.' Merz and Reilly also made a recce of Nasiriyeh and again their report assisted in

Above and below: Caudron G.III with the Indian Flying Corps number IFC3. It was eventually lost on 16 September 1915, and the crew of Lt Treloar and Lt Atkins became PoWs.

the taking of that city on the 24th. These recces were carried out between a quarter and half a mile over the Turkish lines. No wireless was installed (the sets would have been too heavy to carry anyway) so reports had to be brought back or dropped in film canisters with a streamer attached.

As well as the extremes of weather, the men had to watch out for marauding Arabs. Cpl Bill Wheeler, one of the first reinforcements, recalled the precautions they had to take:[16]

A small section of the Half-Flight when stationed at Amara were 'camped' in a small mud walled enclosure (called a compound) quite possibly the site of an early village since it was fairly close to the River Tigris. The mud wall would have been about eight feet high and about three feet thick at the base. While sentries were posted at night for protection against thieving Arabs, Warrant Officer Heath in charge of the workshops arranged for the barbed wire fence on top of the wall to be electrified by means of a magneto driven all night. Probably the first electric fence in the world.

These precautions were not possible at advanced landing grounds and in March 1916, 30 Squadron recruited from various Hampshire Territorial units, one NCO and three men to act as guards and police. Their presence paid off on 4 May 1916 when at 00.30 an Arab thief was shot dead and two more wounded. Blood trails were followed into the desert, but the culprits were never found.

Adding to the mechanics' woes was the flimsy construction of the obsolete aircraft which meant accidents were both common and also costly. Very quickly, the Farmans were reduced to one and the two Caudrons were lost to enemy action.

On the first occasion, on 30 July, after completing a reconnaissance of Nasiriyeh in Caudron IFC4, Lts Merz and Burn landed in the desert near Abu Salibiq (midway between Basra and Nasiriyeh) with engine trouble. The other Caudron, IFC3, piloted by Major Reilly (with Sgt Sid Player, a mechanic as passenger) also force landed, but they saved themselves by later fixing their aircraft and flying back.

Not so for Merz and Burn. They went missing and after sighting flares, Lt Wills together with Staff Sgt Cyril Heath, an Arab river pilot and two Indian soldiers, used a 'bellum' – a local type of boat – to investigate. For this effort, Sgt Heath was later awarded the only Australian Flying Corps Distinguished Conduct Medal for the war. His citation read; *For considerable pluck and determination in Mesopotamia on 1st August 1915, when he assisted to pole a bellum 28 miles in 12 hours, in most intense heat, in order to rescue aviators who had been forced to descend in the enemy's territory.* Despite his and Wills' efforts, Merz and Burn were never found.

The remains of Caudron G.III IFC3 of the Australian Half-Flight, recovered two days after the crew, Lt Merz and Lt Burn, were killed by hostile Arabs.

According to later Arab reports, the missing aviators were attacked by marauding Arabs and although the pair put up a good running fight covering over five miles using their service revolvers in defence, eventually they were overcome and killed. Their bodies were never found, but the hacked-apart aircraft was located by Reilly two days later and was returned to the depot for salvage.

While much is made of the Gallipoli ANZAC spirit, unnoticed is the fact that Australia's and New Zealand's first air casualties – Merz, Australian, and Burn, New Zealander – died together, beginning the close relationship the two air forces share today. Merz's loss was doubly felt as he was also a medical doctor who had received his degree from the University of Melbourne in 1914.

By August, Force 'D' had expanded to Divisional strength and had commenced its advance up the Tigris. On the 6th, the decision was made to continue the advance to Kut-el-Amara. As the first stage of a mini reorganisation of the flying service in Mesopotamia, in late August the Half-Flight received four single-seat Martinsyde S1 scouts and was re-designated 'A' Flight of 30 Squadron, RFC.[17] All officers were then gazetted into the RFC on 5 August 1915. War Office promises continued with further assurances of a complete squadron of three flights arriving 'in the near future'. However, while the Martinsydes were delivered to the Basra depot in working order, they were still obsolete aircraft unwanted on other fronts. The rest of 30 Sqn was in Ismailia, Egypt, yet to join up in Basra, but this would not happen until the end of the year.

Martinsyde S1, 4243 (IFC5) of the Half-Flight/'A' Flight 30 Squadron, with engine running up.

The RNAS Contribution

Sqn Cdr R. Gordon

Lt V.G. Blackburn

On 21 August 1915, Squadron Commander Robert Gordon RNAS, Lt Vivian Gaskell Blackburn, Flt Lt Alan George Bishop and Lt Gilbert Dirk Nelson together with 25 personnel, three Short Type 827 seaplanes (822, 825 and 827) sailed from East Africa on the SS *Elephanta* bound for the Persian Gulf to reinforce the RFC. Gordon, born in 1882, had gained his RAeC certificate No. 166 as early as 1911, becoming CO Dundee Air Station in 1913. Nelson, a civilian mechanic with Short Brothers, was commissioned into the RNAS and accompanied the unit to the Gulf.

By 18 June 1915, Gordon had arrived in East Africa, part of the RNAS contingent that would destroy the German raider *Königsberg* in the Rufiji Delta, and was awarded a DSO for this work.

Lt Vivian Blackburn had already had a remarkable war. He had been mentioned in despatches (MID) for his actions during the Cuxhaven Raid on Christmas day 1914, then the destruction of the *Königsberg* and would be Mentioned a third time for his work during the siege of Kut. Three awards in nine months! It would be followed by the award of the DSC (gazetted 21 January 1916) for his work in Mesopotamia, particularly for air reconnaissance in September 1915.

The unit arrived at Basra on 5 September 1915, and located themselves in the grounds of a former Turkish hospital on the Shatt-al-Arab. A Bessonneau hangar was erected in December with a second added in February 1916. Short 827 was assembled on 8 September as a seaplane and first flown on the 10th. A day later Short 825 was ready and the last aircraft, Short 822, was ready to fly by the 16th, but water trials proved unsuccessful and all aircraft would be converted

A scene of great activity on the Shatt-al-Arab on 24 February 1916 at Basra.
The two BE2c fuselages on a barge were destined for 30 Squadron, then at Ora on the Tigris not far from Kut. There are four aircraft packing cases on the larger RFC barge. In the foreground the Bessonneau hangar shipped in by Sqn Cdr Bowhill's RNAS detachment from East Africa is being assembled just in front of their HQ, and the large vessel at anchor on the right is HMT Huntscastle *on which the RNAS unit had just arrived.*

Short 827 was erected on 8 September 1915 and flown on the 10th. However, following unsuccesful water trials, it and both 822 and 825 (below) were converted to landplanes.

Left: Maurice Farman IFC7, converted to a seaplane in August 1915, does not appear to have been any more successful than the Shorts.

Bottom: Short 827 outside the Bessonneau hangar in front of the former Turkish hospital used as the RNAS HQ.

Indian Army troops come to see two of the converted RNAS machines at Basra.

Sqn Cdr R. Gordon sits looking to his right in the middle of this group of the first RNAS Detachment in Mesopotamia. They arrived from East Africa on 5 September 1915.

to land machines at various times.

It was the intention that the RNAS unit would work with the RFC and two of the seaplanes arrived at Sannaiyat on 23 September fitted with wireless, together with Farman MF7 and Martinsyde Scout MH8, before a move to Nukhailat.

It became obvious that the Army had little or no experience of working with aircraft when on the 28th, the crew of Blackburn/Arnold flying Short 827 noted that despite the artillery receiving their W/T reports, they paid them no heed unless they agreed with the spotting of the battery forward observing officer.

Four more seaplanes arrived in February 1916 to assist with the delivery of supplies to Kut.

Short Floatplane 827 on the Tigris in November 1915.

Short 825 undergoing conversion to a landplane.

Short 822 during its conversion to a landplane on 13 October 1915, before being sent to Ora to assist in operations to relieve Kut.

The wreckage of Short 822 at Ora following FSL W.H. Dunn's crash on 14 February 1916, in which his observer, CPO Herbert Chaplin, was injured and had to be invalided to India.

The remains of 822 after being shipped back to the main base at Basra, a journey of about 450 miles which took ten days. The framework of the second Bessonneau is just visible behind.

The Advance

This fine illustration of the organisation developed by the Inland Water Transport Department in Mesopotamia shows how much of the movement of personnel and equipment was undertaken. A tug, such as T.28 on the right, could take two barges, one secured to each side, up and down river. Progress was slow, with frequent strandings, but nevertheless a valuable alternative to the roads, despite distances between any two places being greater on the winding rivers than by land. The coracle-like boat in the foreground is a gufa, waterproofed with bitumen from the oilfields, the type of local craft used in the shallowest parts of the rivers and marshes. The scene also hints at another important service provided to the Expeditionary Forces by both naval and air arms: wireless communication in a land with no established telegraph or telephone network

Meanwhile, in early September 1915, Force 'D' again began moving north, concentrating on Ali Gharbi, which was to be the mounting point for the Kut attack. Ali Gharbi also became the advance landing ground and a detachment was sent up river by barge to support the forward operations from 7 September onwards. Townshend pushed on and by mid-September his forces had reached Sannaiyat, aided by the fine work of the airmen. On the 9th, Farman IFC1, Caudron IFC3 and Scouts IFC5 and IFC6 flew up to Ali Gharbi in support. Within two days, a British pilot wrote-off the Shorthorn IFC1 in a bad landing. On the 13th, Scout IFC5 crashed on the same ground during a test flight and on the 16th, the sand and heat took their usual toll as on this date, Treloar's number came up while flying IFC3. Years later he recounted what happened:[18]

Martinsyde S.1 4243 (IFC5) of 30 Squadron. It was destroyed at Ali Gharbi on 13 September 1915.

I was just landing at Headquarters after an hour-and-a-half flight from our temporary aerodrome at Sheikh Saad where I had received an order from the flight commander to join Divisional HQ on the Tigris River nine miles above Arak when I espied my observer, Captain Atkins making his way towards me with his usual bright smile lighting up his tanned face. We start at daybreak tomorrow he commenced; to reconnoitre the position supposed to be held by the Turks about 14 miles to our front and we are to find out at any cost whether they still hold the place and several other minor matters. Our ships went within 6,000 yards of their position today and there was not a single shot fired at them. The Arab spies say that they are there in force but reports from other sources contradicted them saying the Turks have retired before our advance. If that is the case, our force must follow rapidly in pursuit.

They went off to plan the flight…

…We came to the conclusion we would make for the Turkish left flank and fly down their line getting necessary information we required and then come home by the river signalling to the 'Shaitun' [a command vessel] as we passed them that we had finished. Now we are just over their front line on its left flank, there we find redoubts, trenches and information enough to keep Atkins sketching and writing at his fastest rate. A little puff of smoke over to our left quickly followed by others shows us plainly that we have succeeded in our mission and that the Turk has betrayed himself by using his artillery on us.

…I fancy the engine is slowing up and I glance at the indicator to find the revs are indeed dying down fast. I tell my observer who has also noticed the failure and we decide to make for a dry piece of ground on the left bank of the river, well in the Turkish Front where possibly I may be able to make a hurried repair and still get away. A few shrapnel shots burst here and there but as before their shooting is very bad. I see the Gunboat and know that I cannot reach it against the rising wind.

A long slow glide during which we are able to tear up our notes and maps and cast them over the side keeping a careful watch for any stray patrol parties which may

30 Squadron's camp at Sheikh Saad, the Advanced Landing Ground for Ali Gharbi in 1915, with four aircraft visible on the ground behind the lines of tents, and river transport moored at the jetties.

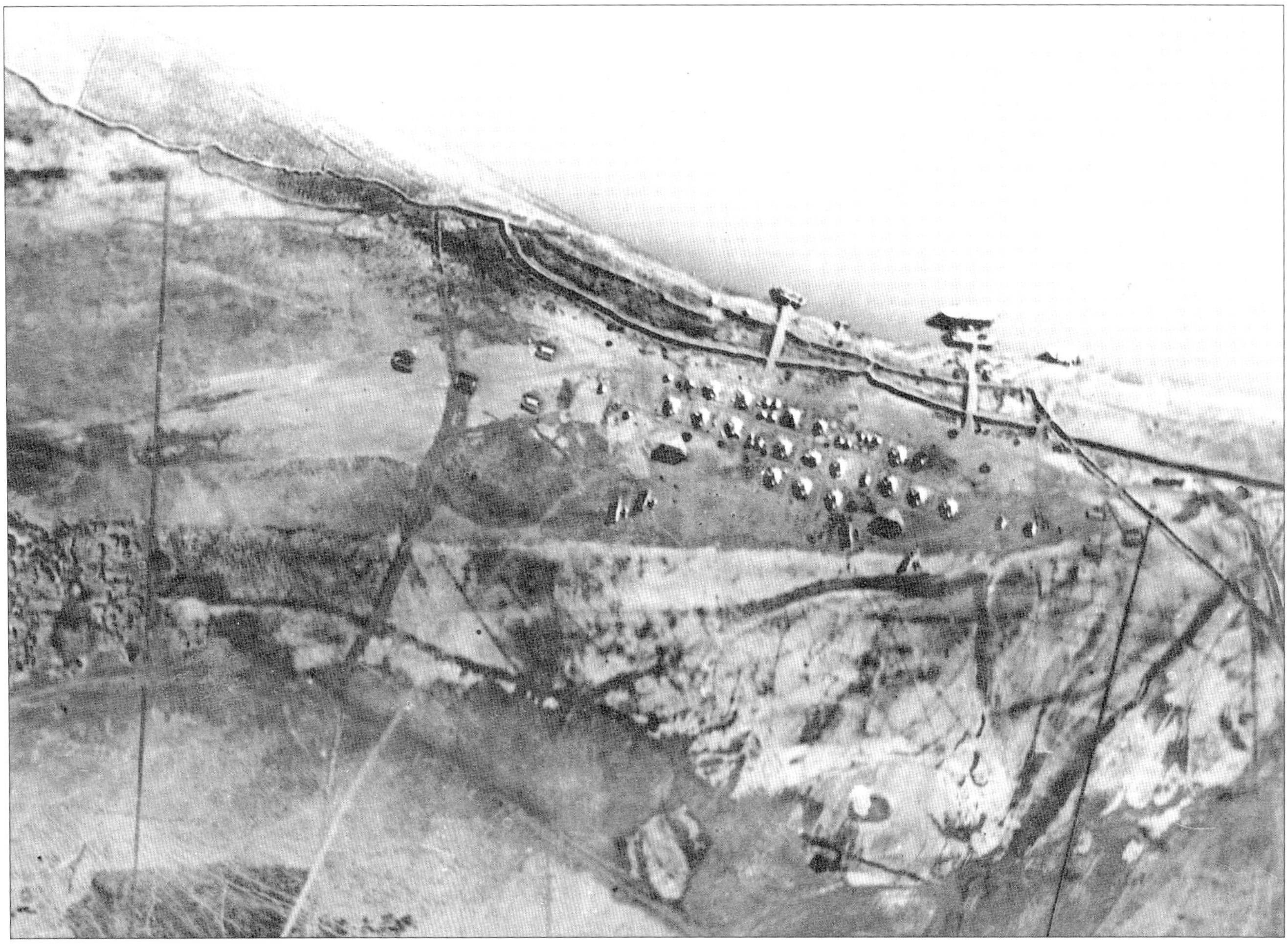

Martinsyde S.1 SCout 4250 (IFC8) ready for take-off. This machine had a hard life, having been damaged twice, in crashes when flown by Petre, before Fulton was shot down and made POW when flying it on 22 November 1915.

be out in front and now we are about to land.
… we are now about 200ft up and I see the irrigation channel which we are just going to skim over is full of men. From a calm, we glide into a perfect hail of rifle fire to land about 80 yards in front of this trench, which was full of Arabs. Turkish irregulars.
The bullets were whizzing past our heads, going through the bracing wires. We jumped out of the machine quickly and placed our hands up but as the firing continued, we took what cover we could eventually daring to try and run to the boat but before going many paces we were surrounded by some cavalry and in a minute or two by an excited crowd of Arab fanatics and Turkish irregulars who started to loot us at once, tearing off most of our clothes and equipment.

Just when things seemed grim, a Turkish officer appeared and they both went into captivity. Initially transported to Baghdad, and although badly treated, they survived the war as POWs.

Within a week of the Flight's arrival at Ali Gharbi, three of the four aircraft were gone leaving a single Martinsyde IFC6 to support the advance on Es-Sinn, a Turkish stronghold before Kut. Given the need for air support, Scout IFC9 was crated and together with the three seaplanes was sent up river on a pair of barges. But the first barge became stranded on a sandbank and it was well into October before it was freed. So Petre flew Scout IFC8 up to support the advance, unfortunately damaging it at Sannaiyat, which caused further delays as well as injuring his left foot. The other Shorthorn, IFC7, was flown up by White, arriving safely making only two aircraft available for Townshend's 26 September assault on Kut (IFC6 and IFC7). By the 30th, Petre's IFC8 arrived, but on 2 October, he crashed it again.[19]

This sketch, published by General Townshend after the war, of the view up the Tigris from Qurna, with Turkish steamers in the distance, shows how vessels on the river could be visible from many miles away across the low-lying land and marshes.

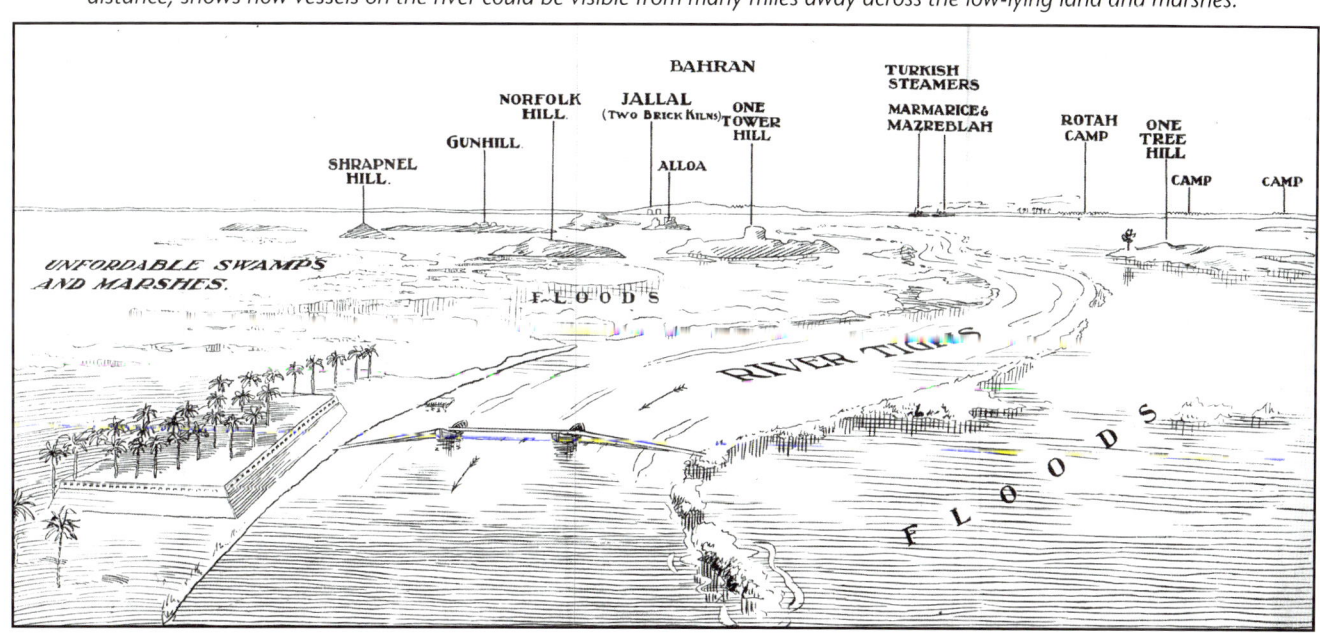

The Move Towards Kut

The RFC airfield at Sheikh Saad from ground level, with the smoke of a river steamer rising in the background.

Townshend now set his mind to take Kut, and to do so he required knowledge of the Turkish defences. In 1915, Kut-el-Amara was a native town of about 6,000 inhabitants nestled in a tight bend on the left bank of the Tigris. The town, built predominantly of mud brick, was of strategic significance because it controlled the river traffic. On the 14th and 15th of September, aerial and naval reconnaissance of the Turkish lines had been carried out, showing the Turks were in strength and digging in. When Treloar and Atkins failed to return, Reilly in the Caudron made an evening flight, bringing back a hand drawn map of the Turkish positions which Townshend in his memoirs described as 'fine work' and by the 17th, all was ready. White had also tried aerial photography, but the poor quality film combined with the weather conditions meant the shots he took were of little use. However, the subsequent assault on Kut on the 27th of September was successful, the Turks withdrawing three days later. Townshend's eagerness to capture Kut extended his lines of communication, and as we shall see, it was later to be his downfall.

The RFC flight moved up to Kut on 30 September and daily flights by Major Reilly followed the Turks' withdrawal to Ctesiphon. The first flight to Baghdad was carried out by Capt Petre on MH8 on 6th October, but he unfortunately crashed on landing. With all these crashes, it was surprising that he was not badly hurt.

By October, the Army advance had reached within 50 miles of Baghdad, but it would be at much cost. Although operations had resulted in 4,000 Turkish casualties including 1,153 POWs, Townshend's force was tired and stressed by the heat and poor provisions. The Flight (now with two of the Shorts converted to land machines) flew repeated reconnaissance missions and the occasional bombing sortie. Since the battle of Qurna, two-pound hand-bombs were tossed over the side, causing panic amongst the enemy soldiers. Later 20lb bombs arrived in theatre, but the inadequate bomb racks meant crews preferred to drop them through a hole cut in the cockpit floor. Most operations were carried out up and down the Tigris and Euphrates Rivers, as that was the most likely place to observe troop movement and the easiest method of getting around was by river transport. As well as bombs, crews

Kut-al-Amara, located in a loop of the Tigris, which was 200/300 yards wide in this area.

Ground troops pause to watch work in progress on two of the Short Seaplanes, now converted to land machines.

also dropped messages to troop commanders thereby assisting them in their task, giving descriptions of the terrain and maps of Turkish troop positions.

Meanwhile problems with aircraft serviceability improved slightly and by 13 October, Farman IFC2 had been repaired making four aircraft to continue reconnaissance and bombing missions. On the 22nd, engine trouble forced down Capt Thomas White with Capt Frank Yeats-Brown, an Indian Army observer, near Zeur and as Yeats-Brown armed with only a rifle, acted as guard and navigator, White taxied the aircraft back across the rocky ground until safe over the British lines. The audacity of the move must have stunned the Turks, who never fired a shot. After taxying for 17 miles, the engine picked up and they were able to fly home. It was a remarkable escape.

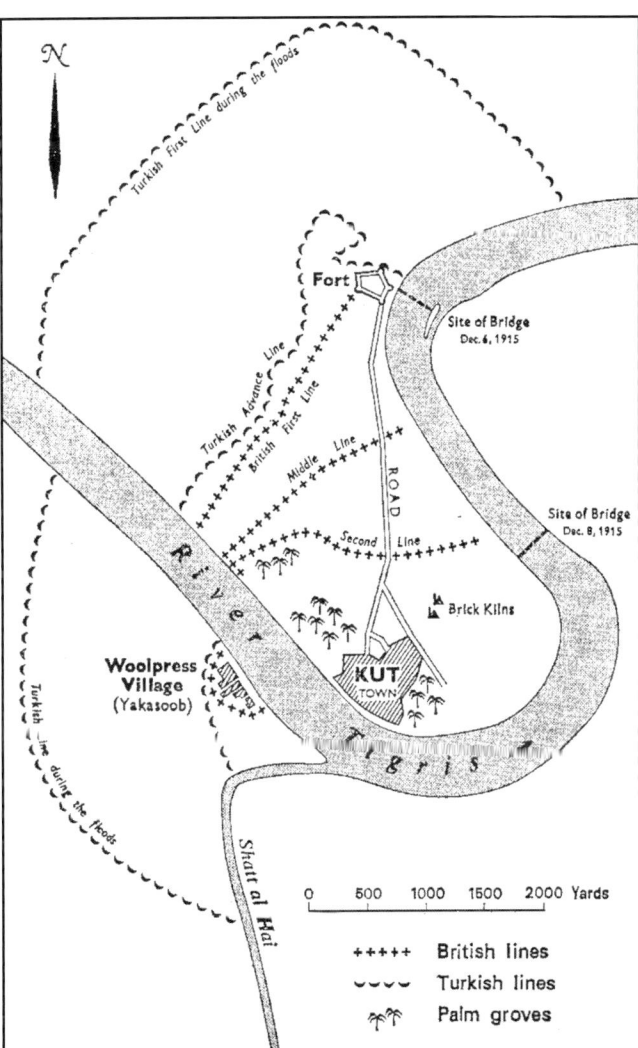

A plan of Kut, showing the opposing lines that developed later. The Shatt-al-Hai is an ancient canal, cut to link the Tigris and the Euphrates.

An official photograph of Air Mechanics at work on a Maurice Farman 'somewhere in Mesopotamia' – probably Basra.

A view inside the town of Kut.

The Mesopotamia Aircraft Park

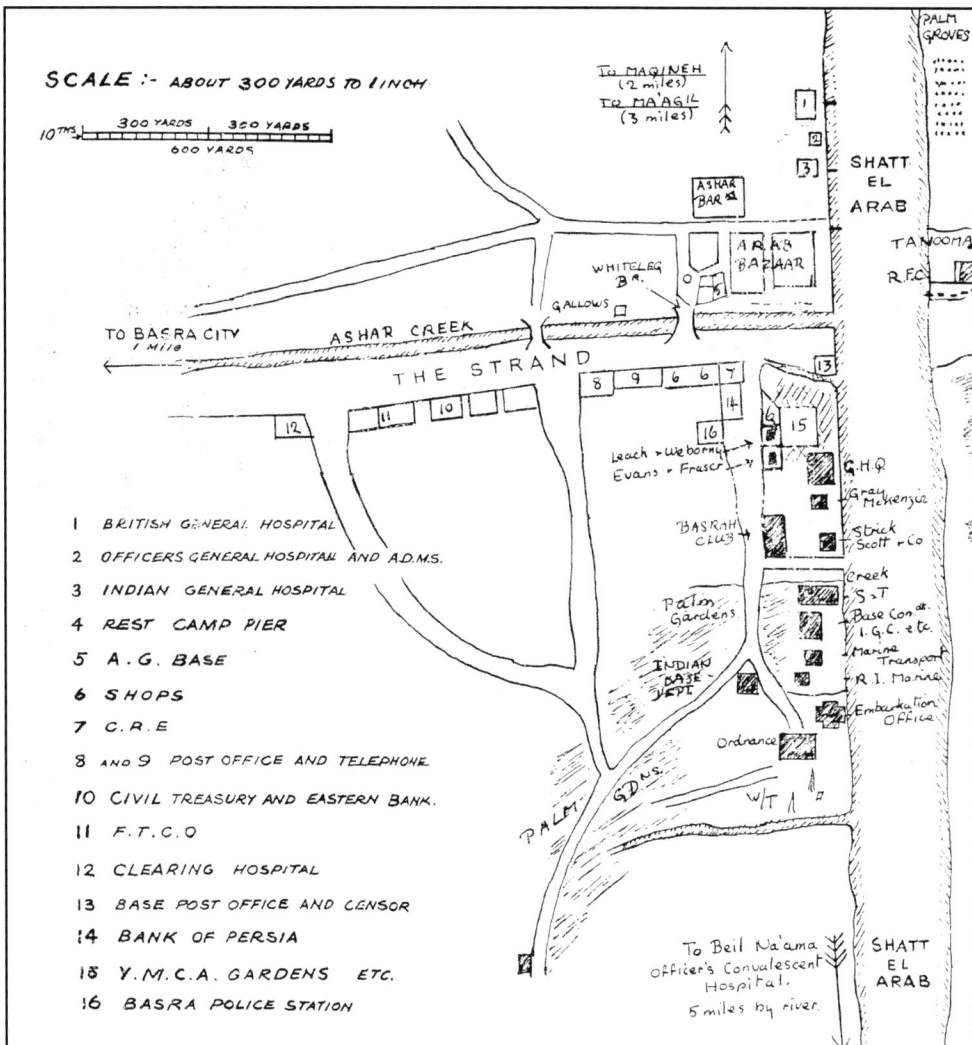

The main British base at Basra, located on the Ashar Creek, about a mile from the city itself, with the original RFC site at Tanooma on the opposite bank of the Shatt-al-Arab. The Australian base at Ma'qil was further upstream, as indicated on this sketch-plan.

Capt A.F.A. Hooper, who commanded the Aircraft Park until March 1916.

On 22 October 1915 a complete RFC Aircraft Park, (the first sent out from the UK) arrived at Basra under the command of Capt Alexander Francis Anderson Hooper. The other officers were 2Lt (Later Capt) Geoffrey Somers-Clarke EO (Rigging) and 2Lt Norman Pellew EO (Workshops). The aircraft park had been formed at Farnborough on 1 September 1915 and within a fortnight three Sergeants and 42 other ranks had joined. The park boasted four RAF hangars, two BE2cs, two workshop trucks and about 100 tons of tools and equipment.

A lack of facilities at Basra caused many problems in unloading the cargo and many packing cases had to be opened before they could be transferred to the AFC site at Tanooma/Tanumah. About the unloading, the unit historian recorded:

Great difficulties were experienced in unloading the workshops' plant, stores etc., there being no facilities at the time for discharging cargo from lighters, and a great many cases had to be broken open and the content removed piecemeal before the material could be landed; the workshop lorries had also to be dismantled to enable them to be got on shore.

By the end of December 1915, all plant had been erected, stores put into place, and an Advanced Aircraft Park (AAP) at Amara (about halfway between Basra and Kut) established under the command of Capt Wills. Early in January, 1916, three 100ft barges and one 60ft barge arrived and were converted into floating workshops, one for each flight, using the equipment from the workshop lorries. Rain storms and high winds in January flooded the camp, blew the roofs off three permanent hangars and destroyed other tented ones. They were repaired in time for the arrival of four BE2cs at the end of February.

Early in March 1916 Capt Hooper was posted to take over as CO India AP, Capt Wills taking charge until 17 March when Capt Parr transferred from 30 Squadron to become CO. Parr was replaced by 2Lt John Alexander Gibson as EO2. At the end of March, thirteen BE2cs arrived from the UK, the SS *Bahmashir* was taken over, and steamer T3 took a permanent hangar to Amara.

June 1916 saw extreme weather conditions decimate the park personnel, leaving only 15 men able to work during the month. 2Lt Pellew was invalided out of the country, but replacements from England arrived, Capt Walter Wood Tullis EO1, and Lt (Later Capt) Frederick Hibberd Songhurst EO2. Capt Tullis commanded the Air Park from 29 August 1916, and Capt Eric Francis Hirtzel EO3 (Stores) arrived on 18 October to take charge of the motor transport and port duties.

By January 1917, a 100ft storage barge (given the

Matting huts, the original primitive living and working conditions at the main Base Depot, Tanooma, Basra.

Capt W.R. Wills, who took over command of the Aircraft Park from Capt Hooper.

The only permanent RFC hangars at Basra, 1915. It was not until the fall of Baghdad that more were constructed at an enlarged Aircraft Park.

The steam yacht Bahmashir, previously owned by the Sheikh of Muhammerah, proved to be a real floating workhorse of the Mesopotamia campaign.

Lt F.H. Songhurst.

Caudron G.III C2 IFC4 outside the permanent hangars, with Maurice Farman IFC2 visible under cover on the right.

Two Martinsyde S.1 Scouts (4243 on the left) a Caudron G.III and a Maurice Farman Shorthorn. Martinsyde 4243/IFC5 crashed at Ali Gharbi on 15 September 1915.

Another traveller by water transport. Martinsyde S1 Scout 4244, also known as IFC6, with the Indian Flying Corps number MH6 above the serial on the rudder, seen here on an RFC barge, on its way from Basra to Ali Gharbi It was lost on 21 November 1915 when Major H.L. Reilly was shot down and made POW.

BE2c fuselages on an RFC barge at Basra 24.2.1916: 4361, 4412 and 4459. The new aircraft had been delivered from Ascot AP in the UK.

Problems: Martinsyde G.100 Scouts at Basra Aircraft Park in September 1916. They had arrived without engines and spares, and had been so badly damaged in transit as to be almost unusable.

nickname 'Noah's Ark') was permanently at Amara plus a small group of mechanics and two months' supply of spares. 2Lt Arthur Evelyn Young EO3(Engines) arrived on 10 January to replace Somers-Clarke who proceeded up river as the new wing EO following the formation of the new 31st Wing established on 1 February.

Following the fall of Baghdad, the Amara depot moved to Sheikh Saad, which was now the Army's advanced base, Amara being retained as a petrol dump. Finally, the RFC was able to improve living conditions for its personnel, EP Tents with fans and electric lights helping to reduce the casualties caused by heatstroke and other ailments.

Up until May 1917, the RFC command in Egypt had been responsible for all aviation supplies, but in reality, Egypt and Palestine units had first call. Demands for more squadrons in Mesopotamia and lack of support from Cairo now saw RFC HQ London take control of supplies, and that resulted in the holding of six months of supplies at Basra, two months at the Advanced Air Park at Amara and one month by 30 Squadron.

In September, the AAP moved to Baghdad, where new buildings were established for stores, and engine and aircraft repair shops, and the former German wireless station building was also commandeered. As the depots expanded, additional tradesmen were recruited from Army units and by the end of the year, the Park was capable of completely rebuilding damaged machines, including repairs to fuselages, mainplanes, propellers and engines.

The role of the main Aircraft Park at Basra was expanded in January 1918 with the establishment of a local flying school. Fresh pilots arriving in the theatre with less than 20 hours flying time had further instruction and became acclimatized to local conditions. The school continued to operate until the arrival of 72 Squadron in March.

In March 1918 the main AP moved to Baghdad and Lt (later Capt) Francis Mapleton Iremonger Watts (Worcester Regt & RFC) took command. Five Bessonneau and seven permanent hangars were erected, the stores barges were dismantled, and stores and equipment moved into the German wireless station building during the summer of 1918

The workforce by September numbered some 330, made up of mechanics, carpenters, electricians, instrument repairers, armourers and coppersmiths. Climatic conditions would still take their toll, and in May

Ravages of the climate: Martinsyde G.100 7467 undergoing a complete overhaul and change of fabric at Basra Aircraft Park.

'... the old BEs and Martinsydes shrivelled in the sun and their engines choked with desert sand. Their fabric became bleached and loose, one could poke one's finger through it: to have looped one of these machines would have been courting disaster. A machine in Egypt had collapsed in the air owing to the dryness of the wood.'

LtCol J.E. Tennant
In the Clouds above Baghdad

of 1918 Lt Frederick Edward Leach EO3(Stores) who had arrived on 25 June 1917 would be invalided to India, later dying of heatstroke in Bombay.

By the end of the war, despite the climate and shortages, the Air Park had been able to fulfil all the demands the aviators had placed on it.

The barges, some large enough to carry one or more aircraft crates, were often lashed to the side of a powered vessel. The steamer T3 with RFC Barge No 3, represent typical transport in the area. Navigating such a combination around the many bends of the Tigris, which might be shallow or strong-flowing depending on location and season, was often a matter of controlled bumping against the banks to change direction.

Below: On 31 January 1916, Lt H.P.S. Glogstoun, 30 Sqn, managed to wreck Voisin 8505 on Basra Aircraft Park.

The Basra Aircraft Park in 1917 with the original hangar in the centre, now surrounded by base hospitals and a Turkish POW camp.

Townshend's Push North

Meanwhile, in early November 1915, Capt White in Longhorn IF2 rescued Maj-Gen George Kemball, the Chief of Staff to Nixon, who had been forced down in enemy territory when one of the Short seaplanes in which he was a passenger developed engine trouble. Landing close by, White returned the General to camp leaving the seaplane pilot and a salvage crew to get the seaplane out.

Townshend's thrust into the Mesopotamian heartland continued with a gathering enthusiasm to capture Baghdad. Blinded by success and for fame, he pushed onwards, requiring more and more from his aviators. On 13 November 1915 White in Longhorn IFC2, again with Yeats-Brown, volunteered for a mission to cut the main telegraph line into Baghdad. Carrying necklaces of guncotton and extra tins of fuel and oil, the pair discovered that the telegraph wire ran westward from Baghdad along the main road and not out into the desert as the maps depicted. As Turkish troops were constantly moving along the road, it was inevitable they would be caught. Although landing in a spot where the surface looked smooth, the aircraft crashed into a telegraph pole damaging it irreparably for flight. Despite the arrival of an armed party, Yeats-Brown managed to blow up the wires while under fire as White refuelled the aircraft, hoping to taxi it to safety as he had done previously. But his efforts were to no avail, and they were captured and interned. White later escaped after two-and-a-half years in captivity, recalling his story in his book *Guests of the Unspeakable*.

After the war, he turned to politics and after serving as a Wing Commander in World War II ended his working life as Australia's High Commissioner in London. General Nixon who had arrived at Aziziya the same day, and fearing the loss of further precious aircraft, forbade the long-distance flights, effectively denying himself any intelligence on Turkish reinforcements – it would be a crucial mistake.

A week later, Major Hugh Reilly and Capt Edmund James Fulton became the final casualties of the Half-

Capt Thomas Walter White in a Maurice Farman.

Flight. On 21 November, while reconnoitring Ctesiphon in Scout IFC6, Reilly was shot down by ground fire and taken prisoner. His latest report of Turkish reinforcements at Ctesiphon never reached Townshend – a misfortune that would signal the end for Townshend's force. Had it done so, the Campaign outcomes may have been different. Reilly's maps, however, fell into Turkish hands where they were a godsend. According to translated documents quoted in the Official History:[20]

Major Reilly's greatest gift to us was a sketch showing the course of the Tigris from Diyala to Aziziya. This little sketch, probably of small account to the enemy, was an important map in the eyes of the Iraq command. For the Headquarters and with the troops, there was no such thing as a map.

The next day, Fulton received the same treatment in Scout IFC8. By now, the Flight had only one Scout (IFC9), one Shorthorn (IFC7) and three BE2cs (IFC12, 12A and 14) remaining. Petre was the only pilot.

The dream of an early and triumphal entry into Baghdad evaporated in late November. The Battle of Ctesiphon (Suliman Pak to the Turks, 22-24 November 1915) did not go well, with the infliction of severe casualties on the overstretched and outnumbered

In Turkish hands. Martinsyde S.1 4244 which was shot down by ground fire on 21 November 1915, the pilot, 30 Squadron's CO, Major H.L. Reilly becoming a POW.

British forces, and was the first reverse of the Campaign. Although only the Farman IFC7, two seaplanes and later, a BE2 were all that was available, the aircraft were used to constantly monitor the situation, dropping messages on the 6th Division HQ. On the 25th, they reported a large Turkish force, some of whom they bombed with 100lb bombs, advancing towards the British from Diyala. The British had marched to within 24 miles of their target, Baghdad, but it would be another year-and-a-half before that prize would be claimed. They were now forced to retire. After Townshend's failure to secure the town, on 3 December, his 3,000 British and 10,000 Indian troops and their camp followers[21] withdrew back to Kut-el-Amara. Here, they were to be besieged for five months while Nixon attempted to organise a rescue. Major Seaton Massy who had arrived from Egypt during the battle, took command of the unit from 28 November, replacing Reilly.

After it became clear that there was no escape from Kut, Townshend ordered all serviceable aircraft back to Basra, and so on 7 December Petre flew Farman IFC7 out with Major Massy to continue operations out of Ali Gharbi. BE2c IFC11,[22] also departed, flown by Capt Eric MacKay Murray with Lt Granville Spain. The two river barges and mobile workshops had also been lost in the retreat, so there were no spare parts and no

The unique brick arch of the palace at Ctesiphon, marking the great achievements of ancient Mesopotamia, and the end of the first advance on Baghdad.

way of repairing the grounded aircraft. Scout IFC9 and two BE2cs were abandoned. More unfortunately for the Squadron, observers Capt R.D. Corbett, 2Lt C.H. Courthope-Munro, and Capt S.C.B. Mundy, also pilots Capt T.R. Wells and Capt S.C. Winfield-Smith, together with 44 Australian and RFC other ranks were now trapped in Kut.

Many months later, the German mechanics succeeded in rebuilding a single aircraft from the remains in Kut and it joined the aircraft of their flying squadron. Meanwhile, back at Basra, and with a decision that

30 Squadron, end of November 1915

Commanding Officer	Major Seaton Massy	
Equipment Officer	Capt Wilfred Wills	
'A' Flight		**Machines**
Flight Commander	Capt Henry A. Petre	MF Shorthorn IFC1
Flying Officers	Capt Thomas Wells	MF Longhorn IFC7
Observers	Capt Stanley Munday 2Lt Caryl Henry Courthope-Munro	Martinsyde Scout IFC9 4250
'B' Flight		**Machines**
Flight Commander	Capt Eric Murray	BE2c IFC11 4500
Flying Officers	Capt Stephen Winfield-Smith Lt Arnold Graves	BE2c IFC12A 4361 BE2c IFC14 4363
Observers	Capt Robert Corbett Lt Granville Spain	

'B' Flight, 30 Squadron RFC, Sheikh Saad, Mesopotamia, 1915-16.

BE2c 4500 (IFC11) was a stalwart of the advance in November 1915. Standing on the left is Capt E. Murray MC, 'B' Flight commander who, together with Capt Petre in the Farman, flew daily reconnaissance for the battles of Ctesiphon and Wadi, and also covered the retreat to Kut, from where he escaped to Basra with Lt Granville Spain as the Turks closed in on 7 December 1915.

would presage the formation of the RAF in April 1918, the RNAS Short seaplanes and the RFC's Farman IFC7 and BE2c IFC11 were combined into a single identity – The RNAS had aircraft and few pilots, the RFC had pilots and few aircraft. Only when two 140hp Voisins arrived at Basra on 17 January for use of the RNAS, did the pilots have the ability to resume regular patrols.

With the virtual loss of all air support, on 27 December 1915, 'C' Flight arrived at Basra from Egypt both completing the unit establishment and adding vital reinforcements.

Meanwhile, Townshend's force was now cut off and surrounded by the 18th Turkish Corps and while English reinforcements were being rushed up to assist, they were held off at Fallujah by the 13th Turkish Corps in a flanking move. Had Townshend known the real extent of the Turkish 6th Army and the fact that it was a shallow force, he might have seized the initiative and been prepared for a breakout. Aerial reconnaissance was uncoordinated and aerial photography and interpretation methods only in their infancy, so the true extent of the enemy's position was not appreciated. The Siege of Kut, which lasted from 7 December 1915 to 28 April 1916, would be a disaster of monumental proportions, eclipsed only by the fall of Singapore some 26 years later.

From January 1916, attempts were made to relieve the beleaguered garrison using a revamped British force, the 'Tigris Corps'. Under newly appointed Lt-Gen Fenton Aylmer,[23] it was to be hamstrung on three counts. First, the Turks were by now well established and knew the ground. Second, the Tigris floods prevented outflanking manoeuvres and third, Townshend made no offer to help with a co-ordinated assault out of Kut (despite frequent requests to do so). The first attempt to relieve the garrison commenced on the 4th when Maj-Gen Sir George Younghusband's[24] 7th (Meerut) Division advanced from Ali Gharbi to Sheikh Saad. His force would go no further. The airmen continuously moved up with the troops operating from Ali Gharbi, Musandeg, and Sheikh Saad, finally arriving at Ora on the 16th.

One of the Voisins being towed out for a reconnaissance by a Crossley tender.

The German Air Service Arrives in Theatre

As the Turkish Commanders were considering their own position, in late November 1915, the Germans and Turks agreed to the creation of a new flying squadron after they had successfully secured the Dardanelles. On 1 December, *Fleigerabteilung 2* left San Stefano under command of *Hauptmann* Franz von Aulock. The unit was essentially German crewed with ten aircraft, including four Pfalz Parasol monoplanes for fighter duties. After a tortuous journey by wagon, ship, rail and river steamer, the procession arrived in Baghdad nine weeks after departure where an aircraft depot, *Flugpark 6* was established.[25]

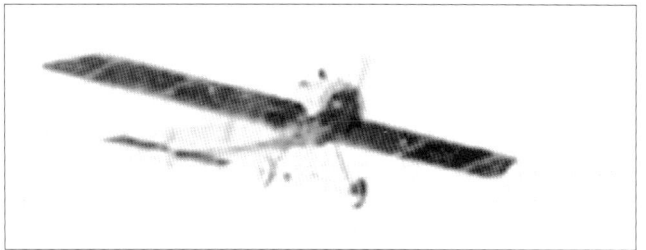

Officers almost certainly from Fliegerabteilung 2 which arrived in Mesopotamia in January 1916. This damaged photograph of German and Turkish flying personnel was discovered at Imam-Mahdi during the advance on Baghdad in February 1917.

The first Turkish aeroplane, however, appeared in the Baghdad skies on 27 November and reported the British occupation of Lajj, but this event went unreported through the British chain of command.[26] It was no doubt one of the two captured British aircraft (IFC3 or Shorthorn IFC7) which a Turkish crew had managed to get airworthy. Later, Townshend casually considered the arrival of enemy aircraft on 1 January with a note on a Cable, which read:

'An aeroplane passed over here in the forenoon reported by a look-out man. As I understand yours did not go out from Ali Gharbi, it would appear to be a hostile one'.[27] Indeed four aircraft had also been brought forward and for the next six weeks, the German fliers now in theatre merely reconnoitred the British lines. The British Air Historical Branch publication *The Royal Air Force in the Great War* states that these were three Fokker monoplanes and an Aviatik.[28]

However, on 13 February 1916, the Kut garrison experienced their first bombing raid, an action which greatly improved the morale of the Turkish troops and firmed their resolve. At 09.15, the enemy aircraft appeared overhead dropping four bombs into the town and flying away unscathed. It was to be the beginning of a new phase. So close was the enemy aerodrome at Shumran Bend that lookouts in Kut could watch them take off and thus sound the alarm. Despite the regular arrival of the enemy aircraft overhead, few casualties were recorded from the bombing, as most of the garrison was living underground, the German 30lb bombs having little effect. So the siege continued.

Turkish aviation troops with a Pfalz and an Albatros at an unknown location.

A view looking south, showing the loop of the Tigris around Kut in the flood season. The Shatt-al-Hai runs off south-west towards the Euphrates at the top left of the photo. The Turkish airfield was located near the Tigris Shumran Bend to the west, just off the top right-hand side of the photograph.
Below: Halberstadt D.V in Turkish markings.

The garrison responded by placing machine-guns on the roofs of houses and by converting one of their 13-pounder guns for anti-aircraft operations, but this only forced the enemy to fly higher. According to the British Official Historian, Brig-Gen Fred Moberly, those left in Kut *suffered from further periodical bombardments, which at times did considerable damage.*[29]

Hauptmann Hans Schüz who flew with *FlAbt 2* later recalled that *day and night the 'Parasol' monoplane hummed over Kut, dropping bomb after bomb upon the crowded troops below, who previously had been secure against all bombing.*[30] The Germans established an aircraft depot at Baghdad, and like their English and Australian counterparts, found it very difficult to keep their aircraft serviceable. They too were only provided leftovers from the other fronts. Schüz continued:

Gunners looking out for hostile aircraft taking off from Shumran bend, while observers on the northern defences of Kut watch for activity by the besieging Turkish ground forces.

Fokker E.III 381/16, flown by the Turkish Air Service.

BE2c 4303, flown by 30 Squadron in late 1915/early 1916.

One of our greatest difficulties was the manufacture of bombs, but with the assistance of cast-iron pipes inserted one inside the other, filled with high explosives, and detonated by a cartridge, we succeeded in producing an efficient substitute.

Not so fortunate were the British. Moberly was later to write:

For the greater part of February, General Aylmer had only one serviceable aeroplane (BE2c) at his disposal and although by the end of the month three machines of the RNAS had joined him, he no longer had superiority in the air. The Turkish aeroplanes were increasing in number and efficiency and were greatly faster and better fighting machines than those of the British. In addition to bombing Kut periodically, three of them also bombed General Aylmer's camp on 22 February.[31]

Henry Farman 1540 at the Aircraft Park some time after its arrival on 8 February 1916. It would be used for supply dropping missions during the siege of Kut.

Short 827 and a Henry Farman at Ora to support the troops at Kut. They would soon face German-led opposition.

Officers and ratings of the RNAS Detachment at their main base at Basra, March 1916. The building was formerly a Turkish hospital. Identified officers seated in the centre of the group are (l-r) Lt John Douglas Hume, FSL Humphrey de Verd Leigh, Lt Gilbert Dirk Nelson, Sqn Cdr Frederick William Bowhill, Wg Cdr Robert Gordon, FSL Wilfred Henry Dunn, Lt Alan George Bishop.

The February reinforcements were an RNAS Flight commanded by Sqn Cdr Frederick Bowhill comprising four 250hp Sunbeam Short Type 827 seaplanes and three Henry Farman F27s. Four BE2cs arrived on the 21st and were allotted to 'A' Flight.

By the beginning of March the new RNAS flight had joined the Tigris Column (three active seaplanes, others in reserve) and on the 6th, GHQ Force 'D' reorganized the column's air support. 30 Squadron 'A' flight with BE2cs also joined followed by 'B' flight's BE2cs at the end of the month. Also this month gun spotting work was developed, under the overall command of Cdr Robert Gordon. With a now desperate need for aircraft reinforcements, 13 BE2s had been shipped to Mesopotamia (Arrived 20 March) in a belated effort to support the beleaguered Army, but these would arrive too late.

Adding to the perilous aircraft situation, on 5 March, the Turkish machine-gunners succeeded in shooting down a Voisin V1541 near Es Sinn, with recent arrivals, pilot Lt Roland Peck and observer Capt Walter Palmer both killed.

Short Type 827 Seaplane 8046 being prepared for service at the RNAS main base, Basra, April/May 1916.

Disaster at Kut

No escape for man or beast: burning dead horses during the siege. Towards the end, surviving horses were slaughtered for food.

By now, the weather was also turning, becoming very hot during the day and the high sun glare and dust adding to the misery. To top it all, the mosquitoes and flies became unbearable and appeared in plague proportions, maddening horses and men alike. After Younghusband's first attempt to break through in January, another was set for 7 March. The Battle of the Dujaila Redoubt was likewise a failure, the British losing over 4,000 men. Aylmer was subsequently replaced by Gorringe as Commander of the Tigris Corps, now newly promoted Lieutenant-General.

Attempts to relieve Kut were becoming desperate, and on 15 April the RFC (from their base at Camp Wadi) were ordered to start dropping food, medical supplies, money (£10,000 in gold, silver and notes) and spare parts for the garrison wireless. Also on one occasion, a 70lb millstone was dropped to grind corn, parachutes being made from old aeroplane fabric and shipped up river from the Basra AP.

Flies – most numerous of the 'minor horrors of war' at Kut.

Capt E.M. Murray, designer of supply-drop equipment.

After several experiments Capt E.M. Murray was able to build a food dropping attachment for the aircraft which consisted of a long bar fitted to a bomb frame from which the bomb guides and fittings had been removed. The bar was pivoted at one end while at the other end a quick-relase mechanism enabled a BE2c to drop two 25lb bags while a further two 50lb bags (one on each wing) could be released by the pilot via a simple slip knot. Each bag was made up of a tight inner and loose outer, which absorbed the impact well. All drops were made from about seven thousand feet, but

Left: One of the BE2cs which carried food supplies, showing bags carried on the wing and under the fuselage.

Below: FSL W.H. Dunn at the controls of Voisin 8506, in which he made seven supply flights.

Although there had been an exchange of sick and wounded at the beginning of the siege, demands on the medical service continued to grow. Above: Capt King carrying out an operation.

Right: BE2c 4323 of 30 Sqn fully loaded with food bags is wheeled out for a supply mission to Kut.

Below: Some of the patients in one of the makeshift hospital wards at Kut.

the BE2cs proved difficult to handle, the Voisins being much better suited and carrying the most food (150lb per trip). The Henry Farman could carry 200lb without an observer. The distance from the landing ground at Ora to Kut was 23.5 miles. It was not just the Kut garrison that was suffering: everyone in 30 Squadron was showing the signs of short rations and fever and dysentery were common.

Evacuating the hospital at Kut before the siege; and trenches at Kut, from the album of FSL C.B. Gasson.

On the first day of food drops, 15 April, 3,350lb of stores were dropped, below the stated daily requirement the garrison had requested, but considering the machines and pilots available a creditable result. The aircraft and RNAS pilots who flew many of the missions were as follows:

FSL W.H. Dunn	(Voisin 8506)	7 flights	850lb
FSL J.D. Hume	(HF 1540)	10 flights	2000lb
FltLt W.H. Elliott	(Short 8047)	3 flights	540lb
FSL H. de V. Leigh	(Short 8043)	3 flights	700lb
FSL L.E.R. Murray	(Short 8046)	6 flights	840lb
FSL C.B. Gasson	(Short 8044)	8 flights	1580lb

Detail of supply dropping gear fitted to a Short Type 827.

Above: Lt J.R. McCrindle (30 Squadron) in BE2c 4362, in which he flew 16 missions, showing a food bag carried on the wing.

Below: FSL Gasson taxies Short 827, 8044, up to the slipway at Basra. It has been fitted with release gear for supply dropping.

Combined operations. Short Seaplane 8043, usually flown by FSL H.deV. Leigh, on the Tigris at Ora, preparing for a supply flight to Kut, with support from two of the Royal Navy's river monitors.

Also, 500lb were dropped by RFC machines flown by RNAS pilots who completed 47 food dropping flights. On 26 April two aircraft were shot down. First, Short 184 seaplane (No 8044) flown by 2Lt Cecil Gasson and 2Lt Archibald Cecil Thouless who was killed. The other was a BE2c (probably IFC11) flown by Lt Donald Davidson, who was severely wounded, but escaped. His unarmed aircraft was delivering supplies and had 32 bullet holes plus the right aileron shot away. Although over 19,000lb of supplies were dropped in 61 sorties, it was to be to no avail.

Two days before the RFC casualties – on 24 April – the river steamer the SS *Julnar* loaded with 270 tons of food, and a volunteer crew commanded by Lt Humphrey Osbaldston Brooke Firman VC, RN tried to break the Turkish blockade. Steaming 25 miles up the Tigris, under cover of darkness, the steamer was halted eight and a half miles downstream of Kut, by steel hawsers stretched across the river. Under heavy fire, most of the crew were killed, wounded or captured and Firman was posthumously awarded the Victoria Cross. He has no known grave. (Basra Memorial, panels 1 & 60.)

On 27 April 1916, one last desperate act took place that would remain in the secret files of the British and India Office for years. Under a flag of truce, Maj-Gen Townshend, accompanied by T.E. Lawrence and Aubrey Herbert of the Arab Bureau in Cairo, sailed upstream to negotiate with Khalil, the Turkish Army commander. Their proposal was that instead of unconditional

Short 8044 was brought down on 26 April 1916. The pilot FSL Gasson, was injured and taken prisoner, but his observer, 2Lt Thouless, was killed.

River monitor HMS Stonefly *supporting the Short seaplanes in April 1916 during the operation to drop supplies.*

The SS Julnar, *and her commander, Lt H.O.B. Firman VC, RN.*

Buildings on the bank of the Tigris used as General Townshend's Headquarters during the extended siege.

Left: *Representing the mixed crews who flew the supply dropping missions: FSL W.H. Dunn RNAS (left) and Lt T.M. Dickinson 16th Cavalry, Indian Army/RFC.*

THE FORTUNES OF WAR

Above right: *Some of the sick and injured caught up in the siege of Kut found themselves very much more fortunate than most, when they were included in an exchange of prisoners which took place on 29 April 1916.*
The postcard, from the album of C.B. Gasson, of the hospital ship Sikkim, *was sent to Mrs Gasson in London, and reflects the empire-wide effort that was made to provide transport for Mesopotamia. The message on the back reads in part 'This is the p.c. sent to me by Lady Pentland. It is the boat Cecil came down on after being exchanged...'*

Below: *A group of officers on board the hospital ship. FSL Gasson is fourth from the left in the front row. The others are unidentified.*

Below: *C.B. Gasson recovering at home with his brother in Upper Norwood.*

A long hard march into captivity awaited the survivors of Kut, but Gen Townshend, seated centre right with Turkish commander Khalil Pasha on his left, fared rather better.

surrender as demanded, they would offer the Turks two million pounds for the parole of the army, plus guns and ammunition. Enver Pasha rejected the offer suggesting instead that Townshend alone would be paroled to India for a payment of one million pounds plus the guns and stores held in Kut. It was an offer rejected by the British and doomed the troops to incarceration.

Despite attempts by Gorringe and Aylmer to mount a land rescue, finally they failed due to Turkish entrenchments, lack of river transport and the floods. On 29 April 1916, and almost starving, the garrison surrendered after 146 days. Private John Brown an original Half-Flight member, later stated that only 12 of the original mechanics from the Half-Flight at Kut escaped to Basra to be absorbed into 30 Squadron.[32] Despite its apparent failure, this air re-supply was notable, however, as it was the first time in history that aircraft had been used to carry and drop supplies of any significance.

Townshend's Force 'D' had been decimated through disease, heat and starvation, but this was to be only the start of their suffering. A forced march into captivity from Kut to Anatolia, a distance of over 700 miles, meant many perished on the journey and in scenes to be repeated in Burma-Thailand in the next war, the survivors were forced to work on the railway in the Taurus mountains. Left behind were the 30 Squadron pilots and observers plus the other ranks as already noted. The NCOs and men included nine Australians. Of those nine, only two survived. Cpl Jim Sloss and AM Keith Hudson, because of their skills as mechanics, were put to work servicing German staff cars. Despite their deliberate 'go-slow' the work under German supervision probably saved their lives. British RFC losses were likewise significant.

A memorial plaque to those who suffered at Kut now lies in the crypt under St Paul's Cathedral. It reads:

KUT-EL-AMARA
5th December 1915 to 29th April 1916
TO THE MEMORY OF
5746 OF THE GARRISON
WHO DIED IN THE SIEGE
OR AFTERWARDS IN CAPTIVITY

British officers made POWs by the Turks. The only man identified in this group is Capt R.D. de la Cour Corbett, an observer with 30 Squadron, sitting on the ground fifth from the left.

The End of the Australian Half Flight

A group of unidentified Australian Half-Flight personnel with a Maurice Farman.

The disaster at Kut was also to be the end of the Australian Flying Corps' contribution to the air war over Mesopotamia, although Australians later served with the RFC and ground forces that eventually repelled the Turks. On 23 May 1916, Capt Petre was invalided to India after a bad bout of enteritis, where he recovered, eventually to take command of 75 (Home Defence) Squadron RFC back in his English homeland. Awarded a Military Cross for his efforts in resupplying Kut, and after several RAF postings, upon discharge, he resettled in England as a solicitor, before passing away in April 1962.

As to the remainder of the Half-Flight, of the remaining 49, two were invalided prior to the fall of Kut, at least 22 went to Egypt to join 1 and 2 Squadrons AFC, and the remainder were dispersed to other units or returned to Australia later in 1916. Stress, poor food and extreme living conditions no doubt all contributed to the ill health of many of the survivors. In October 1916, the Half-Flight was officially disbanded.

As a postscript to the Half-Flight story, on 5 June 1915, the Australian authorities received a further call from the Viceroy of India for reinforcements. They subsequently commissioned a second Half-Flight of another four officers (commanded by Lt Richard Williams with Lts Alan Murray Jones, David Manwell and Vince Hall) and twenty mechanics, but in the end it was not required.

Apparently, the first reinforcements and 30 Squadron's arrival sufficed and so after doing some advanced flying training in preparation, the second Half-Flight was disbanded at the end of 1915, allowing Williams to go to Egypt to join 1 Squadron AFC in early 1916 and on to greater things.[33] Thus ended Australia's Mesopotamian Half Flight, but this was only the beginning of the Royal Flying Corps' push to take Mesopotamia.

After Kut, there was a lull on both sides and eventually, the British brought up reinforcements and prepared a new offensive beginning in November 1916. With newer aircraft types and the cooler conditions, they quickly regained control of the air, but it would be a long fight before Baghdad was captured and the victory won.

HALF-FLIGHT AND 30 SQN AIRFIELDS 1915-1916

Locations/ Fwd Landing Grounds	Dates
Bombay	18 May 15–21 May 15
Basra	26 May 15–1918
FLG Qurna (Chirish)	31 May 15–2 Jun15
FLG Abu Aran (Bahrein)	2–3 Jun 15
FLG Abu Rabah	3–9 Jun 15
FLG Abu Salabig	20-24 Jul 15
FLG Amara	5 Jun 15 - 23 Sep 15
FLG Asani (2 a/c)	14 Jul 15 - 30 Jul 15
FLG Ali-al-Gharbi (Sheikh Saad)	7 Sep 15 - 6 Oct 15
FLG Sannaiyat	23–30 Sep 15
FLG Kut-el-Amara	30 Sep 15–29 Apr 16
Aziziya ('B' Flight)	8 Oct 15 - 30 Nov 15
FLG Lajj (4 a/c)	20-24 Nov 15
FLG Ali-al-Gharbi	7 Dec 15–29 Apr 16
Musandeg	6 Jan 16–10 Jan 16
Sheikh Saad	10 Jan 16–16 Jan 16
FLG Ora	16 Jan 16–29 Apr 16
FLG Camp Wadi	1 Apr 16–6 May 16

Kut – the Aftermath

With the fall of Kut on 29 April 1916 came the dashing of British hopes for a swift and decisive victory in Mesopotamia. Coming so soon after the disastrous defeat that was Gallipoli, there were immediate calls in the British Parliament for tabling of papers and investigative commissions into what went wrong on both counts. On the Kut issue, Lord Kitchener, the British Minister for War was compelled to speak to the House amid uproar. In what can only be described at best positive spin and at worst blatant propaganda, he addressed the members on 4 May 1916 trying to defuse the 'mess pot' issue as it had become known:

Lt-Gen F. Aylmer, whose Tigris Corps failed to raise the siege of Kut.

Gen von der Goltz who left an effective military legacy to the Turks.

I am glad that the noble and gallant Lord has offered me this opportunity of paying tribute to General Townshend and his troops, whose dogged determination and splendid courage have earned for them so honourable a record.

It is well known how, after a series of brilliantly fought engagements, General Townshend decided to hold the strategically important position at Kut-el-Amara, and it will not be forgotten that his dispositions for the defences of that place were so excellent and so complete that the enemy, notwithstanding large numerical superiority, was wholly unable to penetrate his lines... General Townshend and his troops in their honourable captivity will have the satisfaction of knowing that, in the opinion of their comrades, which I think I may say this House and the country fully share, they did all that was humanly possible to resist to the last, and that their surrender reflects no discredit on themselves or on the record of the British and Indian armies.

Kitchener may have believed these words, but history was later to prove them shallow. Regardless of a certain level of military incompetence by those in command, particularly Townshend and Nixon, Army HQ at Simla in India had to shoulder some if not much of the blame. Poor or insufficient supplies, insufficient river transport, a total lack of adequate medical support, extremely poor rations, an overly bureaucratic administration and a complete ignorance of field conditions all contributed. Official Inquiries into both Kut and the Dardanelles were eventually set up, with Parliament and the Press out for blood – but the Mesopotamian Commission report took time. Tabled over a year later on 17 May 1917, as well as failing to identify the 'culprits', the war had moved on, but not before a thorough overhaul of the Indian Army organisation had taken place and command returned to the War Office in London.

Unfortunately, worse was still to come for the British and Indian troops who went into captivity. Their treatment was nothing short of appalling. While Townshend was feted in Constantinople, of the 11,800 men who left Kut-al-Amara with their captors on 6 May 1916, 4,250 died either on their way to Anatolia or in the camps that awaited them at the journey's end.[34] Theirs, however, is another story.

Meanwhile, General Nixon had resigned and been replaced by another aged general, Lt-Gen Sir Percy Lake, and he and Gen Gorringe were left to take stock. As well as Townshend's 6th Division being now gone, the air service also was virtually non-existent. The remnants of the Australian Half-Flight had already merged with elements of 30 Squadron. They had effectively lost a complete flight of aircraft, pilots and airmen and were badly in need of rebuilding. Operations would now pause while both sides regrouped and waited out the terrible heat of the summer.

There was trouble too for the German High Command. The elderly but respected General Freiherr Kolmar von der Goltz[35] appointed by Enver Pasha in 1915 to lead the Turkish forces, died of typhus in Baghdad on 19 April 1916, aged 72. He was to be replaced by Halil Pasha whom we shall meet later, but not before Goltz had set the Turks on a winning streak.

The strategic situation was now thus. From an allied perspective, Mesopotamia was always seen a valueless side-show once the oil supply in the south had been secured, so this theatre would not draw much needed modern equipment and troops from others, let alone the Western Front. The expected German push into the oil-rich Middle-East had not eventuated, but national pride, revenge for Kut and possible post-war division of land spoils meant the British could not withdraw. The Turks and their German backers had to be defeated. And then there were the Russians. So new commander, General Sir Percy Lake,[36] took the lull to reorganise and better equip his men. He reduced the role of the Tigris Corps to one of protection of the Ahwaz-Amara-Nasiriya corridor, built up flood banks around Basra and conducted an administrative reorganisation. Most pressing was the need for river transport, hospitals and better rations for the troops.

From the Turko-German side, things looked quite different. The Turks were keen to maintain their empire and saw their German allies as able to counter the British, especially in Egypt and on Turkey's northern approaches. The Germans were not only keen on capturing the oil, but longed for the possibility of making a push towards Britain's greatest prize – India. Control of the Egypt-Palestine cross roads (the Suez Canal) and Mesopotamia (entry to both Persia and the sub-Continent) would ensure a collapse of British power in the East.

RFC Flying Services Rebuild

A BE2c of 30 Squadron, at Sheikh Saad in August 1916, armed with two 112lb bombs and a rearward-firing Lewis gun.

What of the Flying Corps during this interregnum? By 1 May 1916, 30 Squadron RFC could muster six BE2cs (with three pilots) and three Maurice Farmans, and by the 6th, the three flights had moved to Sheikh Saad Aerodrome. Meanwhile, eleven Australians were at Amara and three attached to 30 Squadron at the Sheik Saad aerodrome.[37] The three (Sgts Jack Stubbs, Chief Mechanic Bill Wheeler and Sgt Sid Player) would eventually transfer to 1 Squadron AFC (67 Squadron RFC) in Egypt in late December 1916 while others would return home or transfer to the Western Front. For the Half-Flight contingent, their role in Mesopotamia was effectively over and so too any Australian airman presence.

As part of the initial reorganisation of the air services, the RNAS seaplane detachment now under Cdr Frederick Bowhill, were ordered back to Egypt[38] due to their limited utility in the Mesopotamia theatre, and departed on 20 June. In their place, 14 Kite Balloon Section RNAS under the command of Cdr Francis Wrottesley, RN arrived with four balloons for artillery spotting duties.

Above: 14 KB Section RNAS at Arab Village near Sheikh Saad, 1916.
Left: RFC and RNAS aircraft at Sheikh Saad.
Below: The German wireless sation at Baghdad aerodrome, which became the main RFC/RAF Aircraft Park in April 1918.

Turks Maintain Air Superiority

At the same time, the Turkish 2nd Squadron (*2nci Tayyare Bölük*, also called *Fliegerabteilung* 2) was gaining in strength. Still based at Shumran Bend, more aircraft arrived and although not an impressive air force,[39] nonetheless it kept the British at bay for most of 1916. The CO, *Hauptmann* Franz von Aulock[40] now had four crews and a small group of mechanics at his disposal. He had established an aircraft park in Baghdad (*Flugpark 6*) and was conscious of preserving his valuable air assets.[41]

His airmen, few though they were, held and maintained air superiority which hindered the British from conducting their much needed reconnaissance of the Turkish lines and the approaches to Baghdad, which in turn made planning for a further offensive extremely difficult.

Around this time, the Germans selected Mosul as the site for a new aircraft park (*Flugzeugetappenpark*) and placed *Hptm* Artur Faller in command. He would oversee site construction and coordinate supplies and aircraft repairs. Aircraft would be flown directly from the Baghdad rail head, the Germans having chosen to abandon shipment via the unpredictable Euphrates River system.[42]

But the heat, sand and primitive conditions that had so affected the Australian and British airmen in 1915 also hit the German flying service too. At any one time, the most von Aulock could muster was four aircraft, one of which was the Fokker E.1 flown by *Hptm* Hans Schüz who became the only German ace in the theatre and the nemesis of 30 Squadron. During this hiatus of the land campaign, Schüz, who had already claimed two seaplanes and a BE2c during the siege of Kut, would claim a further five before the war's end. He ended as a ten victory ace only to be lost in a flight from Africa to Sicily in 1941.

After the Kut success, the Turkish army in Mesopotamia had been weakened by the withdrawal of the XIII Corps to bolster forces against the emerging Russian push into Persia towards Kermanshah.

The Turks could not afford to let the Russians join up with the British, so they depleted their Mesopotamia-based troops and were reliant upon air reconnaissance to ensure the British did not counter-attack. Control of the air became essential and was keenly contested. A record of successful air combats during the remainder of 1916 exists and is telling as there were so few, with most engagements being little more than a draw:

7 May 16 – BE2c 4558 shot up by Schüz and forced to land. Capts Eric Murray and John Thomson-Glover uninjured. Schüz also claims a second BE2c, but it was forced to land through engine failure.

13 Aug 16 – BE2c 4141 shot up, again by Schüz and damaged - forced to land. Lt (the Hon) James Rodney wounded. Schüz was also forced down by another BE2c 2690. See later commentary.

23 Sep 16 – Voisin shot up and damaged. Capts Justin Howard Herring and Lawrence King-Harman OK.

The weather claimed as many of the RFC as the enemy. On 2 May, a violent storm wrecked F.27 Farmans 5909, 7308 and 7346 at the advanced landing ground at Ora while the machines were pegged out in the open. Despite the best efforts of nine men trying to hold one of the Farmans down, it finally broke free, took off, and smashed into the other two machines.

Three Maurice Farmans of 'C' Flight, 30 Squadron, serials 5909, 7436 and 7308, were wrecked by high winds and a dust storm on 2 May 1916.

The remains of the damaged Farmans are loaded aboard an RFC barge and its parent steamer T3 at Camp Wadi on the Tigris, on 5 May 1916, These machines had only arrived in Mesopotamia in April, but were now on their way back to Basra for repair.

'C' Flight took the wrecks with them when they departed to Basra to re-fit. The heat also took its toll. Capt Murray wrote despairingly in the Unit History:

From eight pilots in April, the Squadron flights in the field suddenly dwindled to two pilots and finally to one pilot each. All the others went into hospital more or less 'knocked up' directly after the strain due to the feeding of Kut was over. The hot weather came on apace and there were many admissions to hospital among the rank and file.

Other aircraft had propellers split in the heat and wings warp. It was a constant struggle for the mechanics to keep the engines serviceable. But most sapping of morale was Mother Nature herself. With the summer came the swarms of flies, searing heat and disease – fever and dysentery the worst. It was not unusual to get temperatures above 45°C daily, dropping only to 30°C at night. The advance on Baghdad would now have to wait until early 1917. Of the conditions, the newly arrived Commander of 30 Squadron, Major John

Left: Maj J. E. Tennant became CO of 30 Squadron in 1916 and remained in command until promoted to to take charge of 31 Wing early in 1917.

Right: Capt H. de Havilland and Lt C.J. Chabot have evidently tried to escape the extreme heat at Sheikh Saad by swimming in the rather unappealing waters of the Tigris.

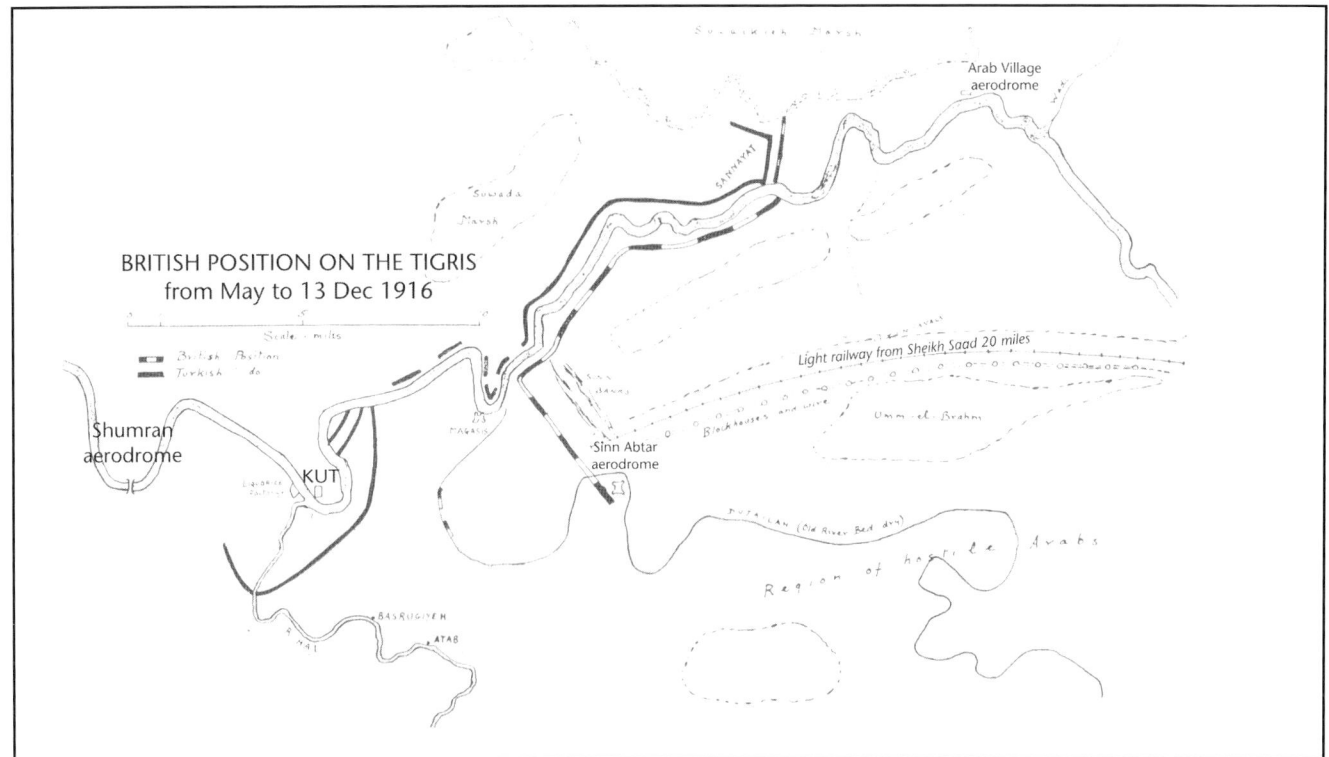

Edward Tennant, was later to write:

The heat during the whole journey up-stream [towards Sheikh Saad] had been terrific; the two boatmen who had started with us were both down, one with dysentery, the other with heat stroke. One's apparel consisted of shorts, shirt sleeves and a 'topi' without shoes or stockings...

...The sand flies at Sheikh Saad defied description, and mosquito nets were of no avail, the net especially designed against these pests entailing a mesh so small as to make ventilation impossible.[43]

Tennant had arrived in Basra on 31 July 1916 as part of the reorganisation of the RFC. He assumed command of 30 Squadron on 7 August from Capt Eric Murray. On 11 January 1917, Tennant was promoted to Wing Commander with the temporary rank of Lieutenant Colonel, subsequently taking command of the newly formed 31st Wing from 1 February. As a result, the post of Assistant Director Aviation, Indian Army, was abolished, a post that had been held by Lt Col Norman Duckworth Kerr MacEwen[32] from 16 August 1916 following the departure of Lt Col William Broke-Smith to India on the same date.

Also during the high summer lull the Fokker's engine failed during a dogfight on 13 August and it was lost in the subsequent forced landing. After driving down Lt Rodney in BE2c 4141, Schüz put the Fokker down in no-man's land and while he made it safely back to his own lines, the fighter was shelled by British artillery and destroyed. Schüz was claimed by Lt Tom Lander and 2Lt Eric Barr in BE2c 2690 after a 20 minute struggle. It was the first enemy aircraft claim lodged by the British in the theatre.

The next evening, Major Tennant with Capts Hereward de Havilland and Justin Herring each flying a BE2c without observer, bombed the German aerodrome at Shumran Bend in a daring moonlit raid. Despite heavy ground fire, all returned safely. Captain de Havilland's nonchalant post-flight report completes the story.

Above: Sketch map based on one published by Lt Col Tennant, showing the position of the Turkish aerodrome at Shumran Bend, the British aerodromes at Arab Village and Sinn Abtar, and also the British and Turkish lines, including the strong position of Sannayat, which thwarted the relief of Kut and delayed Gen Maude's later advance.

Capt de Havilland's BE2c, 2702, converted to a single-seat scout. Its front cockpit has been covered, the sides of the pilot's cockpit raised, and a second Lewis gun installed. It was nicknamed 'Ooo-er'.

BE2c 4322 was on the strength of 30 Squadron from April to September 1916. The crew are showing off its heavy armament and message-dropping release lever.

Left the ground at 11.10 pm and keeping to the south and in sight of the river, approached Shumran at a height of 6000 feet. Started coming down when about three miles to the south of the pontoon bridge and arrived at the hangar on the aerodrome at a height of about eighty feet. Eight bombs bracketed about the hangar, damage uncertain. Some rifle shots were fired from the left bank of the river... Returned and landed at Sheikh Saad at 1.30 am.

De Havilland was known as Mk2 being the younger brother of the well-known Geoffrey. He had arrived at 30 Squadron on 1 August 1916 and soon gained a reputation for being fearless and flamboyant – flying his reportedly, personalised, vermillion painted BE2c 2702 nick-named *Ooo-er* by his colleagues.

Fortunately for the German airmen, it was also during August that their much-needed replacements arrived: four new Albatros C.1s and a more potent Fokker E.III fighter.[44] Together with the aircraft arrived an observer, *Hptm* Wilhelm Niemeyer who took command of the squadron. Meanwhile, *Hptm* Franz von Aulock was appointed chief of Turkish 6th Army air operations and commander of *Flugpark* 6 in Baghdad.

The RFC had been rebuilding as well. At the end of June they could boast 17 BE2cs, seven Shorthorns and three Voisins (which had been left by the departing RNAS). But most importantly, a steady trickle of flying officers and observers began to arrive with 77 mechanics and riggers to replace those lost at Kut and those suffering illness. Given the sporadic contact with the enemy both on the ground as well as in the air, the majority of the flying was reconnaissance, photography and artillery observation. Most valuable was the production of accurate maps, which hitherto were virtually non-existent and these would be crucial for the coming advance on Baghdad. At the end of August, a further change of senior Army command had taken place with Lt-Gen Sir Percy Lake handing over command of the Mesopotamian Expeditionary Force to Lt-Gen Sir Stanley Maude[45] on the 28th. Maude, like his German Army predecessor von der Goltz, would not survive the campaign, dying of cholera in November 1917.

Gen Sir Percy Lake.   *Gen Sir Stanley Maude.*

During September 1916, the RFC carried out daily reconnaissance flights, 51 in total, the longest being over a distance of 95 miles. More than 400 photos were taken and eight bombing raids carried out, six of which were aimed at the enemy aerodrome at Shumran Bend onto which eight 20lb, two 100lb and four 112lb bombs fell. During one raid on 23 September, the Hon Lt J.H.B. Rodney descended to 100ft to drop his bombs and Lt John Stephen Windsor descended to less than that to drop two 20lb bombs within 10 yards of an Albatros machine. It was also during September that 30 Squadron received the first of eight Martinsyde G100 Elephants, some of which were still flying into late 1918.

BE2cs and Martinsyde Elephants on the advanced aerodrome at Sheikh Saad in 1916.

Preparing to Advance

BE2c 2702 of 30 Squadron about to leave Sheikh Saad for the new landing ground at Arab Village on 29 October 1916. The hut on wheels was used as a mobile workshop.

In October, the Squadron moved up to Arab Village where flying began in earnest, 258 hours being logged. Seven bombing raids were carried out including one night raid on the enemy aerodrome at Shumran. Reconnaissance flights produced 344 photos essential for the compiling of accurate maps of which there were virtually none.

On the 26th, the RFC lost Capts Sydney Hayward and Lawrence Hope King-Harman (O) killed when their Voisin 8523 crashed just after take-off, cause unknown. While flying operations had been rekindled by fresh crews and newer aircraft on both sides, it was the RFC who won the initiative in the final months of 1916. An advanced aircraft park had also been established at Amara which consisted of two engineering officers, 12 other ranks and a 100ft barge fitted out with six months supplies of squadron spares to supply the expanding RFC unit.

Meanwhile, General Maude used the run-up to Christmas 1916 as a preparatory phase (something none of his predecessors had done) for his coming land operations. In his dispatch to the War Office dated 10 July 1916, Maude had explained his plan:

> It was of paramount importance, in view of the approach of the rainy season, that no undue delay should take place in regard to the resumption of active operations, but before these could be undertaken with reasonable prospect of success it was necessary:
> (a) To improve the health and training of the troops, who had suffered severely from the intense heat during the summer months.
> (b) To perfect our somewhat precarious lines of communications.
> (c) To develop our resources.
> (d) To amass reserves of supplies, ammunition and stores at the front.
> It was therefore considered desirable to retain General Headquarters at Basra till the end of October, in order to systematise, coordinate and expand (b) and (c), whilst (a) and (d) continued concurrently and subsequently.

As the days of 1916 came to a close and the weather cooled, the RFC crews became more daring with bombing raids carried out on a more regular basis. Combats in the air remained indecisive. By now, Maude was intent on consolidating his position on the Hai (river salient near Kut) from 13 December 1916 to 4 January 1917 to allow him to position for an advance on Baghdad towards the end of February. Lines of communication back to Basra had been strengthened and adequate supplies brought up. Maude now had suitable numbers of ground troops and the RFC had regained control of the air.

BE2c 4487 at Sheikh Saad. The crumpled mass in front of the aircraft is the remains of Voisin 8523 which crashed on 26 October 1916, killing the crew.

Given the preparations for an advance, 30 Squadron were tasked from October to carry out reconnaissance to ascertain if there were any hostile reinforcements within 30 miles of Kut and to prevent the enemy from carrying out its own observations. In addition, regular updates of friendly force movements were also required.

In November 290 hours flying time was logged, including five more raids on the Shumran aerodrome. Three 112lb, five 100lb two 65lb and 175 20lb bombs being dropped. On one such raid, Capt de Havilland scored a direct hit on an Albatros with a 20lb bomb. A Williamson Aero Camera also arrived at the end of November, the squadron producing 807 photos, compared with the previous monthly total of 340.

In December there was a daring night attack on the 15th/16th during which Capt J.H. Herring proceeded to bomb a Turkish pontoon bridge strung across the Tigris River. Twice he returned to base to re-arm until he had completed his task while under heavy fire. The pontoons eventually slipped their moorings and the barges drifted onto the river bank preventing the Turks from moving troops and supplies across the river. For this action, he was later awarded the DSO. Further air combat success was recorded on the 20th when Lt Gerald Merton and Lt

William Allen Forsyth in BE2c 4423 attacked an Albatros C.III serial AK.11, sending it earthwards. The observer, *Leutnant* Back was killed and pilot *Vizfeldwebel* Max Konrad wounded.[46]

The Christmas period was quiet for both sides, but it was the lull before the British storm. And a storm of another kind also appeared. The winter rains set in and the Tigris River rose over eight feet in two weeks, bringing with it flooding of the surrounding areas.

General Maude's push towards Baghdad was slowed between 25 January and 5 February 1917 when he encountered stiff Turkish resistance by about 3,500 troops at the Hai salient. Bitter hand-to-hand fighting ensued before the Turks retreated. By the 9th, at the battle of Dahra Bend, the Turks began to surrender. The stage was now set for a reversal of fortune for the British with the capture of Baghdad in March 1917 and afterwards the push to Mosul and lands to the north.

Left: A BE2c of 30 Squadron at Arab Villlage, December 1916, being prepared for a raid like that carried out by Capt Herring. It has two 112lb bombs and a rearward-firing Lewis gun.

Below: In the mainly very flat and mirage-prone areas near the Tigris, only aerial photography could offer the kind of revelation of complex trench systems seen here.

30 SQN LOCATIONS APRIL 1916 – MARCH 1917

Date	HQ	A Flight	B Flight	C Flight
29 Apr 16	Camp Wadi	Camp Wadi	Camp Wadi	Basra
30 May 16	Sheikh Saad	Sheikh Saad	Sheikh Saad	Sheikh Saad
1 Oct 16	Arab Village	Arab Village	Arab Village	Arab Village
3 Mar 17	Aziziya	Aziziya	Aziziya	Sinn Abtar
5 Mar 17	Zeur	Zeur	Zeur	Zeur
8 Mar 17	Bustan	Bustan	Bustan	Bustan
11 Mar 17	Baghdad	Baghdad	Baghdad	Baghdad

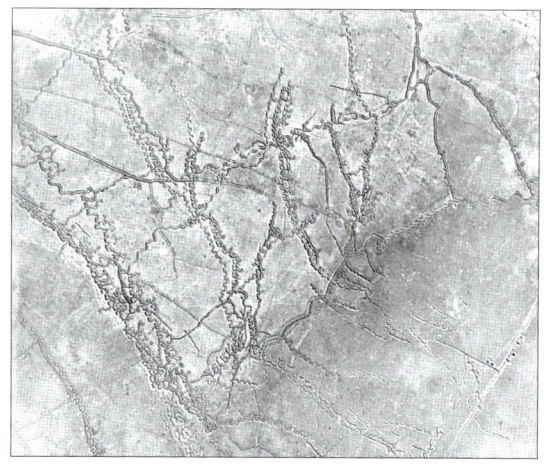

Transport and communications: RFC wireless and equipment barges on the Tigris alongside Arab Village aerodrome, summer 1916.

On To Baghdad

Air power and the army. Advancing British troops stir up the dust as they pass by the side of an airfield. Aircraft were sometimes able to land beside ground troops to pass on information on enemy movements or even give them accurate details of their own position in the generally featureless landscape.

The year 1917 would usher in new fortunes for the British in Mesopotamia, but the struggle in the air would continue right to war's end. For the Turkish Air Service, the year got off to a bad start with the death in action of the CO of *2nci Tayyare Bölük* (2nd Turkish Squadron)[47] *Hptm* Wilhelm Niemeyer, killed on 19 January while flying over Kut as observer in an Albatros with *Feldwebel* Max Konrad at the controls. A Turk, *Hptm* Schadul, replaced him in command.[48] During the period 4 to 10 January, 30 Squadron carried out successful artillery co-op work, seventy targets being registered including two direct hits on an enemy pontoon bridge

This official map Operations of Indian Expeditionary Force 'D' 1914-1917, *was issued in June 1917, complete with 11 small pages of chronology listing the still-unfolding events of the campaign from Brig-Gen Delamain's landing at Fao and capture of the fort in 1914 up to the defeat of Turkish forces on the Shatt-ul-'Adhaim (upper left of map) on 1 May 1917, about six weeks after the capture of Baghdad.*
This fragile and insignificant-looking document, measuring just a pocket-sized 4x6½in when folded, nevertheless speaks volumes for the levels of resourcing and support of Gen Maude's operations. Where Lt Col Tennant's sketch map (p51) indicates the territories of 'hostile Arabs', this map gives the names of different groups, whose allegiance to the Ottoman Turks/Germans, to the British, or indeed to neither side, would need to be generally known at this period.
The experiences of aviation personnel include encounters with local inhabitants of very different persuasions.

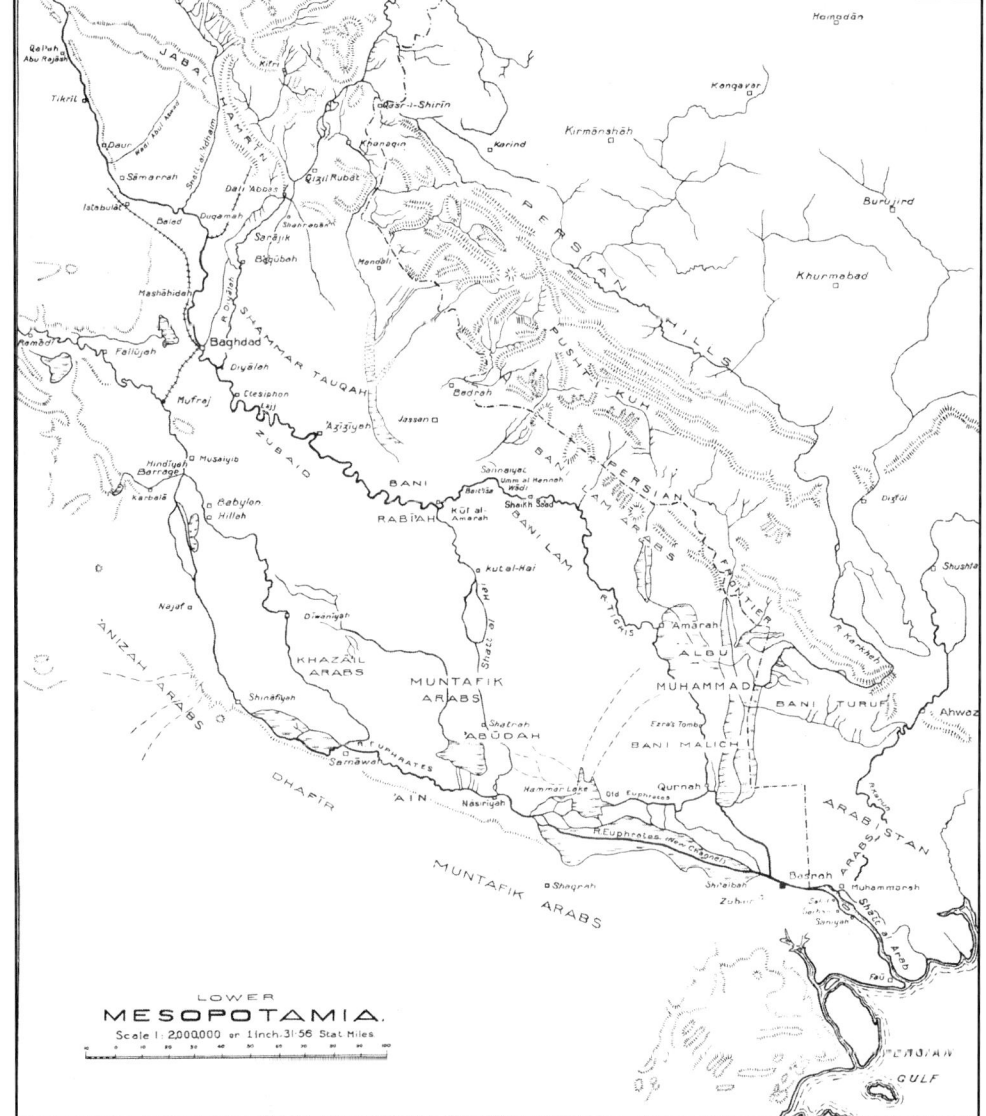

One of the BE2c machines that formed the bulk of the RFC force: 4302, – a presentation aircraft, 'The Maharajah of Rewa-Bandhava'.

from a range of 9,800 yards.

As the air war on the Mesopotamian Front was heating up, the planned RFC expansion took place on 20 January 1917, when 31st Wing was formed at Sinn as a Corps wing under the command of newly promoted Lt-Col John Tennant. Major Hereward de Havilland replaced him as CO of 30 Squadron. Tennant's book, *In the Clouds above Baghdad* records his experiences in both appointments.

By March 1917, the British field force commander, General Sir Stanley Maude, was ready for his assault on Baghdad. Success at the Hai Salient, Dahra Bend (during which four RFC machines had carried out highly successful artillery co-op work) and Shumran in the preceding two months had finally provided the British hope for a culminating win against the Turks. Most pleasing was the successful advance on Kut in February, the recapture of which in some small way avenged the loss of Townshend's garrison force of a year earlier. This advance had seen 30 Squadron (less 'C' Flight with the Euphrates detachment at Sinn Abtar) forced to advance a distance of 150 miles to Arab Village, all to be supplied by three light tenders and two fast motor boats on the Tigris.

Meanwhile, Baghdad was not only a symbol of Ottoman pride but a prized possession for the conqueror that had been seized from the Mongols by Suleiman the Magnificent and had been in Turkish hands ever since. Now it would be the British Empire's turn to be the occupiers.

By now, Maude had at his disposal two corps and five divisions – an impressive force of nearly 65,000 men – a force that comprised fresh British but mostly Indian Army troops. Maude's careful analysis of his situation and preparation of secure logistics support; transport, food supplies, and medical facilities, ensured there would be no repeat of the ill-fated adventures of Generals Nixon, Townshend and Gorringe. To counter this build up, the Turks could only muster their XIII Corps of two divisions – no more than 18,000 men.

At the end of February, the advance began in earnest. Within a week, Maude was past Ctesiphon which was found deserted, and after a long march through a dust storm, the British Army reached Bustan, about 120km south of Baghdad. Then, without a major engagement, he outflanked 11,000 Turkish troops entrenched south of Baghdad and directly threatened the town. With this situation unfolding, Halil Pasha withdrew his remaining army north of the city to concentrate at Samarra. Neither side was prepared for urban warfare, so Baghdad was there for the taking.

Maude's air component was the now reinforced 30 Squadron and 14 Kite Balloon Section, RNAS under Cdr Frank Wrottesley. The Squadron moved up from Arab Village in early March to advanced aerodromes at Al Aziziya, Zeur and Bustan. They concentrated on providing much needed reconnaissance of enemy locations and the prevention of the enemy from doing the same. In the haste to move up, two Martinsydes were wrecked on landing in strong winds at Zeur, but

Observers FSL G.F. Brown and Flt Lt M.C. Gill of 14 Kite Balloon Section RNAS about to make an ascent.

Gen Maude poses in front of a group of Turkish prisoners.

Indian Army troops at Baghdad railway staion after the capture of the city. This was the terminus of the still-unfinished Berlin-Baghdad railway. The name board offers one example of the various transcriptions from Arabic to English that can be found in maps and reports of the period.

this still left over a dozen BE2cs, three Farmans and a single Martinsyde Scout available for use.

As the British marched towards Baghdad, skirmishes in the air became more common. On 3 March, *Unteroffizer* Bop while escorting two Albatros observation planes flying the Turk's only Fokker E.III fighter F12, was shot down and killed. It was a huge setback for the Turks as they no longer could conduct reconnaissance over the British lines. From now on they required a fighter escort.

On 2 March a reconnaissance to Baghdad revealed the enemy preparing a position on the Diyala River. In order to try and prevent the evacuation of guns and stores to Samarra via the Baghdad railway, 2Lts John Stephen Windsor and Robert Kay Morris set out on the 7th with two officers from the Royal Engineers in an attempt to destroy the railway bridge at Sumaikcheh. Landing within 200 yards of the bridge, they discovered that it was built of reinforced concrete and the attempt was abandoned.

On 9 March, Major de Havilland tried once again to interrupt rail traffic, successfully hitting a railway station near Kazimain, scoring a direct hit with a 65lb bomb, which blew off the station roof and destroyed a train sitting underneath. It was the start of the Turkish rout. On the night of 10/11 March 1917, the Turks evacuated their positions on the right banks of the Tigris and the Diyala Rivers, and as dawn broke, the leading British troops entered the fabled city. A further 9,000 Turks were captured and although the Kurds and Arabs had looted what they could, Baghdad, now there for the taking, was otherwise intact.

When Maude entered the city, he uttered the now famous quote: 'Our armies do not come into your cities and lands as conquerors or enemies, but as liberators'. Baghdad was now British and would become the base from which to launch Maude's final campaign.

While the Turks moved up to Samarra to regroup, Maude spent the next four months of the sweltering Mesopotamian summer consolidating and reinforcing

The British airfield next to Baghdad railway station immediately became the base for air operations as ground forces continued to move north.

Capt J. Everidge of 63 Squadron noted the airfield dimensions as 650x216 yards on this photograph taken in the autumn of 1917.

Lt-Col J.E. Tennant (2nd left in front of Martinsyde Scout 7493) landed 24 miles east of Kasr-i-Shirin near the Pai Tak Pass in the Persian mountains to deliver dispatches to the Russian forces under Gen Baratoff on 2 April 1917.

his position. At the same time, 30 Squadron moved up to Baghdad where they found a quantity of aero engines (including six of their own captured at Kut) and five damaged machines[49] left by the Turks at Kazimain, north of the city. The official report of the capture of Baghdad later commented:

> The Royal Flying Corps maintained the closest co-operation with the 1st and 3rd Corps and despite the high wind (at times 40mph) carried out successful shoots with artillery, as well as reconnaissance work with the cavalry and reporting enemy positions on the Diyala and south-west of Baghdad.[50]

Meanwhile, *Hptm* Hans Schüz of *2nci Tayyare Bölük*, had earlier decided he needed to reinforce the Turkish air arm. He personally travelled to Germany to lobby for new machines, but meagre resupplies would not begin to arrive until early April. Eleven scouts, including three Halberstadt D.V single-seater fighters[51] would replace their losses, but on the day they arrived, 3 April, the old workhorse 'Baghdad No 1' an Albatros C.III, was forced down 35km behind the British lines. The crew, *Feldwebel* Max Dürre and *Leutnant* Unroch, removed the machine guns, and in an amazing feat of physical endurance, walked back to their own lines over the next three days!

Lt-Col John Tennant also was busy, this time on more strategic matters. On 2 April he was asked by Army commander General Maude to make contact with allied Russian forces under General Nicolas Baratoff whose Cossacks were moving into Persia from the east. This force had travelled from the Caucasus past the Caspian Sea and into Persia, a trek of over 1,000 miles. Flying Martinsyde 7493 he landed near Kasr-i-Shrin after three hours to be met by 'this wild looking group of Cossacks, clustered around me in their picturesque long coats and sheepskin hats cocked at a rakish angle'.[52] With neither side able to speak the other's language, Tennant handed over messages from GHQ and returned to report his find.

3 April would end up being a busy and eventful day. Schüz took off in Fokker E.III F13 and soon engaged BE2c 4585 flown by Lts Lancelot Harold Page and Arthur Rattray. In the melée, the two aircraft collided over Balad. Schüz returned over his lines with part of the BE2's wing attached and claimed a kill, but the BE landed safely at Kasirin despite the damage. Regardless of intercepted Turkish reports stating that the Fokker

A soldier of the Indian Army stands beside the wreck of an Albatros C.1 two-seater of the German/Turkish air service that was found on Baghdad aerodrome after the capture of the city on 11 March 1917. Someone from the victorious forces has added a patriotic inscription 'God save the King' to the fuselage.

BE2c 4585 of 30 Squadron, in which Lt L.StA.M. Page and Lt A.R. Rattray survived a mid-air collision with Hptm H. Schüz, who not surprisingly claimed a victory. The BE however returned safely, with some damage to the wingtips.

BE2c 4500/IFC11 first arrived at Basra on 13 September 1915. Having been flown out of Kut on 7 December 1915, it later took part in the food dropping missions during the siege, before going to the AP at Amara for repair. Flown back up-country on 13.4.17, with operations 17.4.17, 6.5.17, was still on 30 Squadron charge by 15.6.17.

had returned, it was later found to have crashed in the desert and been destroyed, although Schüz survived to fight again. That same day, the CO of the aircraft park, *Hptm* Franz von Aulock, took off in Halberstadt HK2 to fly to Samarra: however, his aircraft stalled after take-off and crashed, and von Aulock was killed. Schüz became the new CO.

On 5 April the first Bristol Scout D (7033) arrived at the Squadron and Major de Havilland flew from Baghdad to Basra and back to collect it, a distance of 750 miles, completed in eight and a quarter hours of actual flying time – a record for its day.

Schüz continued to lead from the front. Flying a new Halberstadt D.V single-seater fighter, on 15 April he shot down BE2c 4194, this time killing the crew of Capt Charles Pickering and 2Lt Hedley Craig. Testament to the chivalry of the day, Schüz personally conducted the funeral service which was attended by many Turkish and German dignitaries, and ensured the graves were marked by a propeller.

In retaliation, 2Lt Matthew 'Paddy' Maguire shot down *Vzfw* Max Konrad in Halberstadt HK6 on the 22nd. Flying a new Bristol Scout, Maguire spotted the Halberstadt over Istabulat, near Samarra, and shot it to pieces, the Halberstadt's port wings ripping off in the dive. Maguire was awarded the Military Cross for this action, his citation reading: *For conspicuous gallantry. With great courage and skill he attacked and completely destroyed an enemy aeroplane, which crashed to the ground from 4,000 feet.*[53]

But as fate would have it, Maguire, flying Bristol Scout 7034, would himself be shot down six days later. Again, Schüz was the victor. Badly wounded, Maguire was taken prisoner, but died in hospital a few days later. On 28 April, 2Lt Kenneth Buchanan Lloyd was also claimed by Schüz, his ninth and final victory in Mesopotamia. Lloyd survived the crash but left the Squadron for India soon afterwards.

In his later memoirs, Schüz recalled after the fall of Baghdad this contact with his British foes:

At that time a very singular exchange of letters was in progress, which relieved the monotony of desert warfare in a most welcome fashion. The limit was reached one day when the English airmen proposed that we should all land at some neutral spot to meet over a cup of tea, and exchange news papers [sic] and gramophone records. However, we were unable to see eye-to-eye with them on this conception of warfare.[54]

On the ground, the British had commenced a further offensive to secure the banks of the Tigris. Here Maude split his force into two – the right bank column being led by Maj-Gen Sir Vere Fane, with Lt-Gen Sir William Marshall taking the left. Consequently, a flight of 30 Squadron was attached to each flank. 'B' Flight was withdrawn from Baqubah and joined Fane's column

The carefully marked graves of both Capt C.L. Pickering (above) and his observer 2Lt W.H. Craig.

Vzfw Konrad lies beside the remains of his Halberstadt D.V of Flt Abt 2. His victor, 2Lt M.L. Maguire, was himself shot down six days later.

at Fort Kermea while 'C' Flight at Kasirin joined with Marshall. By now, the Squadron could boast 21 BE2c and BE2es, seven Martinsyde Scouts, and three Bristol Scouts.[55]

The British columns made steady progress although facing stiff opposition at times. By 23 April, Samarra had been captured with 30 Squadron elements providing much needed reconnaissance, artillery co-operation and airborne patrols. By early May, the Turkish XIII Corps had moved into the Jebel Hamrin hills on their way up to Tikrit where they dug in. Meanwhile *2nci Tayyare Bölük* also moved to Tikrit to reorganise and wait out the summer heat.

The last engagement of the spring occurred on 6 May when Lt Lionel Skinner flying BE2c 4191 and Lt Thomas Eaton Lander in Martinsyde 7466 were intercepted by a Halberstadt flown by *Feldwebel* Johannes Pommrich.[56] Lander was shot down and became a POW. While he survived the engagement, unfortunately Pommrich would die of typhoid in July, testament that disease was still a major cause of casualties to both sides.

Martinsyde G.100 7466 at Nasiriya in the spring of 1917. Lt T.E. Lander was wounded in combat and force-landed near Tikrit to become a POW on 6 May 1917.

The Martinsyde was later re-captured by British forces when Tikrit fell on 6 November 1917, the Turks evidently having at least tried to use it themselves.

Changes over the Summer

The hot desert summer effectively put paid to any further advances but it gave both sides the opportunity to take stock. The Turks were by no means finished: there would be 18 months of further fighting before the Mespot war came to a close.

After the loss of Baghdad and now with reinforcements, the Turks divided into three separate forces, thereby forming three fronts. On the Tigris was an army of three divisions of war-weary troops who had retreated up from Kut. On the Euphrates, a detachment of about 2,000 troops were near Ramadi. While on the Diyala River (Khanikin front), stood the XIII Turkish Army Corps of three divisions of fairly fresh troops. But the Turks lacked air power, and this they would need to rectify.

The fall of Baghdad shocked the Ottomans and in response, as well as sending army reinforcements, interim measures were put in place to bolster the air service. In May, a fresh shipment of Albatros C.IIIs was received at the Mosul *Flugpark* and the *13nci Tayyare Bölük* (No. 13 Turkish Sqn) was resurrected under the command of *Hptm* Max Prechter to be based at Kifri. Indeed, further air reinforcements were also forthcoming. The *11nci Topçu Tarrassut Tayyare*

Hptm Schüz, a German pilot with the Turkish Air Service, the leading ace in Mesopotamia, who claimed ten British aircraft. This Albatros D.III, which he flew later in the war, was fitted with double radiators and carried Turkish markings.

Bölük (11th Artillery Director Aircraft Company) under the command of *Hptm* Heidrich and comprising five Albatros C.IIIs left Istanbul on 17 June for the Iraq front, but upon arrival crews and aircraft were dispersed between the 2nd and 13th Squadrons, bringing both those units up to full strength.

Both to bring in reinforcements, and also to obtain information on the British advance, on 7 July, *Fw* Max Dürre and *Hptm* Hans Grone in AK.64, with *Flgr* Arnold Hopff and *Ltn* Walther Teich in AK.68, flew to Ramadi to form a new detachment. The engine of one Albatros overheated and seized and the crew were forced to land in the desert. When the other aircraft landed to assist, its engine also quit, and all four airmen attempted to walk out. Dürre and Grone were picked up by a British patrol three days later and became prisoners, but Hopff and Teich were never found. Presumably they had died of exposure.

At the close of summer, the Turkish squadrons soon began intensive reconnaissance flights to monitor the anticipated Russian advance to reinforce the British in the Suleymaniye area, an enclave well to the north-east. During one such flight on 11 August, *Fw* Nolle[57] piloting AK.54 with *Hptm* Prechter as observer, ground looped on landing and flipped killing Prechter. Nolle survived the impact but was badly wounded.

However under the new CO, *Hptm* von Plates, the Squadron continued its work unabated, resulting in the disruption of the Russians' attempt to link with their British allies.

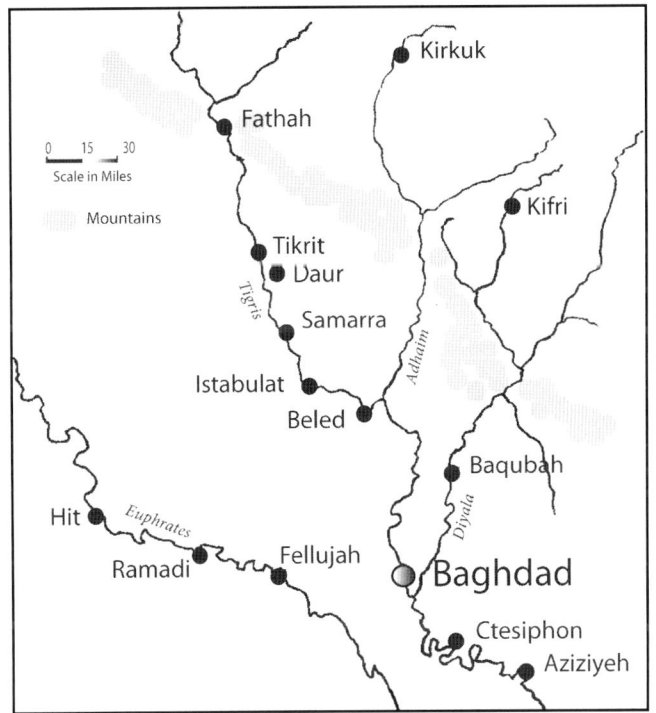

The area of operations north of Baghdad, including both the Euphrates and regions to the east.

30 SQUADRON LOCATIONS APRIL – JULY 1917

Date	HQ	A Flight	B Flight	C Flight
1 April 17	Baghdad	Baghdad	Baquba	Kasirin
7 April 17	Fort Kermea	Fort Kermea	Fort Kermea	Sindiya (Kuwar Reach)
20 April 17	Barurah	Barurah	Barurah	Barurah
4 May 17	Baghdad	Baghdad	Baghdad	Sindiya
26 June 17 (Till September)	Baghdad	Baghdad	Kahn Jadida	Baghdad

RFC Reinforcements Arrive

A line-up of RE8s and a single Spad S.VII of 'A' Flight, 63 Squadron at Samarra in the autumn of 1917.

For Maude, it was now obvious that RFC reinforcements were badly needed and sanction was given for a further squadron plus a kite balloon company, No. 23, to replace the now departed RNAS unit.

63 Squadron had been formed at Stirling Scotland on 31 August 1916 under the command of Major Arthur Courtney Boddam-Whetham. Towards the end of October, the unit was transferred to Cramlington near Newcastle-upon-Tyne and would remain there for nearly seven months, essentially as a training unit, but with many officers being warned for overseas service.

In late April 1917, Boddham-Whetham was posted, and Capt John Charles Quinnell took command from the 27th. Quinnell had transferred in from 83 Squadron where he had been CO. During his time at 83, Quinnell had worked with four highly experienced pilots: Capt James Everidge who had accumulated 199 hours flying time, first as an observer with 9 Squadron, and later as a Flight Commander instructor in the UK; and Capt Ronald Davidson Simpson had also served in 9 Squadron, first as an observer and then a pilot. On return to the UK a 3 Wing report noted: 'during his time in France as a pilot Simpson had become exceptionally efficient at artillery observation – an expert'. The other two ex-9 Squadron personnel were Lt Malcolm Glassford Begg who had been with the unit as an observer in February 1916 before pilot training, and Lt Arthur Styran.

But getting them was another matter. In a letter dated 30 April 1917 to OC 19th Wing, Quinnell requested all four personnel be transferred to 63 Squadron because: 'the pilots were all old observers and would be invaluable in training pilots in artillery observation'. There was a delay in a response from Wing HQ but on 19 May 1917, Quinnell sent a note to Everidge to '…come along as soon as you are ready. Herbert (the OC 19th Wing) has promised me that he will let me have you and Simpson as Flight Commanders so everything should be alright'. Ten days later Everidge received a second letter from Quinnell. 'I am afraid that I have some rotten news for you. Despite the efforts of Burdett (Major A. B. Burdett, formerly CO of 9 Squadron in March 1916), the OC of this wing has refused to make either of you flight commanders until you go overseas again. Under these circumstances I do not know if you will be pleased to come to me?'

A 13pdr AA gun guarding a kite balloon of 52 Section, 23 KB Company RFC on the Euphrates front.

When Quinnell wrote these letters, Capt Cedric Yeats McDonald had been appointed as a flight commander in 63 Squadron (from April 1917) and would sail with the Squadron as such, together with Capt John Philpott and Capt Frank Robinson as the other two flight commanders, both of whom had only been posted in to the squadron ten days previously. McDonald had seen previous service with 31 Squadron in India, but there was obviously some tension between him and Quinnell; either that or MacDonald's appointment had been forced upon him, because on 2 June 1917 Everidge arrived at 63 following Begg, Simpson and Styran in May. Everidge also noted in his log book his appointment as OC 'B' Flight from June 5th!

Despite persistent rumours that the squadron was bound for France to fly DH4s, a decision was made to allocate the unit to Mesopotamia almost at the eleventh hour. They embarked on 23 June 1917 on the SS *Dunvegan Castle* bound for the Persian Gulf with stop-overs at Cape Town and Durban, South Africa. At Cape Town, MacDonald left the ship, being posted back to home establishment, and Everidge became CO 'B' flight as noted! The squadron's aircraft went separately on the SS *Nizam*.

The squadron was lucky as it was equipped with more 'modern' aircraft in the form of the RE8 and the Spad VII, with the promise of less mechanical trouble in the hot weather. The RE8s had air cooled engines and their performance was much superior in the oppressive conditions. They disembarked at Basra on 13 August 1917, stepping into the blast furnace that was a Mesopotamian summer. After the cool climate of Northumberland, the personnel found the summer heat unbearable and many succumbed to heat stress and sand fly fever, even while still in transit. Temperatures of over 50°C decimated the officers and men alike, with three men dying and over 30 of all ranks being evacuated to hospital in India almost immediately upon arrival at the depot at Basra.[58]

63 Sqn was allotted to the 1st Indian Army Corps under the command of Lt-Gen Sir Alexander Cobbe VC who was holding the Tigris front. There was little time to acclimatise while Basra Air Park repaired the warped

Lucky to be alive. Capt James Everidge, OC 'B' Flight, 63 Squadron, on his first flight at Basra in BE2c 4421, crashed into palm trees after the engine failed at 40ft in the heat.

wings and split propellers damaged during the voyage, plus overcoming carburettor problems associated with the RE8's 140hp RAF engines. It was therefore 10 September before two RE8s, piloted by Capt Philpott and Lt Begg, flew the 400 miles to Baghdad. 63 Sqn's eventual location would be a landing ground at Samarra next to the railway station on the Berlin-Baghdad line. During October the squadron machines made their way northwards with one stop at Amarah, with only two or three mishaps along the way.

On 30 October the remaining four RE8s and a Spad VII left Basra. The Spad returned with engine trouble, while the RE8s attempted to land in a dust storm at Samarra, two being successful, the other two force-landing some miles away.

Before the squadron arrived at Samarra, 'A' flight, at the RFC's Baghdad airfield began reconnaissance work. The first flight against the enemy on 25 September ended in disaster with the pair of RE8s both coming down behind enemy lines. They were attacked by *Feldwebel* Reiners in a Halberstadt D.V HK.3 over Tikrit and although he claimed both, it transpired that one RE8 suffered engine failure and the other lost a section of its wing extension while so engaged. Philpott flying with observer Cpl Oliver Grant, and Begg with Lt Noel Baillon all became prisoners, but Philpott's loss was the most sadly felt.[59] Malcolm Begg left a diary in which he described the action:[60]

RE8 A4335 was flown by Capt J. Everidge of 63 Squadron at Samarra in September/October 1917. It was one of the first batch of 24 which arrived in Mesopotamia on 11 August and was eventually flown by both 63 and by 30 Squadron.

Tikrit. 9 a.m. Tuesday 25th September 1917.
Returning from a flight up the Tigris, we both spotted a Halberstadt at our own height over Tikrit. We went straight for him; me on the right, Phil on the left, and as he came across our bows we both opened fire. He dived away towards his aerodrome; we followed him down firing at intervals, but at 5,000 feet my extensions folded up and I came down fairly under control until within 100 feet of the ground, when I side slipped in attempting to turn avoiding a Turkish camp and crashed. Baillon was slightly bent but otherwise no personal damage. Turkish soldiers came up at once and took us away to the camp close by.

Meanwhile, Phil's engine practically failed and he came down about two miles away and tried to taxi on but as his engine gave out and the Turks were sniping in fairly large numbers, he had to give up.

…Although we were quite near the aerodrome, none of them [the Germans] came to see us, but we learnt that the Halberstadt pilot was on his first Halberstadt solo and had his engine done in.

'Ready to rise …' Balloon of 52 Section.

Also in September, 30 Squadron would be joined by 23 Kite Balloon Company RFC (51 & 52 Sections). The CO, Major Harold Jensen, had previously been CO of 17 KBS in October 1916.

Concentrating on photography, 30 Squadron, meanwhile, flew over 400 square miles of country on the Euphrates and Diyala River front around Turkish entrenchments at Ramadi, Daur and the Jebel Hamrin Hills. 'B' Flight had moved up to Fallujah to work with the 15th Division. This allowed the surveyors to produce new and accurate maps for the Army commanders in preparation for the next ground assault. After General Maude moved his forces up and between 27 and 29 September, Maj-Gen Sir Harry Brooking encircled the Turks at Ramadi. Unable to escape, the Turks were overwhelmed by Brooking's force and more than 3,000 surrendered, effectively clearing the Euphrates River of Turkish positions up to this northern point.

With October came the withdrawal from the war of the Russians after their September Revolution, so some pressure was relieved on the Turkish north-eastern front. As the cooler weather arrived, the land campaign

RE8 A4343 of 'A' Flight. 63 Squadron. It was normally flown by Capt E.D. Simpson and 2Lt H.W. Underhill.

Spad A8811 is being ignored by everyone in this scene. It arrived at Baghdad on 12 September 1917 and was sent first to 30 Squadron, then to 63. Lt J.H. Caldwell was killed in action when flying this aircraft on 12 January 1918.

Martinsyde Elephant 7494 at Basra AP. On 16 October 1917 Lt A.E.L. Skinner force landed this machine 20 miles inside enemy territory during a raid on the Turkish airfield at Kifri, and was rescued by Lt Welman as described below.

recommenced. This necessitated further reconnaissance and aerial photography work. Most of the action was on the Tigris front and 63 Sqn was in the thick of it. They lost RE8 A4336,[61] forced to land behind enemy lines on the 5th and a pair of Martinsydes on the 16th during a three-aircraft strike against the Turkish airfield at Kifri. The bombs hit two of the Unit's five Albatros C.IIIs, but all three Martinsydes were also hit by ground fire. Lt Lionel Skinner, with his fuel tank holed, was forced to land. On seeing Skinner's predicament, 2Lt John B. Welman landed alongside and picked him up, while Lt Frank Nuttall flying above machine-gunned hostile Arabs as they approached the downed airman.

General Maude now turned to the Diyala and Tigris front and after ground skirmishes between 18 and 20 October, the enemy was again driven back further into the Jebal Hamrin Hills. Again, the RFC provided vital air support and some sporadic bombing of the enemy. On 21 October, 63 Squadron's Major Quinnell was posted home, and Capt Frank Robinson took command. During the last days of October, aerial reconnaissance discovered a Turkish force advancing down the Tigris and a watch was placed on their movement. Such observation would not go unchallenged and both 30 and 63 Sqn recorded engagements. On 31 October, a repeat attempt was made to bomb the 13th Turkish Squadron at Kifri, this time involving six aircraft. That date would be remembered as eventful for the airmen on both sides.

First to be hit was Welman who was shot down in his Martinsyde G100. He was wounded and became a POW. BE2e 6804 was hit next and 2Lt Allen Adams was forced down. He burnt his aircraft and was picked up by Nuttall in a Martinsyde. They both returned to the Squadron lines. A third Martinsyde (A3940) was shot down by Archie and landed 18 miles inside the Turkish lines. The pilot, Lt Charles Cox, 30 Sqn, burnt the machine to prevent capture and eventually took nearly seven hours to walk out and make it back to the Squadron – a singularly remarkable feat.

It was during this period that a number of unfortunate accidents also occurred. On 22 October, BE2e A3088 (overseas presentation aircraft *The Seven Seas*) crashed on take-off while crewed by 2Lt Harold Gardner, who was injured, and his observer Lt Alex Leeson, who was burned to death when the petrol tank caught fire, spilling its contents over Leeson. Meanwhile,

63 Squadron had begun to receive more Spad VIIs.

On 30 October 2Lt Ninian Hyslop, from Hawkes Bay New Zealand, left Basra en-route to Baghdad flying Spad A8809. He crashed in thick mist at Qurna 70 miles up-river and was killed. Hyslop had, according to the Court of Inquiry, 'inadvertently closed the throttle instead of opening it as the Hispano throttle works in reverse action to most machines'.[62]

Meanwhile the British ground troops were pressing steadily forward. By the end of October the Turks had been forced back to Daur, and by early November they were at Tikrit. In order to avoid an encirclement as had happened on the Euphrates front, the Turkish XVIII Corps withdrew further up the Tigris Valley to Fathah. For the first time since the start of the war, the two Ottoman Army Corps (XIII and XVIII) were joined on a single front. The 2nd Squadron moved up to Humr under *Hptm* Gebhard while the 13th remained at Kifri under *Hptm* von Plates. By autumn 1917, Turkish plans to send the *Yildirim Ordu* (Lightning Army) consisting of the 7th and 8th Armies had to be abandoned as they were needed in Palestine. Only the 50th Division was sent down the Euphrates to bolster the Mesopotamian front. As well as this force of about 8,000 men came a detachment of three Rumpler C.Is which had been withdrawn from Palestine – most likely ex-*Fliegerabteilung 300 Pasha* aircraft of early 1916 vintage.

Two pilots of 30 Squadron. 2Lt Charles Cox (left) and Lt Arthur William Hawkins.

Two New Zealanders with 63 Squadron: Lt G.L. Steadman (left) and 2Lt N.S. Hyslop.

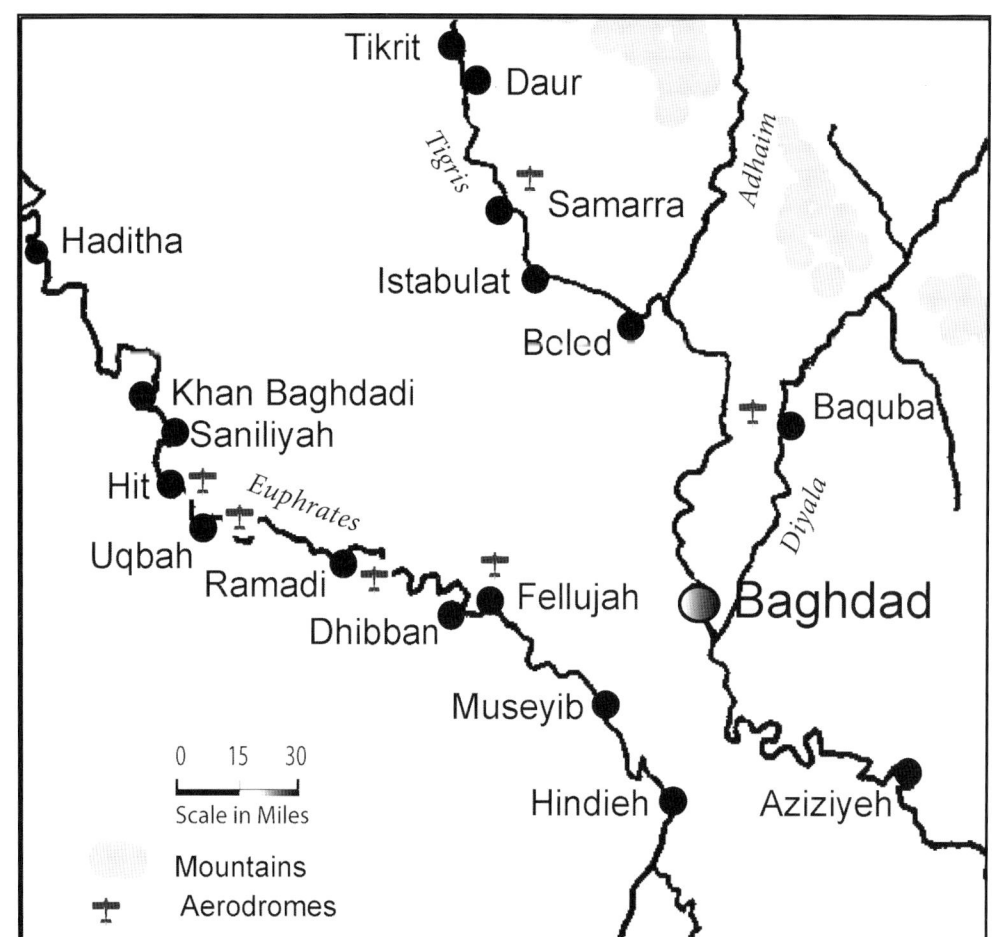

Lt-Gen Sir William Marshall.

Lt J.H. Caldwell.

RFC UNIT LOCATIONS
OCTOBER – NOVEMBER 1917

Unit	Location
31 Wing HQ	Baghdad
30 Squadron	Baqubah
'B' Flight, 30 Squadron	Fellujah
63 Squadron	Samarra
23 Kite Balloon Company	Baghdad
Aircraft Park	Basra
Advanced Aircraft Park	Baghdad

TURKISH AIR SERVICE UNIT LOCATIONS

Unit	Location
2nd Squadron	Humr
13th Squadron	Kifri
Flugpark 6	Mosul

Then came a tragedy for the British. On 18 November, the Mesopotamian Force was shocked by the news that Lt-Gen Sir Frederick Stanley Maude KCB, CMG, DSO had died of cholera, suspected to be due to drinking contaminated milk. Especially hard hit by the news were the men of the 13th Division which he had commanded at Gallipoli and before Kut. For the first time in the campaign, the British had had an intelligent leader who was well versed in land warfare strategy and tactics and now he was gone. Maude was replaced by Lt-Gen Sir William Marshall,[63] a careful and meticulous man, who remained in command of the British Forces in Mesopotamia till the end of the war.

For support to the now combined Turkish army, the Aircraft Park at Mosul received 10 new Halberstadt D.V fighters in November and 12 new AEG C.IVs in December.[64] They were reinforced by 12 battle-hardened pilots and 10 observers. With the fighting on the ground at a standstill, the air war began to heat up again. On 17 December, two British formations consisting of seven RE8s and one Martinsyde attacked the Turkish airfield at Humr, north of Tikrit, during the day. They were met by three enemy machines. After the first pair of RE8s turned back, another pair was met by *Ltn* Klaus in Halberstadt HK.14. Klaus engaged the second pair and although he claimed to have shot an RE8 down, the pilot, Lt John Caldwell, managed to limp the aircraft home. The official history best describes what happened next.

Meanwhile the third E.A. [enemy aircraft] had confined his attention to the two 63 Squadron RE8s piloted by Capt F.L. Robinson MC with 2Lt W.R. McMenan (observer) and Capt H.G. Ffiske who had with him an aerial gunner. The enemy pilot proved himself possessed of a highly offensive spirit. Twice he comfortably established himself beneath the tail of Capt Ffiske's machine, and each time was thrown off before he could get in a burst of fire. Capt Ffiske's only means of escape was to spin, which he did with complete success. The E.A. kept up a furious attack for 30 minutes, when he dived steeply and was last observed very near to the ground on the right side of the Jebel Hamrins.[65]

After this, Klaus was awarded the German War Medal in silver and 50 Livres for his effort.[66]

Retaliation for the attack on the Turkish airfield came that afternoon when four aircraft dropped 24 bombs

Two Rolls Royce armoured cars of the 13th LAMBs (Light Armoured Mobile Batteries) used extensively in Mesopotamia in the latter stages of the campaign.

on the British airfield at Samarra, the army HQ and the railway, but little damage was done. As a consequence, a further raid on Humr took place on the night of 27 December, with aircraft provided from both 30 and 63 Squadrons. Three enemy aircraft were destroyed on the ground. To end the year, on 31 December, the British aerodrome at Samarra was again attacked – a tit-for-tat war had broken out. Hits were made on the Officers' Mess, but there were no casualties. Of the incident, 63 Squadron's new commanding officer, Major Robert Bradley, who had served previously with 30 Sqn before transfer to Egypt to command 58 (Reserve) Sqn, had cause to write:

We had a good dosing last night by the Huns. The waiter was just heralding in the New Year on an empty shell case and I was proposing the health of all in a glass of stout when they came over. They made very good shooting; one bomb twenty yards from my pony; one near 'A' Flight Mess, another ten yards from the M/T park and one by the cookhouse door, which destroyed our cookers, dixies, water carts etc. and nearly got some NCOs in a trench. A large piece of bomb went through the orderly room tent. Altogether a pleasant New Year's evening.[67]

Thus the 1917 campaigning of both sides ended in Mesopotamia. Throughout the final months, 30 Squadron had concentrated on photographic reconnaissance, particularly of the Jebel Hamrin Hills, and map work. 63 Squadron worked closely with the Corps HQ conducting artillery spotting, reconnaissance and contact patrols.

The Kite Balloon Company had been particularly hard hit by sickness and their first ascent was not until the end of November. According to Tennant, the ground crew were men deemed unfit for the infantry and sending them was 'a false economy in Mesopotamia'. The 51 Kite Balloon Section commander, Capt Philip George Bateman, 18th London Regt and RFC, agreed.

It was later reported that the section had employed sixty balloon hands, natives of Samarra, plus three Turkish NCOs (presumably POWs). It was stated that 'they were quite efficient on parade, with all commands given in Turkish'! In December, 51 Kite Balloon Section, hampered by high winds and low visibility were aloft between 14–24 December to make five special ascents to act as landmarks for the LAMBs, Light Armoured Mobile Battery armoured cars, carrying out reconnaissance of the Tigris River. On 30 December 1917 the Section moved to Ramadi on the Euphrates. Meanwhile the Turkish Squadrons concentrated on the reconnaissance of the British advance and attempted to deny the British control of the air. The result was an even match, with both sides suffering losses and neither side getting the better of the other.

A BE2c and BE2e of 30 Squadron prepared for a reconnaissance mission from the airfield at Baquba in December 1917. The last BE2c was not struck off charge until February 1918, while the BE2es remained until 1919.

Capt E.G. Baxter, 30 Sqn.

2Lt A.C. Guyer, 63 Sqn.

2Lt H.E. Wortley, 63 Sqn.

On 28 December 1917, 2Lt R. Beresford and Capt N.A. MacFarlane of 63 Squadron struck the windsock pole when taking off in an RE8 from Samarra. Both were thrown clear before the 112lb bomb their machine was carrying exploded.

2Lt A.A. Tigar, 63 Sqn.

Capt C.H.M. Dennys, Recording officer (left) and Major H. de Havilland. 30 Sqn.

Lt W.N. Sherlock, observer, (left) and 2Lt T.J. West, pilot, of 63 Sqn.

Beyond Baghdad

Baquba aerodrome 30 December 1917. A DH4 and three RE8s from 30 Squadron prepare for a bombing raid on the enemy airfield at Kifri. Maj H. de Havilland, CO, supervises work on the DH4 which had arrived on 24 December.

63 Squadron spent New Year's Day 1918 cleaning up their aerodrome at Samarra after the surprise New Year's Eve visit by the Ottoman Air Service. Both the RFC and Ottoman Air Service made return raids on each other's aerodrome during January as there was little movement on the ground, because of the winter floods, and so little else to do. Thus began what would become an eventful year and the struggle for air supremacy would last to the end of the war.

In retaliation for the New Year's bombing raid, three machines of 30 Squadron, and nine from 63 Squadron, took off on 3 January to bomb Humr, the enemy aerodrome. The weather was bad, and according to Turkish reports, most of their bombs exploded harmlessly in the Tigris providing the Germans and Turks with a large haul of fresh fish. In appreciation, the Germans dropped a photo of their catch with a letter of thanks.

The situation on the ground at the turn of the year was rather static. Following the fall of Baghdad a slow move northwest had begun. Whitehall was satisfied with the taking of Baghdad and as *Hptm* Hans Schüz later wrote:[68]

The English did not press far beyond Baghdad. Their principal object had been to restore their prestige, which had suffered seriously owing to the fall of Kut, by the capture of Baghdad. Consequently, in the summer of 1917, the Turks had rest and time in which to recuperate.

Despite Schüz's assertion, the town of Ramadi was taken in September and Tikrit in November. With the death of Gen Maude that same month and the appointment of Lt-Gen Sir William Marshall as GOC Mesopotamia, the British took stock. It would be March 1918 before offensive operations recommenced with an advance on Hit, and later, in May, towards Kirkuk. Meanwhile, the Turks had taken stock as well.

By early 1918, Mustapha Kemal Pasha held the seat of power in the Pan-Turkish party and was able to dictate policy. He decided that Germany had lost the war so he sought to shore up the Turkish position in the east as a bargaining chip when the war concluded. Kemal still had 100,000 troops at his disposal, so his focus was on the Trans-Caucasia region which required him to hold on to northern Mesopotamia. Persia was needed as a backstop. In the end, his policy was not fully enacted in time as we shall see.

Right: Spad S.VII A8806 tipped over on landing at Samarra, 19 December 1917. The 30 Squadron pilot was Canadian Lt W.L. Haight. This aircraft was also flown by 72 Squadron and remained on RAF charge until 28 January 1919.

Opposite: Spad A8808 at Samarra in autumn 1917. It was flown by 30, 63 and 72 Squadron, and also remained on charge until 28 January 1919.

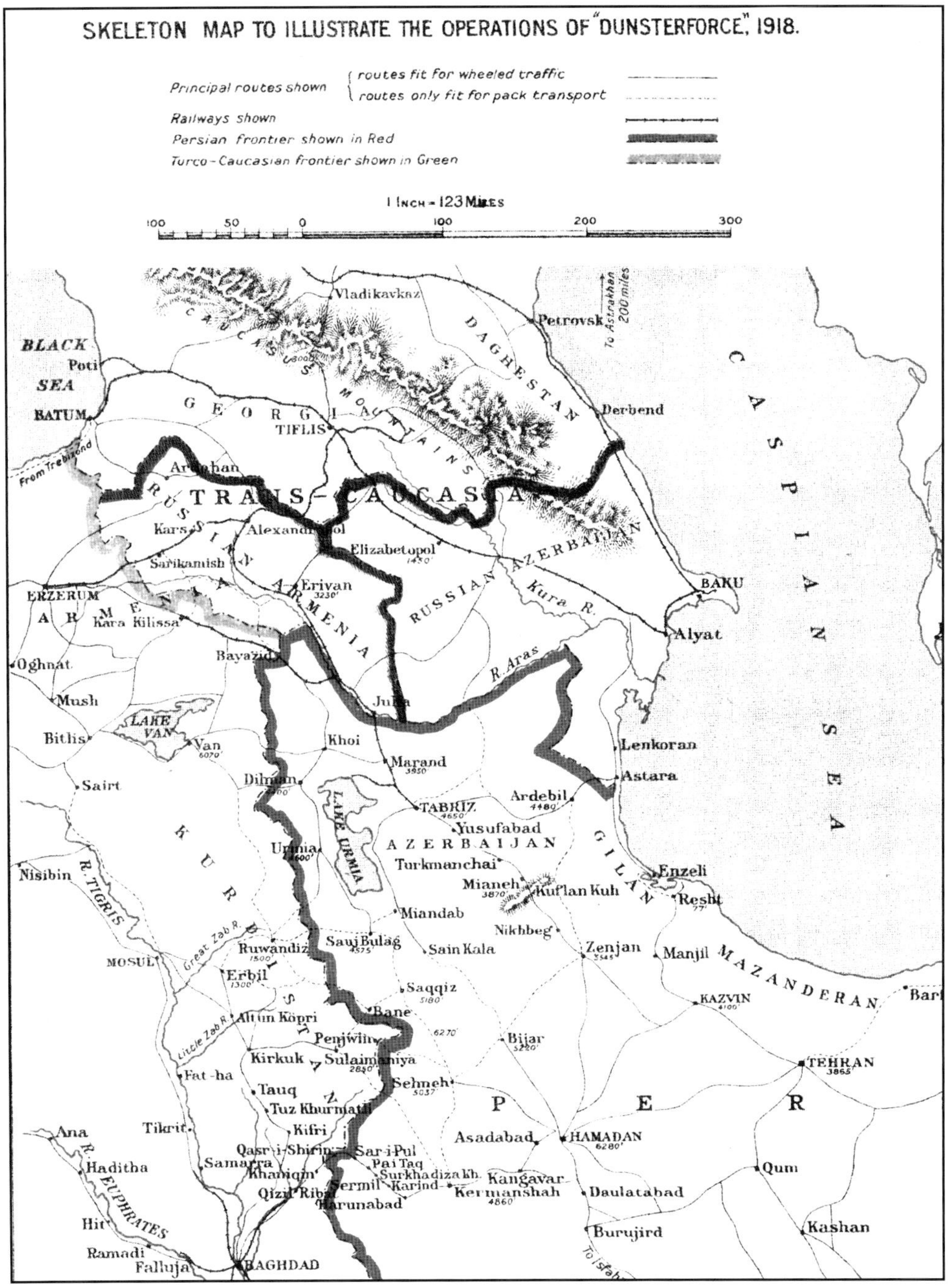

SKELETON MAP TO ILLUSTRATE THE OPERATIONS OF "DUNSTERFORCE", 1918.

Maj-Gen L.C. Dunsterville.

'... by the middle of April our army consisted of 32 officers, 22 NCOs, 50 car drivers, 1 armoured car and 1 aeroplane ... The arrival of the aeroplane caused great excitement as none had previously been seen in this part of Asia, and it consequently added much to our prestige. Throughout the period covered by the expedition the Air Force rendered splendid service; among other fine performances, Lt Pennington's flight to Urumiah deserves recording ...'

The significance of the Caucasus. 'Dunsterforce' was intended to co-operate with Russia to prevent an advance towards India by German/ Turkish forces, which could have destabilised British rule and drawn resources away from the Western Front.

The Russian revolution of October 1917 had resulted in the peace treaty of Brest-Litovsk, the surrender of Romania, and the ceding of three Trans-Caucasian provinces to Turkey. According to the British Foreign Office, and the 'Easterners' in the war cabinet, a combined Turkish and German force had India, Persia and Afghanistan as its objective. Gen Marshall was told to offer all assistance to a new British force under Maj-Gen Lionel Dunsterville,[69] a force made up of an infantry brigade, a cavalry regiment, armoured cars, a force totally independent of the British Army, a force called rather egotistically 'Dunsterforce'.

Despite Marshall's protests, the RFC would also have to be involved, plus over six hundred motor lorries, virtually all the mechanical transport in Mesopotamia. A close examination of maps showed that 330 miles of execrable roads separated Baghdad from Dunsterville's proposed forward base at Hamadan, Persia. Another 150 miles of unpaved, unguarded highway, with a 7,500ft mountain pass, separated Hamadan from Kasvin, then from Kasvin to Enzeli on the Caspian sea was a track only fit for horses and donkeys.

A 'Dunsterforce' advance party left Baghdad for Northwest Persia on 27 January 1918. Its aim was threefold: to force a new front; to prevent German propaganda spreading support for the Central Powers; and to recruit a local force capable of acting as a block to the Bolsheviks who had seized power in Russia. Dunsterville's orders were to eventually proceed as far as Baku on the Caspian Sea, a valuable oil port.

Australians, New Zealanders and British troops made up Dunsterforce. The Australians and New Zealanders were mostly wireless operators and were desperately needed as the Indian government could supply plenty of infantry manpower, but had little in the way of technical men. The wireless troops began to arrive in early 1916 and would build up to full squadron strength by 1918. However theirs is another story.[70]

In December 1917, much-needed modern aircraft had begun to arrive at 30 Squadron in the form of the

DH4 and Spad VII. The DH4 was widely regarded as one of the best medium day bombers of the war and was just what the unit had been asking for. It could cruise at over 130mph and climb to over 20,000ft (on a cooler day). It could carry two 230lb or four 112lb bombs and was well armed with forward and ring mounted machine-guns.[71] The first DH4 was flown up to Baghdad from Basra by Lt Frank Nuttall in four hours, five minutes – the first non-stop flight between the two locations.

The French Spad S.VII scout was sent to Mesopotamia after being replaced on the Western Front by the more capable Spad XIII, but although used as a fighter by the French, to the RFC it was more suited to dive attacks rather than dog-fights.[72] But in Mesopotamia, it was far superior to the BE2s and could match the Albatros D.IIIs and Halberstadts in use by the Germans. But things were slow and by January, only one DH4 and two Spads had arrived.

On the Turkish side, by late 1917, any plan to heavily reinforce the flying units in Mesopotamia had been shelved with the situation in Palestine being given higher priority for both ground and air forces. Consequently a reorganisation of Turkish 6th Army aviation units was required to better prepare for the coming year. A new Command of Aircraft Units was established at Mosul with *Hptm* Schüz in command. His organisation was as follows:

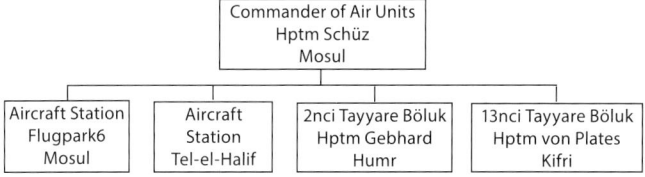

There were only two aircraft engagements of note in January, but a number of losses were incurred by both sides. On the 12th, Lt John Caldwell of 63 Squadron was flying Spad A8811 when he was forced to land in the desert near Tikrit with engine trouble. The Spad was acting as escort to a pair of RE8s, but had departed late and was trying to catch up. Caldwell was last seen flying at about 5,000 feet and heading towards Fathah. His naked and mutilated body was found 12 days later near Daur over 50 miles away from his crashed aircraft. It is not clear how he died: exposure was thought to be the probable cause. Caldwell had walked the 50 miles and eventually succumbed to his wounds and the heat. His body and clothing were likely looted by Bedouins after his death.

On the 17th, 2Lt Walter Taylor flying with his observer Lt Algernon Mills of 30 Squadron, went missing in their RE8 while on a reconnaissance of Haditha. As was often the case, their fate was unknown as the squadron CO wrote in his weekly report:[73]

We have unfortunately lost Lt. Taylor (Pilot) and Lt. Mills (Observer), who have been missing on an RE8 since the 17th. Every possible step is being taken up by Political, and we have not yet given up hope of their eventual return. Arabs are said to have befriended two aviators who came down in a two-seater, and they are said to have concealed them from the Turks and to be bringing them to Samarrah.

They had engine trouble and after a forced landing, burnt their machine and after walking for some 30 miles, were captured by a Turkish patrol and became POWs.

The first major raid for 1918 occurred on 21 January when six aircraft each from 30 and 63 Squadrons accompanied by a pair of Spads for protection carried out a raid on the home of *13nci Tayyare Bölük* (13th Turkish Squadron) at Kifri aerodrome. Eight enemy aircraft were sighted on the ground and two 112lb and 29x20lb bombs were dropped. The bombing proved to be accurate, intelligence reports stating that two enemy machines had been destroyed and three others being damaged and sent to Mosul for repair. During the melée, accurate anti-aircraft fire hit DH4 A7591 piloted by 2Lt William Bean and his observer 2AM Robert Castor.[74] The aircraft was blown to splinters at 7,000 feet and both were killed.

That same day, OC 31 Wing RFC, Lt-Col Tennant, was advised of the approach of an enemy aircraft while he was visiting Fallujah. He and Capt Gerald Merton (30 Squadron) leapt into RE8 A3448 and took off in chase. Although the pair missed the enemy aircraft, it suffered an engine failure and the German crew were forced to land and burn the machine. When Tennant and Merton landed, to their surprise, they found the German airmen comfortably ensconced in the Officers' Mess. The pilot, *Ltn* K.O. Halder, was flying with an unusual observer, *Ltn Doktor* Kruse, a meteorologist.[75] According to Tennant:

Lt John Hay Caldwell was lost in action while flying Spad A8811 on 12 January 1918.

Lt Caldwell's grave.

'the Huns had seen the three British machines pass to cut them off, and thereupon landed near the aerodrome owing to their engine seizing'.[76]

Left: Ltn Halder and Ltn Doktor Kruse with the remains of their aircraft near Fallujah after a forced landing with a seized engine.

Towards the end of January, mishaps became more common. On the 26th, Capt Frank Nuttall with Lt Bob Sievier were flying in DH4 A7621 and were forced to land behind enemy lines. Their engine had caught fire at 1,000 feet, so after a perfect landing, the pair removed the guns, and avoiding enemy patrols, took off with the guns and ammunition slung over their shoulders. Their plan, of course, was to use the guns on any Turkish patrol that came upon them and ride the captured horses to save them the long walk home. Perhaps it was best that no Turks appeared and the pair walked back the 24 miles. Sievier was later awarded the Military Cross for this feat and Nuttall missed out, probably because he already had one!

While on patrol near Abu Jisra on the 31st, Lt Lionel Skinner in Spad A8812 and Lt Robert Morris in Spad A8807 from 30 Squadron attacked an enemy AEG two-seater. A running battle ensued until the AEG was hit in the radiator and fuel tanks and forced to land in the desert within British lines. However, the crew of *Leutnants* Omnos and Schultze burnt their machine and escaped.[77]

Above: DH4 A7621 which caught fire in the air during a bombing raid, forcing the crew to make an emergency landing followed by a 24 mile walk to safety while carrying their machine guns and ammunition.

Left: Another DH4, still unidentified, which was captured and pictured in Turkish hands.

RE8s of 'C' Flight, 63 Squadron, seen here lined up at Samarra north of Baghdad in the spring of 1918. The nearest aircraft are A4344, in service with the Squadron until February 1919; and A4355, written off in December 1918.

During February, 63 Squadron spent almost the entire month on reconnaissance and photography in support of the Corps Brigades and flying contact patrols with the infantry, cavalry and armoured cars while 30 Squadron concentrated on bombing and reconnaissance. The expected British advance up the Euphrates began on the 19th, with a move against the town of Hit, hitherto a Turkish stronghold. Meanwhile, the Turkish commander, Nazim Bey, set about his defences with positions around Hit and another set around Khan Baghdadi. Also, on the 19th 63 Squadron suffered further casualties, when Capt Charles Parker and 1AM John Nelson[78] were killed when their heavily loaded RE8, B5875, stalled and crashed from 300 feet at Basra. Fortunately for the clean-up crew, the bombs on board did not explode.

Right: Remains of another AEG two-seater, this one shot down by Lts E.L. Skinner and R.K. Morris of 30 Squadron on 31 January 1918. The German crew set fire to the machine and escaped.

Spad A8807, at Baquba with Lt R.K. Morris in the cockpit.

Spad A8812, in which Lt Skinner shot down the AEG, photographed at Baquba in 1918. The Lewis gun mounting on the top wing was devised by Capt Nuttall and Maj de Havilland of 30 Squadron.

The Last RFC Unit reaches Mesopotamia

In March, 1918, the third and final RFC squadron to be sent to Mesopotamia arrived in theatre. The decision to reinforce had partly been based on intelligence reports sent to GHQ Egypt in December 1917 from 31 Wing HQ Baghdad, that the enemy air service would be increased from 24 to 44 aircraft. Another squadron would be needed to even the scales.

72 Squadron landed at Basra equipped with a mixture of aircraft types which included Bristol M.1Cs, SE5as, DH4s, Spad VIIs and Martinsyde Elephants. Such variety indicated a dumping of aircraft not wanted elsewhere. Mesopotamia was about as far away from the 'real action' on the Western Front as one could go and consequently was at the end of the supply line as far as stores were concerned. Tennant in his memoirs recalled that: 'in response to many appeals, an additional squadron could finally be spared for Mesopotamia and General Maude [also] accepted the offer of two RFC Kite Balloon Sections'.[79] However, the promised squadron took nearly five months to arrive.

72 Squadron had been formed at Upavon on 2 July 1917 and was to be commanded by Major Herman Walter von Poellnitz. Despite his German sounding name, he had been born in England and educated at Repton and Sandhurst before joining the Lincolnshire Regiment. 'A' Flight was under a Canadian, Capt James Stanley Beatty; the 'B' Flight commander was Capt Norman Berwick Fuller and the 'C' Flight commander was Capt Francis Henry Coleman, a highly experienced pilot who was having a long war. He had served with 32 Sqn in France flying DH2s before joining 72 Squadron in August 1917. He would be still in Iraq between 1923 and 1928 as a Squadron leader in the RAF.

72 Squadron moved to Sedgeford, Norfolk in November 1917, to be equipped with SE5as ready for service in France, but as with 63 Squadron previously, the squadron was switched to Mesopotamia with an assortment of aircraft types as noted. In December, the squadron embarked for the Gulf in two groups, one via an overland route through France and Italy, the second group via Suez, where a number of pilots trained in Egypt would join the unit to bring it to full operational strength. Major von Poellnitz arrived at Basra on 14 February, and the second party under Capt Beatty on 2 March. It was the first time the whole squadron had been together since leaving Sedgeford.

Like its counterparts in Mesopotamia, 72 Squadron would also be distributed: 'A' flight with DH4s, SE5as and Spads was detailed to work with 1st Corps at Samarra; 'B' Flight with Martinsyde G102s was attached to Army GHQ at Baghdad for air defence of the city; while 'C' flight took its Bristol M.1C monoplanes on RFC barge T3 up the Tigris and was attached to III Corps at Mirjana on the Diyala River.

Unfortunately, von Poellnitz was to be CO for only two months. On 10 May, while returning from Baghdad

Top: Working together. Four RE8s of 30 Squadron about to start on a mission from Kirkuk in the summer of 1918, with their escort, a Bristol M.1C from 72 Squadron.

Left: Members of 72 Squadron at Mirjana north-east of Baquba on the Diyala River, in April 1918.
L-r: Lt C.G. Bellord with camera, Lt L.L. Leleu (in the cockpit), Lt H. Izard and Lt C.J.M. Evans, with Spad S.VII A8813.

The grave of Major von Poellnitz.
Aerial view of Baghdad aerodrome showing the site of the fatal crash.

aerodrome to the city, his staff car rolled down an embankment and he was killed, the squadron recording officer Lt Wilfrid Banham being seriously injured but surviving. Poellnitz was replaced by Major Oscar Alfred Westendarp, but he too only lasted six weeks before being posted out to Egypt on 7 July 1918. The third and final CO was Major Owen Tudor Boyd who would remain with the unit until 6 January 1919.

In preparation for a move against the town of Hit, the RFC squadrons increased their reconnaissance, photography and bombing operations. But during this phase, Capt Walter Haight and Lt Harold Hancock flying RE8 B3450, were unfortunately hit by rifle file and forced to land. Both became POWs.

On 8 March, a combined air reconnaissance by 30 and 63 Squadrons brought news that the Turks were evacuating their trenches south of Hit and reinforcing a position north of the town known as

The kite balloon of 52 KB Section, seen bedded down at Sahiliya, between Hit and Khan Baghdadi on the Euphrates, in March 1918.

Martinsyde G.102 Elephant A1594 'PAN-K-KOS'. This machine first flew with 30 Sqn, having arrived on 23 May 1917, but transferred to 63 Sqn in January 1918 before being moved on to 72. Men and machines were spread thinly from the Euphrates in the west to the Diyala front in the east.

A DH4 on the aerodrome at Baghdad on 13 April 1918. Lt R.P.P. Pope of 72 Sqn about to depart for Kufa on the Euphrates with Capt A.T. Wilson, the Civil Commissioner in Mesopotamia from March 1918. His job would be to oversee the administration of captured towns after the declaration of victory.

March/April 1918. Bristol M.1C C4920 of 72 Sqn is prepared for action on the Diyala front, east of the Tigris.

Lower left: A mobile anti-aircraft gun mounted in a wagon on one of the light railways built to enhance supply lines as the army advanced.

Broad Wadi, a small depression. With 52 Kite Balloon Section now at Qubba directing artillery fire, and the combined flights of 30 and 63 Squadrons giving him air support, Gen Marshall took the opportunity to attack. 30 Squadron flew continually over the coming days, with Major Hereward de Havilland 'instructed to undertake a vigorous bombing offensive against the Turks'.[80] This the squadron did, with enemy troops and aircraft bombed and machine-gunned, which caused considerable loss including one enemy aircraft destroyed. Over three tons of bombs were dropped that week.[81] Despite the onslaught, the Turks managed to slip away and reinforce their Khan Baghdadi position some 20 miles further north. The Turkish and German aviators retreated to Haditha, some 50 miles further back. As such, the army took the town and

Below: The German wireless station at Baghdad aerodrome. The main RFC/RAF Aircraft Park was moved to this site in April 1918. Wireless communication was vital in a country with little in the way of established telephone or telegraph networks. Between them, the Army, Navy and RFC/RAF developed a considerable wireless network. Wireless, as well as message-dropping, was also used from air to ground, especially for the direction of artillery. Without spotter aircraft, artillery units had to resort to flimsy contraptions like the observation ladder below right to be able to see anything useful on the flat featureless plains.

SE5a C9564, often flown by Capt J.S. Beatty of 72 Squadron during 1918. As part of operations to conceal details of the army's northward advance, on 21 April he shot down an AEG C.IV that was attempting to observe the base at Samarra. Both crew members were killed.

the RFC moved forward to the rudimentary landing ground at Hit in preparation for the next advance up the Euphrates towards Ana. By the end of March, Ana was taken unopposed. With that, the British declared victory on the Euphrates Front.

At the end of March 1918 and in preparation for the formation of the Royal Air Force on 1 April, the RFC in Mesopotamia was re-organised under Tennant's 31 Wing. Subordinate units were attached to the Army Corps and Divisions as shown below:

Motor transport became more common as time went on, and the firm surface of some desert areas were suitable for rapid movement. This 13pdr 9cwt anti-aircraft gun has been mounted on a lorry, and the open bonnet reveals one of the major problems affecting all engines – overheating. The fine desert sand, stirred up by vehicles or blown by the wind, also caused damage, even to the engines of motor boats on the rivers.

Corps	Army Commander	RFC Squadron/Unit	RFC Commander
1 Corps	Lt-Gen Sir A.S. Cobbe	No. 63 Squadron 'A' Flt, No. 72 Squadron 51 Kite Balloon Sect 59 Anti-Air Artillery Sect 93 Anti-Air Artillery Sect	Maj R.A. Bradley Capt J.S. Beatty
III Corps	Maj-Gen Sir R.G. Egerton	No. 30 Squadron HQ & Flight 'C' Flt, No. 72 Squadron 80 Anti-Air Artillery Sect 92 Anti-Air Artillery Sect	Maj H. de Havilland Capt F.H. Coleman
15th Div	Maj-Gen Sir H.T. Brooking	No. 30 Squadron (Two Flights) 52 Kite Balloon Sect 118 Anti-Air Artillery Sect	Maj H. de Havilland
GHQ	Lt-Gen W.R. Marshall	'B' Flt, No. 72 Squadron	Capt N.B. Fuller

Officers of 31 Wing HQ, February 1918.

Standing l-r: Capt E.F. Hirtzel (EO3 Stores), Lt P.D. Scott (EO3 Gunnery),
Lt J. Durward (EO2 Photo),
Capt V. Buxton (SO3, ex 30 Sqn),
Lt P.L. Hunting (EO2 Wireless).

Seated l-r: Maj J.L. Grinlinton, Maj B.G.M.F. Nixon (Wing Adjt ex 30 Sqn), Lt-Col J.E. Tennant (OC Wing HQ), Capt O.T. Boyd (SO2).

Officers, NCOs and men of 31 Wing HQ, February 1918.

Officers seated l-r: Lt J. Durward,
Capt E.F. Hirtzel, Maj B.G.M.F. Nixon,
Maj J.L. Grinlinton, Lt-Col J.E. Tennant, Capt O.T. Boyd, Capt V. Buxton,
Lt P.L. Hunting, Lt P.D. Scott. Sgt Clerk S.E. Ayling MSM standing between Grinlinton and Tennant.

Group of officers at the farewell dinner for Major Hereward de Havilland, Baghdad, April 1918.
Back row: Lt A.P. Adams (30 Sqn), Capt L.S.A.M. Page (30 Sqn), Lt R.C. Williams (30 Sqn), Capt E.F. Hirtzel (GHQ), Capt P.L. Hunting (GHQ), Capt F. Nuttall (30 Sqn), Capt B.G.M.F. Nixon (GHQ).
2nd row: Lt J. Durward (GHQ), Lt H.A. Dinnage, 2Lt W.G. Lamb (GHQ), Lt E.D. Fanshawe (72 Sqn), Capt G. Cory-Wright (30 Sqn).
Seated: Lt W. Birtwhistle (GHQ), Maj H.D. Jensen (CO, 23 KBC), Maj O.A. Westendarp (CO, 30 Sqn), Maj H. de Havilland, Lt R.B.B. Sievier (30 Sqn), Maj H.W. von Poellnitz (CO, 72 Sqn), Capt O.T. Boyd (GHQ).
Front row: Lt J.B. Case (30 Sqn), Lt J.O. Allison (30 Sqn), Capt N.B. Fuller (72 Sqn), Lt A.G. Lamplugh (72 Sqn), Capt V. Buxton (GHQ).

63 Squadron, Samarra, April/May 1918

'A' Flight (left to right)

2Lt R.C. Mitchell (O)
Lt J.W. Tregale (O)
2Lt H.W. Underhill (O)
2Lt A. Cumming (O).

Lt H.W Price (P)
Lt P. Ainsworth (P)
Capt R.D. Simpson (P)
Flt Cdr N.S. Beswick (P)
Lt F.V. Devonshire (P)

2Lt J.H. Griffiths (O)
2Lt J.L.W. Bacon (P).

'B' Flight (left to right)

Flt Sgt Rhaney
Lt C.W.H. Moller (O)
Lt N.A. MacFarlane (O)
Lt S.L. Matthews (O)
2Lt A.A. Tigar (EO)
2Lt A.E. Evans (P).

2Lt E.J. Bailey (P)
Lt S.G. Frogley (P)
Capt J. Everidge (Flt Cdr)
Lt A.C. Lace (P)
Lt E.J. Crichton (P).

'C' Flight (left to right)

Lt W.N. Sherlock (O)
Capt P.A. Smith (O)
Lt C.A. Walker (O)
Lt G.H. Puckle (RO)
2Lt S.R. Blucke (O).

2Lt A.C. Guyer (P)
Lt G.L. Stedman (NZ) (P)
Capt P.L. Robinson (Flt Cdr)
Capt H.G. Ffiske (P)
2Lt H.E. Wortley (P).

Lt G.V. Stewart (P)
2Lt G.W.P. Avery (P).

The Birth of the RAF

Workshops and hangars under construction at Baghdad Aircraft Park in April 1918, between the terminus of the Berlin-Baghdad railway and the recently-built German wireless station. – the large building just right of centre – which the Turks tried to destroy before retreating. Holes in the roof are still visible, but the RAF soon converted the building to engineering workshops.

Before the official birth of the RAF, the RFC in Mesopotamia lost its commander.

On the morning of 25 March, Tennant, together with Major Percy Hobart,[82] Brigade Major of the 8th Infantry Brigade flying a DH4, went on a reconnaissance of Khan Baghdadi. Hit by ground fire, the engine seized. They landed and burned the machine, then were taken prisoner. After personal interrogation by Nazim Bey, they were dispatched north, heading for Aleppo. But on the morning of the 28th, the pair were rescued by British armoured cars, sent by Brig-Gen Robert Cassels,[83] commander of the 11th Cavalry Brigade.

Tennant was an important prisoner, and the British Generals could ill afford him to tell of their plans. As well as rescuing Tennant, the armoured cars also captured Nazim Bey, thus removing the Turkish commander from the fight. Keast Burke later wrote of the rescue:[84]

> They had almost given up hope of release when our armoured cars arrived on the scene. The road running between the hill and the river was full of corners, and the appearance of the cars was sudden and dramatic. They came up stealthily in top gear with very little noise. The first intimation of them was the machine-gun fire they opened on the ground. Happily, the two Englishmen were separated by twenty-five yards from their escort at the moment, and as the Tartars dived for cover, Tennant and Hobart ran for the car, which kept up a hot barrage over them all the time. I met them at Khan Baghdadi the next morning, the happiest men in Mesopotamia.

While Tennant was away, the British 11th Cavalry stormed the Turkish entrenchments at Khan Baghdadi, relieving the town and capturing over 5,000 prisoners. The action cleared the way for the final advance up the Euphrates. As for Tennant, clearly he had become too much of a risk so 'the powers that be' chose to post him to India as Director of Aviation. Three weeks later, he said his farewells and departed, replaced by the newly promoted Lt-Col Robert Bradley. On 30 April de Havilland departed for England and Major James Everidge came over from 63 Squadron to take command of 30 Squadron from the 25th.

On 1 April 1918, the RAF was officially formed by the amalgamation of the RFC and RNAS. That day was purposely chosen, not because it was April Fool's Day as some jesters in the Army claimed, but as it was the start of the British financial year. A budget could only provide for this new service at the start of the next financial year after Parliamentary assent. For those in Mesopotamia, the date would be remembered for other reasons.

That night, a strong desert storm blew up at Samarra where a considerable number of 30 and 63 Squadron machines were parked. A whirlwind wrecked the camp, standing aircraft on their nose, snapping propellers and undercarriages. Three aircraft were beyond local repair.[85] The 63 Squadron diarist went further recording:[86]

> The storm lasted three days, but between 4.45 am and 5.30 am on the 1st inst. it was at its worst. 'A' and 'B' Flight hangars were completely swept away and the 11 machines, though securely pegged down, were all more or less wrecked. One particular machine received sufficient flying speed to lift it high above the hangars from whence it crashed nose down fifty yards from its

An RE8 flies over the route that Dunsterforce had to take from Baghdad to the Caspian.
Left: Troops of the Expeditionary Force inspect the burnt out remains of Tennant's DH4 shortly before he was rescued.

moorings. In all, 11 machines were more or less badly damaged, two of which had to be written off.

Although the British capture of Hit, Khan Baghdadi and Ana was successful, the terrain running north up the Euphrates valley was rough and unsuited to further advance. This created a pause and the British then turned their attention to the Tigris front and set their sights on taking Kirkuk.

Meanwhile British attention was also drawn towards Persia. General Dunsterville had reported that
...Persia was in a melting pot owing to the weak Persian Government and having regard to the Russian situation and evacuation, it seemed necessary, with a view to operations in the Caucasus and to safeguard British interests in Persia, for us to occupy the line Qasr-i-Shirin – Enzeli'.[87]

With Russia out of the war, the Turks and Germans could freely press their claims in Persia and their propaganda was proving to be very effective. Fears grew in London that if the Central Powers could gain control of Persia then Afghanistan might be next. The British always suspected the real prize was to seize India, just a step further away, but a long one at that. Then, there was also the pressing need to protect the British right flank.

While the RE8s had the range to keep an eye on the Persian situation from the air, in order to fully support Dunsterforce, it was decided to clear the way by attacking across the line between Kifri and Qara Tepe. Advanced landing grounds could then be secured allowing further access into Kermanshah and beyond. The landing grounds were established at Hamadan (May), Kasvin (June) then at Zenjan and Enzeli.

Above, right and opposite:
1 April 1918 was marked by a storm at Samarra which destroyed the 'A' and 'B' Flight hangars of 63 Squadron. The RE8 in the foreground left, A4347, managed to survive until April 1919.

A 63 Squadron RE8 from Samarra and its escort, a Bristol M.1C of 'C' Flt, 72 Squadron, at Umr-Maidan in the Jebel Hamrin mountains on the Mesopotamia/Persia border. They have landed on something the aircrew might literally not have seen for months: a grassy meadow full of wild flowers.

At the end of April, flights from all three squadrons were used to reconnoitre and bomb the Turks with the ground manoeuvre commencing on the 26th. It was during these operations that the Bristol M.1Cs were first used in action by 'C' Flight 72 Squadron.

Within three days, the British had seized their objective and the Turks retreated. Qara Tepe, Kifri and Tuz Khurmatli were now in British hands and another advanced aerodrome was quickly established at Umr Maidan from the 27th. The Ottoman 13th Squadron was pulled back to Kirkuk. A halt was now called to reassess the situation.

The only real air action for the month of April was on the 21st when an AEG C.IV was spotted photographing the aerodrome at Samarra. Capt James Beatty took off in chase in an SE5a accompanied by Lts Percy William Spurr and Arthur Armstrong Cullen in Spads. Spurr soon landed with a boiling radiator, and Cullen could not close. Beatty eventually shot down the German aircraft after overhauling it. *Ltn* Eric Petras and his observer, *Oblt* Hans Minckwitz in the AEG were killed.

Not everything went smoothly for the RAF during the fighting. As the operation to take Tuz Khurmatli was winding up on the 27th, Capt Frank Nuttall, with Lt Richard Williams as observer, was hit by ground fire, wounded in the foot, and became covered in petrol from a hole in the rear tank. Regardless, he landed, had his foot dressed then took off again for the advanced landing ground at Umr Maidan. Despite his wound, he was soon back flying again.

Drawn towards Persia ... Lt George Martin Lees, 'C' Flight, 72 Sqn, with his Bristol M.1C at Tuz Khurmatli in May 1918. The RE8s were from 'C' Flight of 30 Sqn, and moved to Kifri on 26 May.
In the background are the first of the mountains that both aircraft and ground forces would have to cross to reach their goal on the shores of the Caspian Sea. Below left is the view looking back from the Persian side.

Two RE8s of 'A' Flight, 30 Squadron, on the airfield at Hamadan, Persia, September/October 1918. A4357, nearest the camera, remained on RAF charge until 5 January 1920.

The RAF airfield at Kasvin in Persia (Iran) first established in June 1918. This view shows the base later in the year with hangars erected at a main crossroads outside the walled town.

German Reinforcements

With fighting at a standstill, the Turks finally received some more modern fighters when in late April, seven Albatros D.IIIs and a single Halberstadt D.V arrived at the *Flugpark* in Mosul.[88] By this time Schüz had been replaced at the Aircraft Park by *Hptm* Hans Hattendorf who decided to pool the fighters and created the 6th Army Fighter Unit. Schüz returned to the 13th Turkish Squadron where he went on to claim his final two kills before the end of the war.[89] Losses, lack of proper reinforcement in men as well as machines, and illness had combined to decimate the Ottoman squadrons.

A Halberstadt D.V that arrived at Mosul in April.

By May, the enemy had fallen back to Kirkuk on the Tigris Front and although it would stretch the British lines of supply, it was decided the town needed to be taken. In that way, pressure would be eased on the Persian Front and the British would be one step closer to the final outpost – Mosul. The advance of the III Corps began on the 4th and the town was captured three days later after heavy fighting. The British found the townsfolk in a near starving condition, evidence of the famine gripping the country, the result of the Turkish requisitioning system. Unable to feed the town and with fears for the safety of the troops, the British withdrew at the end of the month.

As spring turned into summer so too the weather changed for the worse. Around May, Lt Robert Blucke joined 63 Squadron as an observer. In his diary, he noted the 'horrible' weather and how 'thin' the air was:[90]

When gliding down to land the air becomes so thin that it does not give you the same support as when it is denser, of course consequently one seems literally to drop the last 500 feet or so.

Flying biplanes in the full heat of a Mesopotamian summer was certainly not recommended.

On 2 May, the RAF lost another RE8. While making a sketch map of the Tauq to Kirkuk road, Capt Arthur Edwards of 30 Squadron was hit and wounded by machine-gun fire from the ground and forced to land behind enemy lines. His passenger was Major George Beazeley[91] of the Royal Engineers who was along for the ride. Both were taken prisoner.

A week later, on 9 May, Lt Douglas Fairlie Lapraik and 2Lt Thomas Alfred Pitt from 72 Squadron were on an offensive patrol in their Spads when they encountered a Halberstadt which they later described as having a yellow fuselage and camouflaged wings. Pitt's combat report, neatly typed on Army Form W3348 recalled what happened:[92]

While patrolling over Humr, I saw an EA climbing towards us. I dived diagonally and opened fire. The EA seemed to stall in its effort to do a sharp right hand turn. I fired only 10-12 rounds when the Vickers gun jammed. I endeavoured to clear my jam but failed and during my effort lost the EA and Lt Lapraik.

Having realised Pitt's dilemma, Lapraik continued the attack as stated in his combat report:

I then swung around on the tail of the EA and opened fire. He did an Immelmann turn to shake me off, losing at the same time a lot of height. I dived vertically onto him, firing a good burst. The EA went down in a very steep glide and I followed him at about 150 mph and fired a burst of about 20 rounds into him at close range.

Spad S.VII A8813, flown by 72 Squadron in 1918. Its Lewis gun is mounted on the top wing, and the engine cowling panels have been removed in an attempt to stop the engine overheating – though the pilot, Lt S.D. MacDonald, evidently found that he needed less cooling than the engine and chose to wear a long woollen scarf.

Lt Lees stands by the radiator of an armoured car at Kirkuk, which has just retrieved his M.1C after he was forced to land with a broken tappet rod and then walked 18 miles to safety through enemy territory before assisting in the recovery of the aircraft.

The EA went down vertically at terrific speed. When about 3000 feet below me his starboard wing collapsed, bits of struts and fabric falling from his machine. He then crashed to the ground.

He was probably *OffSt* (Warrant Officer) Edwin Klaus.

By mid-May, the Germans had readied their Albatros D.IIIs and one of these became deadly in the hands of Schüz. On the 15th, the British discovered their presence, losing RE8 B5872 to his guns. A raid of six RE8s from 30 Squadron, escorted by the Bristol monoplanes of 'C' Flight 72 Squadron set out to bomb enemy troops and the aerodrome at Altun Kupri. In his weekly report, the CO wrote of the 'discovery' and the fatal engagement during the bombing raid:[93]

The aerodrome was inspected with a view to bombing it, but as only a bell tent and an empty hangar was observed, it was thought desirable to proceed with the bombing of more suitable targets. In consequence of this, machines divided up a good deal. It appears, however, that the enemy had produced six Albatross (sic) D.3 during the preceding day (they certainly were not there before) and these they had put in a field some miles from the aerodrome. If they intended to mislead us into thinking they had no machines they certainly succeeded so far: for during the subsequent individual bombing by our pilots, Lt Allison and Lt Lancelot Harold Browning were attacked – Allison by three Albatross scouts – and at the very outset of the contest burst into flames and crashed to the ground.

Browning with observer Lt Franklin C. Kirk in another RE8, however, turned the tables as the citation to Browning's subsequent Military Cross recorded:[94]

For conspicuous gallantry and daring whilst carrying out independent bombing behind the enemy's lines. He was attacked by a fast enemy scout machine, which by skilful piloting and accurate shooting he drove down to its aerodrome. No sooner had the enemy aeroplane landed than Lt Browning dropped a bomb, completely obliterating the pilot, who had started to run away, and damaging his machine. He then continued bombing, and while doing so was attacked by two more enemy scouts, both of which he drove off. He showed fine skill and courage throughout.

The British had picked on a formidable team. Flying four Albatros scouts were Schüz, Kunze, Schultz and Borman. Schüz would claim his ninth victory and Kunze, his first. In the case of Kunze, his victim was Lt Lance Page in an RE8 who was bounced on his return flight. While Page landed back in the lines, the gunner, 1AM Fred Suthurst[95] was killed by a stray bullet after expending all his ammunition against the attacker. Page's luck also ran out some months later on 20 August. While carrying out a machine gun practice flight, with a newly arrived observer Lt Laird Kirwan, his RE8 B6611 spun in from 600 feet. Both were killed instantly. Page was the senior flight commander in 30 Squadron, having joined in December 1916. Kirwan was there only 19 days.

It was also during May that the RAF returned its attention to the Persian Front and support for General Dunsterville. Flying from the small aerodrome at Hamadan, 6,500 feet above sea level, and in the heat of summer, must have been extremely trying for the airmen. It was reported that machines needed over 400 yards to get airborne from this site.

Aircraft from 30 Squadron and from 72 Squadron 'B' Flight flew bombing and reconnaissance missions over the entire front. On 20 May Lt Charles Gattens, a South African from 72 Squadron, force landed a mile from Altun Kupri, some 80 miles behind enemy lines. His Bristol M.1C C4925 was burnt to prevent capture and Lt Allen Adams of 30 Squadron flying an RE8 was able to land nearby and rescue Gattens as Turkish cavalry appeared. A few days later Lt George Martin Lees also of 72 Squadron, force-landed in the same area with engine failure. Lt William Thomas on the same flight was able to locate Lees, and accurately report his position to the 13th LAMBs who sent out two armoured cars to rescue the pilot.

On 14 June, 2Lt John Warwick with Lt Tom Keating of 63 Squadron left the aerodrome at Samarra in RE8 A4661 to proceed on a photo reconnaissance. At about 300 feet, the machine nose-dived into the ground and both were killed. Warwick had been with the Squadron just four days.

By the mid-year point, *Major* Erich Serno,

Above: Brothers in arms ... Lt T.I.S. Mackay, Madras Sappers & Miners (left) and Lt Moray Sutherland Mackay, 72 Sqn RFC, at Basra in the spring of 1918.

Top right: Martinsyde Elephant 7459. Flown by 30 Squadron in January 1917, then transferred to 72 Squadron.

Right: Martinsydes 7459 and 7493 of 72 Squadron burning at Baku on the Caspian Sea. The pilots, Lts Mackay and Pope, had been operating in support of Dunsterforce, but were ordered to evacuate the town along with the British ground troops.

Commander of the Ottoman Air Service, was able to report on the status of the *Fliegerabteilungen* in Mesopotamia, finding their efforts were appreciated 'unreservedly' by the army command. Furthermore:

The inspection of the units at El Humar and Kifri, as well as the advance flying field at Suleimanije, passed satisfactorily. It was astonishing and admirable how the units here, far away on the edge of the desert, had each set up decent quarters, how they had fulfilled their duties in spite of all difficulties and especially those of supply; what a comradely life was made here, with what ardour they served, and how inventively one learned how, here in this most remote area of war, to become the master of technical difficulties. What is more, all this had to be done in a climate that is extremely debilitating to the health and also often with inadequate nutrition.[96]

The final British offensive began in the autumn when the weather had cooled. By now the Turkish aviation units had been decimated, not just by the overwhelming British superiority, but by the poor conditions in Mesopotamia. After the long hot summer, food supplies had dwindled as the country was in the midst of famine. According to Schüz, this was brought on by 'Turkish indolence and the bitter feeling among the population of the country, who were no longer cultivating their fields, owing to the vigorous system of "requisitions".'

Little flying was done by either side over Mesopotamia during the summer of 1918, with the few flights that were undertaken leading to nothing. The Turkish 2nd and 13th squadrons together flew just two missions in July and three in August. The fighter detachment at Mosul flew none.[97] Only one fatality was recorded, that of Capt Humphrey O'Brien who was accidentally killed on 14 September when struck by a machine that was taking off.

In July 1918, the remaining Russian forces in north Persia left for the Caucasus. The local government in

Martinsyde Elephant A3972 'Gwalior No. 2' force-landed by Lt A.A. Cullen 90 miles north-west of Tabriz in northern Persia.

Baku had urgently requested British assistance and on 4 August, Maj-Gen Dunsterville landed at Baku having sailed from Enzeli with detachments of the Worcesters, Warwicks and North Staffs. It was a remarkable achievement considering the detachment was now 1,000 miles from Basra.

On 18 August two machines (Martinsyde G.100s) from 72 Squadron with pilots Lt Ralph Patrick Phillip Pope and Lt Moray Sutherland MacKay, sailed from Enzeli to Baku. They were ready to fly by the 25th and would operate from a Russian airfield four miles outside the town. The two pilots carried out bombing raids, reconnaissance and the dropping of propaganda leaflets. In September, a large enemy force attacked Baku, Pope and MacKay flying at low level to machine gun the attacking troops. On 14 September the British troops and the two RAF airmen were ordered to evacuate the town, and return to Enzeli. The two Martinsydes (7459 and 7493) were burnt to prevent capture. The machine-guns, camera equipment and photographic plates were also destroyed.

On 31 August, Lt Arthur Armstrong Cullen of 72 Squadron flying Martinsyde A3972 was reported missing, and it was not until 30th December 1918 that it was confirmed that he had force landed at a village near Nakichivan in the Caucasus. He had not been molested by the local people but had to surrender to the Turks and become a POW. Additional air reinforcements were provided by 'A' flight of 30 Squadron on 17 September, when they flew three of their RE8s from Kifri to Hamadan, a direct flight of 200 miles over mountainous country. 'B' flight at Ramadi was relieved by machines of 63 Squadron and joined 'A' flight on the 18th.

On 28 September, Lt Philip John Taylor Baddiley flying a Sopwith Camel, spotted an AEG over the advanced line of British troops, and gave chase. Baddiley closed and gave the enemy a short burst. The 72 Squadron historian recalled what happened next:

> Suddenly, the AEG turned into wind and landed six miles behind our lines. The occupants left the machine and ran away. At this point Lt Baddiley's guns jambed [sic]. He landed near some of our troops five miles away. A car was at once sent out to take over the AEG but when half-a-mile away the machine took off and escaped.

A remarkable adventure was to be experienced by Lt Lewis 'Taffy' Williams of 72 Squadron on 6 October. Leaving Zinjan in Martinsyde 7467 to escort an RE8 of 30 Squadron, he located three large groups of enemy

Lt T.L. 'Taffy' Williams of 72 Squadron as he appeared after escaping in disguise from enemy territory following a forced landing on 6 October 1918.

transport at the Shibli Pass, and dived to attack. At 500 feet, he fired 150 rounds into the largest group, but his engine cut out completely (enemy fire?) and he was forced to land. Williams found himself in a steep mountainous area without food or water, but after walking some distance, he purchased some food and shelter from a local man. The following morning, locals deprived him of his clothes, revolver, watch and goggles, but otherwise left him alone. Dressed in Persian clothes, his head shaven, and with a local guide, Williams began his journey to safety walking mainly by night. His guide deprived him of some of his clothes but three days later, after walking barefoot he was picked

An AEG C.IV as used by the Turkish/German units in Mesopotamia to the end of the war.

Lt P. Phillips stands in front of 30 Sqn RE8 B3449. On 11 October Lts A.E. Morgan and J.C. Chacksfield force-landed this aircraft when attempting to rescue Lt K.M. Pennington.

The remains of Martinsyde G102 Elephant A3973, which was force-landed in enemy territory by Lt K.M. Pennington and was recovered later.

up by a Ghurka officer who nearly shot him before he could explain who he was.

As Williams reached safety on 11 October, another group of RAF officers found themselves caught up in a similar incident. On this morning, three RE8s from 30 Squadron and their escort, an SE5a and Martinsyde G.102 Elephant from 72 Squadron's 'B' flight sat on the landing ground at Zenjan, awaiting pilots and observers for a reconnaissance and bombing mission over the Tabriz area to the north.

RE8 B5883 was to be flown by the 30 Squadron flight commander Capt Frank Nuttall, now into his eighteenth month of active service in 'Mespot'. His observer was Lt J.B. Case. The second RE8 (B6585) was crewed by Lt Henry Anson with Lt Tom Alderton Tindle and the third (B3449) by Lt Albert Edward Morgan with Lt John Chacksfield. The SE5a was piloted by Lt William Thomas, with Lt Kenneth Misson Pennington, a South African, flying Martinsyde A3973.

The aircraft left at 07.35 flying to an advanced landing ground to top-up with petrol and take bombs on board for a flight expected to take over three hours. Flying north west, Capt Nuttall found a large enemy convoy with troops on the north side of the lake at Yusufabad. Here eighteen 20lb Cooper bombs were dropped and the troops strafed from low level.

As Lt Pennington flew low over Mianeh, enemy fire hit the Martinsyde and cut the engine completely. He managed to land without injury. Minutes later Lts Morgan and Chacksfield landed nearby to affect a rescue. Pennington helped to turn the RE8 around, and squeezed into the rear cockpit ready for Morgan to take-off. Unfortunately, the RE8's undercarriage smashed into a large boulder, and the three flyers were now stranded some 120 miles inside enemy territory.

Over the next few days the three climbed the Kuflan Kuh while evading Turkish patrols, lying low during the nights, and managing to steal fruit and berries from a village as they walked an average of twenty miles each day. Finally, on 18 October, the trio, exhausted and dehydrated, were able to reach an area regularly patrolled by LAMBs, and waved down a patrol about midday. Arriving at Zenjan that evening they were informed of 'Taffy' Williams' remarkable adventure.

On 1 October, the RAF dropped surrender leaflets over the Ottoman lines which announced Allenby's victory in Palestine and the surrender of the Ottoman forces fighting there. Consequently and before the final expected British assault on Mosul, the Ottomans were ordered to withdraw, including what was left of the Ottoman flying service.

However, it was not until late October that the British could fully implement a large-scale assault up the Tigris River valley. Problems with the heat and stretched lines of communication meant a lack of necessary supplies. A lack of support from an ambivalent Indian Government comfortably sitting at Simla didn't help either. General Marshall also had to contend with a reduction in his forces as two divisions had previously been withdrawn to support Allenby's final Palestine campaign. Thus, the push to Mosul was on, although the Turks were already a beaten force and sought terms for peace. But Mosul was rich in oil, and the British wanted to secure possession before the armistice could be signed.

So on 6 October, Marshall ordered the taking

Three RE8s and two Martinsydes of 'A' Flight, at Zenjan, Persia. Second from left is B6585, fitted with a Davis gun..

Bristol M.1C C4934 of 72 Sqn. On 14 July Lt S.D. MacDonald force-landed this aircraft at Nijara on the Diyala river after the engine failed at 100ft. Later, on 25 October, he had to force land this same aircraft in enemy territory six miles east of Altun Kupri. The machine was burnt, and Lt MacDonald was then picked up by Lt A.P. Adams and Capt Mellows in an RE8 of 30 Squadron.

of Fathah Gorge, some 35 miles north of Tikrit, as a launching point for Mosul. He directed Brig-Gen Arthur Lewin[98] of the III Corps to cover the right flank, while the I Corps under Lt-Gen Alexander Cobbe[99] would make a frontal assault. Air cover for I Corps was provided by 63 Squadron and 'A' Flight of 72 Squadron, now flying Camels from Samarra. 30 Squadron at Baquba and Kifri plus 'C' flight 72 Squadron at Mirjana, were attached to General Lewin's column. Prior to the assault, aircraft carried out low level machine-gun raids on tented camps, and enemy cavalry, results and observations being dropped by message bags to British troops. The combined armies made their move on the 23rd and by the next morning, the Turks had fled. The war just petered out and the British took Mosul in the first week of November. That ended all offensive operations.

Although the war was coming to an end, the fighting continued. In an incident reminiscent of Lt Frank McNamara's VC escapade in 1917, at the end of October, Lt Somerled Douglas Macdonald of 'C' Flight 72 Squadron force landed six miles from Altun Kopri in Bristol M.1C C4934, hit while low strafing enemy troops. Minutes later Lt Allen Adams and Capt Arthur Mellows of 30 Squadron, in an RE8 landed beside him, burnt his machine and flew him safely back to Tuz Khurmatli. Meanwhile, other aircraft of 30 Squadron circled above to ensure that the Turkish cavalry did not attempt a capture.

On the morning of 30 October 1918, the Turkish Commander, Ismail Hakki Bey surrendered his Tigris force. Faced with this, the enemy at Altun Kopri evacuated their positions and retreated towards Mosul. An armistice was signed the next day and so ended the war in Mesopotamia.

The last airman to die on operations in the Mesopotamian theatre during 'the Great War' was an Australian, Lt Hugh Cannell whose family came from Perth. Cannell was with 72 Squadron and on one of the very last flights at the end of the war on 29 October, he was shot down by ground fire. Unfortunately, he succumbed to his wounds the day of the armistice but he would not be the last RAF casualty in Iraq.

Schüz best summed up the demise of the Ottoman flying units in Mesopotamia when he wrote in 1919 of their evacuation and loss:[100]

At the very last moment our squadron broke away from the enemy, and, since their retreat to Aleppo was cut off, arrived after infinite trouble by way of Mardin, Malatia, Sivas, and Amasia to Samsun on the Black Sea.
All was now lost for the Turkish Air Service. This was particularly tragic to us, who saw ourselves now condemned definitely to remain upon the defensive, and by way of matériel had to content ourselves with any scraps that were left over from the Western Front.

At Samsun, they awaited transport to Germany which finally arrived in January 1919.

Left: Captured Albatros D.III on the aerodrome at Mosul, occupied by 30 Squadron in the first week of December 1918. The cutaway behind the pilot's cockpit may represent an attempt to convert the machine to a two-seater. Right: A British pilot stands in front of a Halberstadt D.II and the Albatros, which now has a cover fastened over the rear cutout.

30 Squadron HQ and 'C' Flight hangars at Baqubah aerodrome, about 35 miles north east from Baghdad on the Diyala River. The squadron were supporting operations in Khurdistan from this location in October 1918.

'A' Flight, 30 Sqn personnel at Zenjan, Persia, October/November 1918. Officers seated, l-r: 2Lt J. Chacksfield (O), Lt T.A. Tindle (O), Lt P. Phillips (P), Lt A.E. Morgan (P), Capt Frank Nuttall (Flt Cdr), Lt A.L.G. Campbell (P), Lt H.A. Anson (P), J.B. Case (O).

'C' Flight, 30 Sqn, October 1918. Standing l-r: Capt A.H. Mellows (O), 2Lt A. Bentley (O), Lt C.H. Holland (O), Lt F.C. de L. Kirk (O), 2Lt E.D.G. Hughes, Lt R.B. Herring (EO3 Photo). Seated: Lt J.W.C.L. Gordon (P), Capt A.P. Adams (P), Capt F.V. Devonshire (P), Lt A.W. Hawkins (P), Lt F.W. Carryer (P). On ground: Lt C.H.E. Ridpath (EO Wireless), Lt W. Birtwhistle (EO3 Wireless), 2Lt E.N. Fletcher (P).

Armistice, but No Peace

The RFC Aircraft Park when relocated to Baghdad, near the terminus of Berlin-Baghdad Railway. The large building behind the hangars was formerly the German wireless station. This view shows the developed state of the Park in 1918.

As the bells rang out across Britain on 11 November 1918 to announce the end of the war in Europe, the RAF in Iraq knew that their operational flying would not end immediately. Following the Turkish surrender, Iraq was under the control of the GOC British forces, but power was exercised through a Civil Commissioner, Sir Arnold Wilson.[101] The civil administration was essentially Western in nature and would remain until October 1920. With reductions in Army units at the end of the war, it fell to the fledgling RAF to continue monitoring the situation with photographic work, artillery co-operation, and bombing raids mounted against hostile tribes.

An aerial view of Baghdad, looking south down the Tigris early in 1918. GHQ, the GOC's building, a hospital and 31 Wing RFC Headquarters on the river frontage are among the features marked. The aerodrome is shown top right.

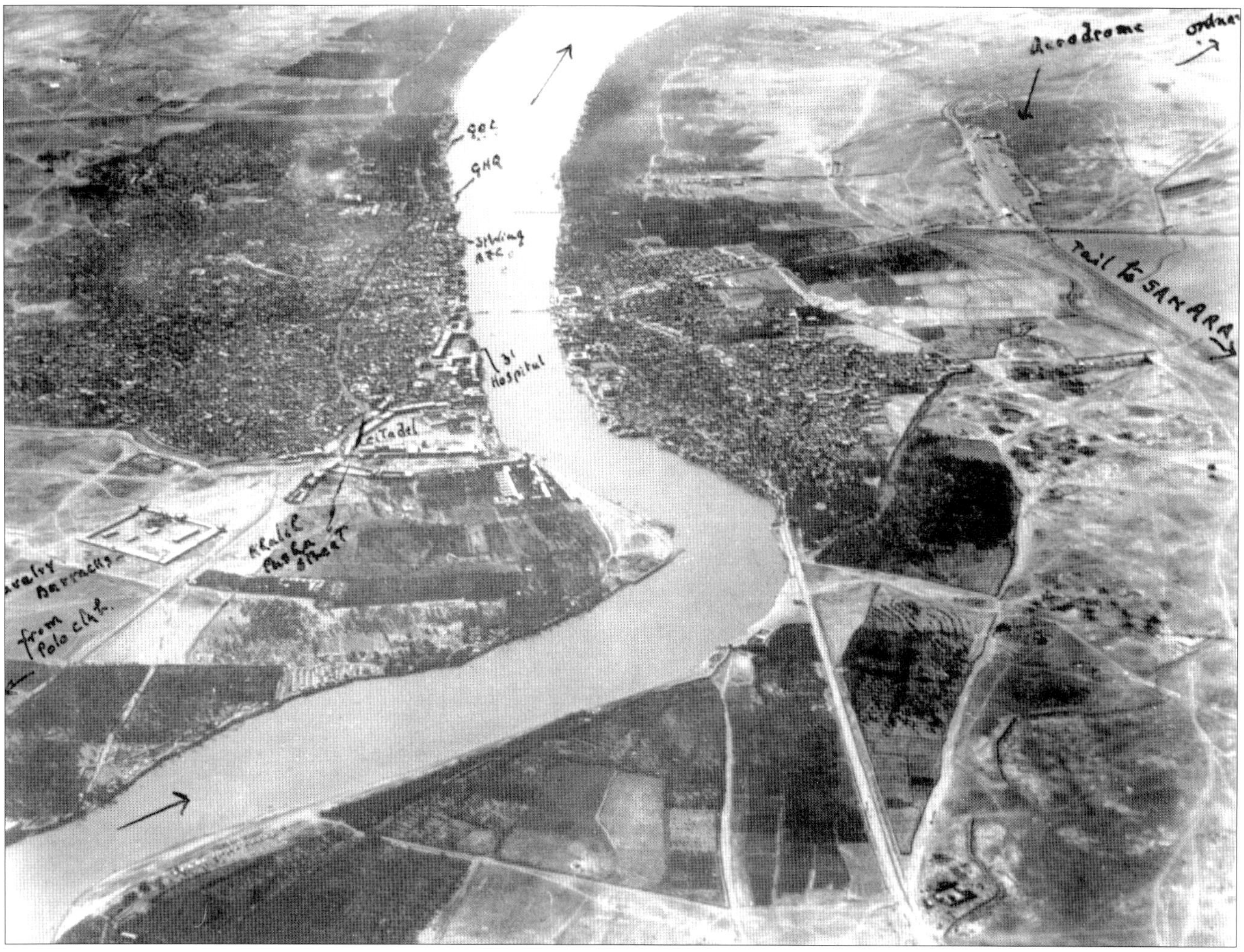

Back to where it all began. An RE8 of 'C' Flight, 30 Squadron, over Bushire province in South Persia where German influence with local tribes had obliged the British to station troops that might otherwise have taken part in operations elsewhere.

30 Squadron and 72 Squadron still operated in Persia and on 12 December, Lt Rodney Beresford of 'A' flight 30 Sqn (previously with 63 Sqn) was reported missing. He was found on the 16th at Kherlieh 40 miles from Hamadan suffering from fever, and was posted home a few weeks later.

On 28 December, 30 Squadron personnel left Baquba for Ahwaz and Bushire, South Persia to arrange a landing ground for operations against the Qashqai Tribe. The first of January 1919 saw 'C' flight making the journey via Baghdad and then to Bushire by river boat and steamer, arriving on the 13th. Also on this date Lt 'Taffy' Williams, flying Spad A8824, was killed at Baghdad when the aircraft broke up in the air while he was attempting a loop. He was just 21.

North from Baghdad, 63 Squadron had supported Army units as they advanced, and reached Mosul by 1 November. Over 700 hours had been flown by 15 machines with many aircraft operating from Tikrit, which was a flight of some eighty miles before the Army front lines were reached. During this period, only one machine was lost, plus one broken undercarriage and one forced landing due to engine trouble. It was a fitting testament to the ground crews from all three squadrons who had carried out their duties in some of the most hostile conditions imaginable. The *London Gazette* of 1 January 1919 reflected this with a long list of Meritorious Service Medal awards, and would do so until at least June. Included on the list were Chief Mechanic Gerald Gardner of 30 Squadron who had served for two years, 11 months in 'Mespot', plus previous service in France; Flt Sgt William Harvey Stewart also of 30 Squadron – two years nine months in 'Mespot' without leave; Sgt Howard Snook, of the Aircraft Park who served between December 1916 and December 1918; and F/Clerk Arthur Charles Waddell Trotman, Aircraft Park between October 1916 and December 1918.

The operations in Bushire would continue until March 1919. On the late afternoon of the 6th, 30 Squadron flew its final offensive operation against

Spad S.VII A8840 and Sopwith Camel D6451, both flown by 72 Sqn during the latter part of 1918.

Officers of 72 Sqn, Baghdad, December 1918, l-r: Lt W.M.W. Thomas, Lt G.S. McKee, Lt T.L. Williams, Lt T.A. Pitt, Lt P.J.T. Baddiley, Lt M.S. Mackay, Capt F.H. Coleman, Lt R.P.P. Pope, Maj O.T. Boyd, CO, Lt S.G. Hollingworth, Lt D.F. Lapraik, Lt E.A. Scales, Lt S.D. MacDonald, Lt G.R.P. Wall

tribesmen located at the village of Khun. Martinsyde 7461 was flown by Capt A.P. Adams, Lt Frederick William Carryer, 2Lt E.D.G. Hughes (RE8 D6709) and Lt Sydney Bull with AM Judge as observer in another RE8. Sixteen 20lb bombs were dropped with six direct hits on houses in the village. In a bitter blow to the squadron, Captain Adams was hit in the head by ground fire, while flying at low level, and crashed. Despite the very rough ground, Lt Bull tried to land beside the wreckage,(the wheels of the RE8 actually touched the ground twelve yards from the Martinsyde) but he was driven off by heavy ground fire. Adams' body was recovered on 12 March. Capt Adams had served with 47 Squadron in Salonika as an observer before joining 30 Squadron on 6 August 1917. His DFC had been gazetted on 1 January 1919, the award being on a list that included seven other flying officers who had served in Mesopotamia. Lt Bull would also receive the DFC for this attempted rescue.

In one final blow to the veterans of the 'Mespot' air war, Flt Lt Frank Nuttall was killed flying RE8 B4698 on 18 September 1920. Nuttall had remained with 30 Squadron until March 1919 before a transfer to 63 Squadron. A further transfer to Egypt followed, but he returned in 1920, commanding 'B' flight of 30 Squadron in February 1920. Nuttall had been awarded the DFC in July 1919 and the AFC in October. Nuttall's courage, and devotion to duty, shown in some of the harshest conditions experienced by a fledgling air service, would set the standard that the RAF would follow in the post-war years.

New Zealander Capt Frank Nuttall, DFC, AFC, OC 'A' Flt 30 Sqn with a Martinsyde Elephant named 'PAN-K-KOS'. (See photo p75.) Nuttall served continuously in Mesopotamia from April 1917 beyond the end of the war. He was briefly posted elsewhere, but soon returned, to meet his end in the area where he had given his greatest service.

Above: SE5as and Sopwith Camel of 'A' Flt, 72 Sqn on Baghdad aerodrome, December 1918.

Top right: 63 Squadron DH9 C6295, seen here ready for a bombing raid, was also used as a mail plane between Baghdad and Cairo early in 1919. The era of regular long distance flights was beginning.

Right: Handley Page O/400 C9700 had arrived at Baghdad on 4 December 1918 on the way to India. One of the passengers on this flight was Lt-Col N.D.K. MacEwen who had been Assistant Director of Aviation Mesopotamia in 1916.

Above: Line-up of 72 sqn aircraft at Baghdad aerodrome on 10 January 1919. Nearest are two SE5as, then two Sopwith Camels, Spad S.VIIs and Bristol M.1C monoplanes. In the background, and below is Handley Page O/400 C9700, which took-off to continue its pioneering flight to India on the following day.

30 SQUADRON LOCATIONS JANUARY – NOVEMBER 1918

	HQ	A Flight	B Flight	C Flight
1 Jan 18	Baquba	Baquba	Fallujah	Baquba
23 Feb 18	Ramadi	Baquba	Ramadi	Baquba
1 Mar 18	Uqbah	Baquba	Ramadi	Uqbah
9 Mar 18	Uqbah	Uqbah	Uqbah	Uqbah
11 Mar 18	Uqbah	Hit	Hit	Baquba
5 Apr 18	Baquba	Baquba	Hit	Baquba
14 Apr 18	Baquba	Baquba	Ramadi	Baquba
2 May 18	Baquba	Baquba	Ramadi	(½) Tuz Khurmatli (½) Kifri
26 May 18	Baquba	Baquba	Ramadi	(½) Tuz Khurmatli (½) Kifri
Early-Jul 18	Baquba	Kifri	Kifri	Kifri
30 Sep 18	Kifri	(½) Kifri (½) Zinjan	Kifri	(½) Kifri (½) Hamadan
Mid-Nov 18	Baquba	Kifri	Kifri	Baquba

63 SQUADRON LOCATIONS JANUARY – NOVEMBER 1918

Date	HQ	A Flight	B Flight	C Flight
1 Jan 18	Samarra	Samarra	Samarra	Samarra
23 Feb 18	Samarra	Samarra Det Ramadi	Samarra	Samarra
25 March 18	Samarra	Samarra	Hit	Hit
29 Mar 18	Samarra	Samarra	Samarra	Samarra
19 Apr 18	Baquba	Samarra	Samarra	Samarra
Mid-May 18	Samarra	Samarra	Samarra	Samarra
15 Oct 18	Tikrit	Tikrit	Tikrit	Tikrit
30 Sep 18	Tikrit	Tikrit	Tikrit	Tikrit
31 Oct 18	Samarra	Mosul	Ramadi	Tikrit

72 SQUADRON LOCATIONS JANUARY – NOVEMBER 1918

Date	HQ	A Flight	B Flight	C Flight
2 Mar 18	Basra	Basra	Basra	Basra
17 Mar 18	Samarra	Samarra	Basra	Mirjana
Mid-Apr 18	Samarra	Samarra	Baghdad	Mirjana
22 May 18	Samarra	Samarra	(½) Hamadan (½) Baghdad	Mirjana
30 May 18	Baghdad	Samarra	Baghdad	Mirjana
30 Sep 18	Zinjan	Samarra	Zinjan	Zinjan

OTHER UNITS IN MESOPOTAMIA JANUARY – OCTOBER 1918

Unit	Location
31st Wing HQ	Baghdad
23rd KB Company HQ	Baghdad
51st KBS	Samarra
52nd KBS	Ramadi
Aircraft Park	Basra
Advanced Aircraft Park	Baghdad

ENDNOTES

1. Maj-Gen (Later Lieutenant General) Sir George Frederick Gorringe KCB, KCMG, DSO.
2. Lt-Gen Sir John Eccles Nixon KCB.
3. Maj-Gen Sir Charles Vere Ferrers Townshend KCB, DSO.
4. Lt/Col Philip William Lilian Broke-Smith Deputy then Assistant Director Aviation for the Indian Army in Mesopotamia. 9 April 1915 – 16 August 1916
5. AWM MSS 511 – MO 199 Table 4. Laverton was then the generic name for the Point Cook location.
6. Cutlack, F.M. *Official History of Australia in the War ... Vol. VIII* 1938, p 2.
7. AWM 224, Item No MSS513. The anonymous author is most likely Private John Brown (based upon commentary about his invalided return to Australia).
8. TNA: 674/21/6/87 – Campaign in Mesopotamia – 1914-18.
9. Also called Tanumah, the location was selected after the original site at Mekina Malsus (2 nm NW of Basra) became flooded.
10. Cutlack, p 5.
11. AWM 224 Item No MS513.
12. AA Series A2023 Item No A38/8/202 – Petre Reports.
13. Moberly, Brig-Gen F.J., *The Campaign in Mesopotamia*, Vol I, HMSO, London, 1924, p 269. It would not be till the end of the year before the promise would be fulfilled.
14. AA Series A2023 Item No A38/8/202.
15. Moberly, Vol I, p 290.
16. Wheeler, CPL W., Formation of First Half-Flight, Unpublished manuscript, RAAF Museum.
17. No 30 Sqn, RFC would relocate to Basra on 7 Dec 15. New arrivals would be 'B' Flight under Captain Arnold Graves and 'C' Flight under Major Seaton Massy. Massy would command the unit from 22 Nov 15.
18. AWM PR84/224 – W.H. Treloar Letters.
19. Flanagan, Dr Brian P., 'The Indian Flying Corps and the Australian Half-Flight', *Cross & Cockade (US) Journal*, Vol 17, No 2, Summer 1976, p 173.
20. Jones, H.A., *The War in the Air*, Vol V, Clarendon Press, Oxford, 1935, p 265. QV. *The Battle of Suliman Pak* by Staff Bimbishi Muhammad Amin.
21. The official numbers were 3152 British, 8455 Indian and 3530 camp followers.
22. Here records differ and are incomplete. One of IFC12, 12A and 14 was apparently flown out by an unnamed British pilot. The other two were abandoned. Henshaw also claims a Voisin was lost, but it must have arrived in Kut after Feb 1916.
23. Lt-Gen Sir Fenton John Aylmer VC, KCB had been sent out from India to command the Meerut Division, but on arrival was given the task of relieving Kut.
24. Maj-Gen Sir George John Younghusband KCMG, KCIE, CB.
25. Flanagan, Dr. Brian P., 'The History of the Ottoman Air Force in the Great War: The Reports of Major Erich Serno', *Cross & Cockade US Journal*, Vol 11, 1970, p 123-124.
26. Moberly, Vol II, p 111.
27. Moberly, Vol II, p 200.
28. *The Royal Air Force in the Great War*, Air Historical Branch, HMSO, London, p 142.
29. Moberly, Vol II, p 307.
30. Schüz quoted in Major Georg Paul Neumann, *The German Air Force in the Great War*, Hodder & Stroughton, London, 1920, p259.
31. Moberly, Vol II, p302.
32. AWM 224 MSS 513.
33. Williams, *These Are Facts*, AWM, Canberra, 1971, p 40 and CRS A2023 Item No A38/8/188.
34. http://www.nationalarchives.gov.uk/pathways/firstworldwar/battles/mesopotamia.htm
35. *Freiherr* (Count) Kolmar von der Goltz. b. Bielkenfeld, Prussia, 12 Aug 1843. d. Baghdad, 19 Apr 1916. Modernised the Turkish Army in the 1880s and 1890s. Although officially died of Typhus fever, he was also reputedly poisoned by assassins from the Young Turk movement.
36. Gen Sir Percy Henry Noel Lake KCB, KCMG. b. 29 June 1855, Preston, Lanc. d. 17 Nov 1940, Victoria, BC, Canada.
37. Copy of a letter by Colin Sutherland (AFC no 437) dated 27 Jul 1973 in Mark Lax collection.
38. TNA. Air 1 505 – *Personnel and Seaplanes, RNAS Stations in Mesopotamia – Proposed withdrawal of, May 1916*. Folio 5A provided Army Council approval dated 16 May.
39. These included one Albatros C.I (AK.5), one Albatros B.I, wireless equipped (A.8) and one Fokker E.I (F.3).
40. Franz von Aulock left the COs job at *2nci Tayyare Bölük* in September 1916 and ran the German Aircraft Park in Baghdad until his untimely death in an aircraft accident at Mosul on 2 April 17.
41. Aircraft included two Albatros C.Is, one Albatros B.I (wireless equipped), and one Fokker E.I. They were also using Farman MF7 and Caudron IFC3 for observation. Aircrew consisted of four pilots and four observers.
42. *History of the Ottoman Air Force in the Great War: The Reports of Major Eric Serno*, pt 1, p 133.
43. Tennant, *In the Clouds Above Baghdad*, The Battery Press, Nashville, 1992 reprint, pp16-17 and 23.
44. One Albatros C.I, three Albatros C.IIIs and a Fokker E.III. With them three pilots and three observers.
45. Lt-Gen Sir Frederick Stanley Maude KCB, CMG, DSO. b. 24 June 1864, Gibraltar. d. 18 Nov 1917, Baghdad.
46. Hamlin in his excellent history of 30 Sqn, *Flat Out*, claims the pilot was (Vzfw Max) Konrad and the observer Capt Wilhelm Niemayer (the CO). This cannot be the case as Niemayer was killed on 19 Jan 1917. Nikolajsen in his seminal study, *Ottoman Aviation 1909-1919*, claims the observer was Ltn.Back. The 30 Sqn *History* by Major Everidge does not give names.
47. We have quoted the Turkish Sqn number and use the vernacular 2nd Turkish Sqn as opposed to *Fliegerabteilung 2* (FlAbt 2 or FA2) to avoid confusion with the German Sqn of the same title. This style is used throughout.
48. Strangely, the 30 Sqn records make no mention of this action, possibly because the Albatros made it back to the Turkish lines.
49. Four Albatros C.III – serials AK13 and AK26, and most probably two of AK29, AK32 or AK33. Fokker E.III – serial F13. Nikolajsen and Yilmazer, p 147.
50. *The Campaign in Mesopotamia*, Operations Section, Air Historical Branch, June 1922.
51. Halberstadt D.V serials HK2, HK3 and HK6. A further eight Albatros C.IIIs serials AK54-57, 64, 66-68 arrived in May.
52. Tennant, *In the Clouds above Baghdad*, p131.
53. *The London Gazette*, 26 July 1917, p 7634. Award dated 1 April 1917.
54. Neumann, p 260.
55. The numbers can be deceiving. Of the 21 BEs, only nine were serviceable. Of the seven Martinsydes only three were serviceable and of the Scouts, only two.
56. Some sources call the pilot Ponrich while others have Pomerich.
57. Sources are unclear. This could also be *Feldwebel* Notte.
58. Air 1/408/15/238/1 – *History of No 63 Sqn RAF Mesopotamia Expeditionary Force*, p 3.
59. Philpott was one of the most experienced pilots in the Sqn. The others were Acting Corporal Oliver William Edward Grant, Lt Malcolm Glassford Begg, MC and Lt Edward Noel Baillon, 24th Canadian Reserve. See *History of No. 63 Sqn*, p 7.
60. RAFM: AC1997/127/9 – *The Diary of Three Officers in the Hands of the Turks from the Date of their Internment to the Arrival at Place of Internment*. Quote altered into first person narrative.
61. By October, 63 Sqn had a mixed bag of eight RE8s, two Spads, two Bristol Scouts and three Martinsyde G.100s. Made prisoner on the 5th were Lt John Duncan George MacRae (sometimes spelt McRae) Seaforth Highlanders & RFC and his observer 2Lt John Wallace Blake, 60th Rifles & RFC.
62. Martyn, Errol W., *For Your Tomorrow*, Vol 1, Volplane Press, Christchurch, 1998, p 45.
63. Lt-Gen Sir William Raine Marshall GCMG, KCB, KCSI.
64. Halberstadt serials HK.11-20 and AEGs serials AEG 4, 6, 8, 9-14, 16 and 7066 and 7068. Nikolajsen p 140.
65. AHB: Air 1/408 *The Campaign in Mesopotamia*, Ch 6, p 16-17.
66. Nikolajsen, p 140.

67 *The Campaign in Mesopotamia*, Ch 6, p 66-67.
68 Major Georg Paul Neumann, *The German Air Force in the Great War*, Naval & Military Press (reprint), Uckfield, 1920, p 2.
69 Maj-Gen Lionel Charles Dunsterville CB, CSI.
70 In all, 558 Australian signallers were sent to Mesopotamia. C.E.W. Bean, 'The Australians in France During the Main German Offensive, 1918', *The Official History of Australia in the War of 1914-1918*, Angus and Robertson, Sydney, 1938, Vol 5, Appendix 5, p 704. For further on Dunsterforce, see Keast Burke, *With the Horse and Morse in Mesopotamia*, Arthur McQuitty & Co, Sydney, 1927.
71 J.M. Bruce, *British Aeroplanes 1914-18*, Putnam, London, 1957, p 179.
72 J.M. Bruce, *The Aeroplanes of the Royal Flying Corps (Military Wing)*, Putnam, London, 1982, pp 557-58.
73 Maj J. Everidge MC RAF, *History of No. 30 Squadron Royal Air Force*, Baghdad, 1919, p 206. Copy held at the Air Historical Branch, London.
74 2AM Robert Gregory Castor RFC, No. 186221. b. Baghdad (North Gate) War Cemetery, grave III.D.4. Castor is also listed in some sources as Lance Sergeant with number P/11439.
75 Peter Wright, 'Captain Gerald Merton, MC', *Cross & Cockade International Journal*, Vol 15, No 1, 1984, p 33.
76 Lt-Col John E. Tennant, *In the Clouds above Baghdad*, The Battery Press (reprint), Nashville, 1992, p 248.
77 Peter Wright, 'Lieutenant A.E. Lionel Skinner, MC', *Cross & Cockade International Journal*, Vol 15, No 2, 1984, pp 59-60.
78 1AM John M. Nelson, RFC. No. 27066. b. Basra War Cemetery, grave III.K.12.
79 Tennant, *In the Clouds above Baghdad*, p 165.
80 H.A. Jones, *The War in the Air*, Vol 5, The Naval and Military Press (reprint), Uckfield, 1935, p 325.
81 *History of No. 30 Squadron*, p 34.
82 Maj (later Maj-Gen Sir) Percy Cleghorn Stanley Hobart KBE, CB, DSO, MC Royal Engineers.
83 Brig (later Gen Sir) Robert Archibald Cassells GCB, GCSI, DSO.
84 Burke, *With the Horse and Morse in Mesopotamia*, p 71.
85 Sir Miles Thomas, 'Mesopotamia: The Air War', *The History of the First World War*, Vol 7, No 5, Purnell, London, p 2831.
86 AHB: Air 1/408/15/238/1 – *History of No. 63 Squadron RAF Mesopotamia Expeditionary Force*.
87 Brig-Gen F.J. Moberly, *The Campaign in Mesopotamia*, Vol IV, HMSO, London, 1924-25, pp 112-13.
88 These were Albatros serials AK1, 2, & 4-8 and Halberstadt HK9. Nikolajsen, *Ottoman Aviation 1909-1919*, p 148.
89 Franks et al in *Above the Lines* claim Schüz was posted to the Palestine Front with Turkish *FliegerAbteilung* 13. This is not correct as the 13th Squadron remained in Mesopotamia for the rest of the war.
90 2Lt Robert Stewart Blucke Dorset Regt & RAF. 63 Sqn 25 May 18 – 20 Sep 18. Peter Liddle, *The Airman's War 1914-18*, Blandford Press, Poole, 1987, p 130. Blucke ended his air force career as Air Vice-Marshal R.S. Blucke CB, CBE, DSO, AFC* MID.
91 Maj George Adam Beazeley DSO, RE. Some sources incorrectly list his name as Beasley.
92 Recorded in *No. 72 Squadron History*, Air Historical Branch, London. A framed copy hangs in the crew room of the current 72 Squadron at RAF Linton-on-Ouse.
93 *History of No. 30 Squadron Royal Air Force*, p 250.
94 *Supplement to the London Gazette*, No. 30950 of 15 October 1918, p 12066.
95 1AM Frederick Suthurst, RAF. No. 12793. b. Baghdad (North Gate) War Cemetery, Spec. Memorial No. 1.
96 Brian P. Flanagan, 'Part 4: Last Days of the Ottoman Air Force', *The Reports of Major Serno*, Cross & Cockade US Journal, 1970, p 351.
97 Nikolajsen, p 146.
98 Brig-Gen Arthur Corrie Lewin CB, CBE, DSO.
99 Lt-Gen Sir Alexander Stanhope Cobbe VC, GCB, KCSI, DSO.
100 Neumann, p 264.
101 Sir Arnold Talbot Wilson KCIE, CSI, CMG, DSO.

Selected Personnel Biographies

ALLEN PERCY ADAMS
Born 1898 son of Percy and Leonie Adams, Halstead Essex. Commis in RFC 2Lt Observer. Posted to 47 Sqn Macedonia 20.10.16. Served until 11.5.17 then to Egypt for pilot training. Joined 30 Sqn 6.8.17. Prom Capt OC 'C' Flt DFC gaz 1.1.1919. Shot down by ground fire at Khun Bushire, South Persia 6.3.1919 and killed.

JOHN OLIVER ALLISON
Born 8 October 1891 Maxwell Ontario Canada. In May 1916 he joined the 162nd Battln Canadian Army as signals Officer. Jnd RFC as a pilot (date not known) and trained Egypt (no details) Posted to 30 Sqn Mesopotamia 17.8.17. On 15.5.18 Allison and his obs Lt F.W. Atherton were shot down in flames by three Albatros scouts while m.g. troops near Altun Kupri, Lesser Zeb River. He was posthumously awarded the MC & Bar for low level work earlier in the campaign.

PERCY AINSWORTH
Born Blackburn Lancashire 14.1.1890 yarn and cloth merchant. Commis in the Manchester Regt later 126 Machine Gun Company 42nd Division. Jnd RFC as an obs and posted to 1 Sqn AFC (67 Sqn RFC) 22.7.16 remaining until 18.12.16. To pilot training 23 RS 20 T Wing Egypt then to UK. Joined 63 Sqn Cramlington 24.4.17 To Mespot with unit Served until 17.8.18 Prom Capt To Egypt as instructor 20 TDS and 38 Wing 8.9.18 then back to 20 TDS 22.9.18. To UK 13 Training Group 4 TDS Jan 1919 demobbed 17.3.19.

HENRY ADELBERT ANSON
Born 21.12.1895 in Texas second son of Hon Francis Anson, grandson of George Anson 2nd Earl of Lichfield Returned to England aged 13 educated Harrow. Gaz 2Lt South Wales Brders 26.8.14 to Aden 12.12.14. Posted India August 1915 Lt 15.10.16. Trans to RFC 23 May 1917 for pilot trg (no details) then joined 30 Sqn 15.7.17. Remained in Mespot until April 1919 including 63 Sqn 'A' Flt CO at Kasvin Persia Feb 1919. To UK 22.4.19

JAMES STANLEY BEATTY
Born Toronto Canada 15.10.1888. Attend University of Toronto studied law, called to the Ontario Bar 1914. Accepted as a Ross-Hume recruited candidate and sailed to UK 27.11.15. Arr 5.12.15 pilot trg on MFLHs 5 RS. Completed 'ticket' after 215min instruction 17.1.16 To 33 TS Bristol on BEs and 7 RS Netheravon. To France with 26hr 46min solo 5.5.16 posted to 5 Sqn Droglandt. Trans to 18 Sqn Bailleul 23.5.16 remaining until 21.12.16. To UK as instructor 43 RS Market Drayton Jan 1917 55 RS Yatesbury March 1917 for two months. Leave to Canada May 1917 then posted to 72 RS Netheravon 27th July 1917. Sqn moved to Sedgeford then Mespot Arr 2.3.18 in charge of Sqn transport and aircraft. Remained with 72 Sqn until 7.11.18 'A' Flt CO. DFC Gaz 15.7.1919.

MALCOLM GLASSFORD BEGG
Date, place of birth not known. Attend Marborough College, and Caius College Cambridge studying medicine at outbreak of war. Commis Rifle Brigade then transfer to RFC as Obs. In 9 Sqn Feb 1916 (together with J. Everidge, A.J.G. Styran and R.D. Simpson all of whom were to serve in 63 Sqn). To UK pilot trg. At 83 Sqn Spittlegate then 63 Cramlington 7.5.17. To Mespot. On 25.9.17 force landed in enemy territory with his obs Lt E.N. Baillon (Canadian) became POWs. Repatriated by the Turks 16.12.18.

CUTHBERT GEORGE BELLORD
Date, place of birth not known. Educated Downside Abbey near Bath (Catholic Public School) then Worcester College Oxford studying law. Taken ill with TB and spent a year in Switzerland, joined father's law firm. Commis 8th Kings Shropshire Light Inftry and later Cyclist Corps. Joined RFC August 1917, pilot trg 21 TS Egypt. Flew MFSHs 7hr dual and 5hr solo. To 22 TS Oct 1917 Avro and Bristol Scouts graduated as scout pilot 22.11.17 with 45hr flying time including 33hr solo. Posted 72 Sqn Mespot 'C' Flt Bristol monoplanes. Admitted to hospital May 1918 after a knee injury and later invalided to India. Admin duties to end of war. Demobbed June 1919.

OWEN TUDOR BOYD
Born 30.8.1889, Marylebone London. Commis 2Lt Indian Army 20.1.1909 to 5th Cavalry I A Rawalpindi 15.3.1910. In India until 1912. To France with Regt then to RFC pilot training, CFS Upavon 14.3.16. To 27 Sqn France 29.5.16, MC for low level attack on enemy train. MC Gaz 9.8.16. Remained with 27 Sqn until 10.10.16 then to UK as instructor, 28 RS Castle Bromwich and Hounslow 42 RS and 28 RS. Prom Temp Major to 66 Sqn Filton Bristol as CO 3.1.17. To France remaining until 22.6.17. Posted to Mespot as Staff Officer (listed as Staff Capt) 31 Wing HQ 25 Nov 1917. To 72 Sqn as CO 7.7.18 until 6.1.1919. Appt OC 31 Wing this date with rank of LtCol. Remained in Mespot until 22.5.1920. OBE awarded 10.10.19. AFC awarded same date.

ROBERT ANSTRUTHER BRADLEY
Born Malta 1879. Joined Argyll & Sutherland Highlanders as a private 1899. Served Boer War. Commis in North Staffs Regt (His father was CO) Capt by 1910. To France 1914 trans to RFC pilot trg and gained RAeC Cert 1237, 12.5.15. Served with 30 Sqn Mespot Nov 1915 until March 1916. Prom Major to Egypt as CO 58 RS. Returned to Mespot as CO 63 Sqn 5.11.17 until 8.4.18. Prom Lt.Col. to OC 31st Wing HQ this date. To HE 6.1.1919.

LANCELOT HAROLD BROWNING
Born 25.9.1897. Educated Wellington College 1911-14. Commis 2Lt Royal Artillery 28.7.15. 2Lt RFC 17.5.16 and posted 30 Sqn as Obs 6.6.16. Remained until 10.1.17 then pilot trg including 57 TS Egypt. Retnd to 30 Sqn 7.12.17, MC May 1918. Prom Capt. To Egypt 3.7.18 posted to 111 Sqn 3.9.18 to 23.11.18. Returned to Mespot post-war with 63 Sqn (May-July 1919). DFC Gaz 10.7.1920. Killed while flying 1928.

HERBERT CHAPLIN
Born 31.1.1880 London. Jnd RNAS as a Petty Officer Engineer Oct 1914 and trained Crystal Palace. Prom to CPO March 1915 posted to France. Wounded and invalided to UK July 1915 (no details). Posted to Major Robert Gordon's RNAS Detachment Mespot Sept 1915. Served until Feb 1916. On 14.2.16 Chaplin was the obs in converted Short 822 which was crashed by FSL W.H. Dunn. To hospital then India. To UK East Fortune, Aug 1916 then Crystal Palace Jan 1917 and Greenwich RN College Aug 17 as Instructor. To Calshot March 1918 Commis 2Lt RAF April 1918 then Alexandria Egypt as Engineer Officer. To HE 1.9.18,

HERBERT PRINSEP SOMERS CLOGSTOUN
Born 19 Sept 1888 India. Went to Clifton School. Learnt to fly Autumn 1914 and gained RAeC Cert 1022, 24.12.14. Commis in the RFC 11.1.15, to Farnborough and Fort Grange. Posted RFC Egypt Detachment 14.8.15. This later became 'C' Flight 30 Sqn. To Mespot reported 30 Sqn 27.12.15 remained until 20.4.16. To 14 Sqn Egypt 7.7.16. Invalided to UK 19.7.16 then ret 27 RS 6.11.16 and 58 RS 11.12.1916. HQ 5 Wing Egypt 15.4.17 as acting Wing Adj then to HQ 40 Wing as Adj 5.10.17. To Staff Officer (3rd Class) 18.5.18 and Palestine Bde HQ as Adj. To UK 18.2.19 demob 2.3.1919.

REGINALD THOMAS COLLEY
Born 1895 India, Greek mother Irish Father. Educated Xaviers College Calcutta, St Josephs College, Darjeeling, Manchester School of Technology, and Owens College 1915. Trained at British Westinghouse Manchester, enlisted 1916. Joined RFC, trained as pilot (no details) Posted to 30 Sqn 19.10.16, served until 17.11.17 then to UK as instructor. 33 TDS Witney, and 24 TDS Collinstown Ireland until 17.10.18. To 55 Wing this date.

FRANCIS HENRY COLEMAN
Born St Peter Port Guernsey 17.8.1894. Educated Elizabeth College Guernsey. Joined Middlesex Regt then trans to RFC 1915. RAeC Cert 2710, 14.1.16. Posted to 32 Sqn (DH2) France 1916. At Farnborough as Inst Jan 17. Joined 72 Sqn as Flt Cdr August 1917 and served in Mespot until 2.4.1919. Acting CO 72 Sqn 6.1.1919 until 13.2.19. Remained in RAF post-war Sqn Leader Iraq 1923-28.

GORDON D. CROWTHER
Born Cobourg Ontario Canada and living in Toronto when his enlisted in the Canadian Field Artillery. Sailed to UK and transferred to RFC pilot trg. Posted to 63 Sqn Cramlington from 61 TS 9.6.17.

To Mespot but invalided out with nerve problems 26.10.17. (No other details known).

ARTHUR ARMSTRONG CULLEN
Date, place of birth not known. An undergraduate at Oxford University Aug 1914. Joined Oxford Sqn King Edwards Horse Cavalry Reserve before trans to Dublin Fusiliers. Served Gallipoli, Serbia and Macedonia before trans to the RFC as an observer. 47 Sqn Salonika April 17 then to Egypt pilot trg 23.9.17. At 58 TS Nov 17 then to 72 Sqn 3.1.18. Went on loan to 30 Sqn 21.3.18 to 12.4.18. On 31.8.18 while flying Martinsyde Elephant A3972 force landed near Mianeh North Persia and became POW. Repatriated by the Turks 30.12.18.

HENRY WYNN DEACON
Born 14.10.1893 Fontainebleau Paris. Educ Malvern School 1905–1911 then Sandhurst. Commis in the Royal Artillery WIA 1917. Trans to RFC posted to 63 Sqn as obs 12.9.18 remaining until 18.12.18. To Egypt No 3 SMA Jan 1919, 111 Sqn March 19. Injured April 1919 but ret to 111 Sqn 23.5.19 until Feb 1920. 14 Sqn 1.2.20 until 15.2.20. Prom Capt 12.9.18 DFC 5.4.1919.

CHARLES BRODERICK MITCALFE DALE
Born 15.4.1893. Educated Sherbourne School. Commis 4th Battln Northumberland Fuslrs 13.5.15. Trans to RFC 5.6.16 pilot trg (no details). Posted to 30 Sqn 17.8.17 until 9.1.18. Invalid to India. To Palestine 17 TDS Oct 18 until 1.7.1919. To 'P' Flight this date then 142 Sqn 1.8.1919.

THOMAS MALCOLM DICKINSON
Born 1893. Ed Wellington College and RMC. Jned 16th Cavalry Indian Army 19.1.12. Trans to RFC pilot trg 5.6.16 (no details). RAeC Cert 1625, 22.8.15. Gaz 2Lt flying officer 10.1.16. Served 30 Sqn 22.12.15 until 31.8.16 as obs. To France 56 Sqn 27.5.17 with 52 hrs solo flying time. Shot down by Jasta 28 on first OP 4.6.17 while flying SE5A A8920. Wounded both legs and POW.

WILFRED HENRY DUNN
Born 19.9.1893 at Cornigliano Genoa Italy. Indentured with the British India Steam Navigation Company for four years from 12.3.1910. 2nd mate 22.4.14. Joined RNAS for pilot training, RAeC Cert 1106 on 11.3.15. Posted Calshot May 1915 then HM Dockyard Portsmouth. Back to Calshot 15.6.15 then to HM seaplane carrier *Empress* 8.7.15. Left 27.11.15 posted Sqn Cdr F.W. Bowhill's detachment with 90hr flying time. To Mespot first flight 12.2.16. Allocated Voisin 8506 and did recce/bombing work including seven food dropping flight to Kut-al-Amara during the siege. Remained Mespot to July 16 then admitted to hospital. Sailed Bombay 16.7.16 then to Ceylon. To Zanzibar to rejoin Bowhill's Sqn Nov 1916. Remained until 5.1.18 DFC Gaz 22.2.18. Rtnd to UK permanent Commis in the RAF.

JAMES EVERIDGE
Born 1881. Joined Surrey Yeomanry (Queen Mary's Regt) prior to the outbreak of war and served five years. Not passed fit for service due to deafness. Learnt to fly at Brooklands pre-war then to Hendon for pilot Cert 1475. On the strength of this accepted in the RFC as an obs and posted 9 Sqn. In France from October 1915 then to UK pilot trg 6.6.16. To 27 RS 15.7.16, to Dover 13 RS 19.7.16. Posted Farnborough test and ferry pilot 31.8.16 then to 83 Sqn Spittlegate as instructor 23.3.17. To 63 Sqn Cramlington 2.6.17 with 199hr flying time. To Mespot as OC 'B' Flight. Remained with Sqn until 25.4.18 when prom Major and CO 30 Sqn. In Mespot until 2.5.1919.

EVELYN DALRYMPLE FANSHAWE
Born 25.5.1895, Peshawar India. Joined Queen's Bays 2nd Dragoon Guards then transfer to the RFC pilot training. RAeC Cert 4480, 13.4.17. Posted 72 Sqn in the UK 7.12.17. Served with squadron until 2.9.18. Prom Capt 23.8.18.

GEOFFREY FIELDEN
Born 4.5.1893, Headington Hall, Oxford. Commis 7th Queen's Own Hussars 1913 and joined Regt in India. Trans to RFC 19.8.17 pilot trg Egypt. 57(Res)Sqn MFSH BE2c BE2e and Avro, total time 8hr 51min including 5hr 4min solo. To No.3 School Military Aeronautics Sept 1917 then 58 TS October. School of Aerial Gunnery, Graduated 21.10.17 with 49hr including 37hr 49min solo. To 144 Sqn Palestine 23.4.18 to 5.7.18 then to Mespot arriv 16.7.18. To 63 Sqn for three days 27/29 August 1918 then 30 Sqn. Served with unit including Bushire, South Persia until reported sick 2.4.1919. Posted to UK and later rejoined Army unit.

CECIL BELL GASSON
Born 3.5.1881, Queenstown South Africa. Joined RNAS for pilot training (no details) RAeC Cert 1618, 20.8.15. Posted to SqnCdr F.W. Bowhill's unit, arr Mespot 8.2.16. Allocated Short Seaplane 8044, carried out 8 food dropping missions to Kut. Attacked by *Hptm* Hans Schuz, 26th April, while dropping food, wounded in head, shoulder and ankle, force landed and became POW. His RFC observer 2Lt A.C. Thouless, 30 Sqn, was killed.

ROBERT GORDON
Born 22.1.1882 Henzedah, Burma. Commis 2Lt Royal Marines 1900. Prom Capt 1911 and learnt to fly in the same year, RAeC Cert 166. In 1912 he was a Sqn Cdr then on 15.8.13 CO Firth of Forth Naval Air Station. CO Eastchurch Flying School Aug 1914 to 30.9.14 then CO Dundee Air Station to May 1915. Trans to East Africa. DSO for his work in destruction of German cruiser *Königsberg*. Prom Wg Cdr, to Mespot arr 5.9.15. Later CO combined RNAS/RFC unit. Left Mespot 11.7.16 and saw service in the Eastern Mediterranean, and Aegean 1917-18. Also South Russia (Caspian Sea) 1918-1919.

WALTER LOCKWOOD HAIGHT
Born 1894. From Perry Sound Ontario Canada. Joined 162nd Bn (Perry Sound Bn) Canadian Army. When Bn broke up joined British Army. Trans to RFC for pilot training in Egypt 27.4.17. Joined 30 Sqn 17.8.17. Reported MIA and POW with his obs 2Lt H.L.W. Hancock 4.3.18. Escaped 8.9.18 but recaptured seven days later. Repatriated 16.12.18.

ARTHUR WILLIAM HAWKINS
Born 4.6.1897, Putney, London. Son of Henry Charlton Hawkins Barrister-at-law. Educated Repton School Burton-upon-Trent 1910-1914, and RMC Sandhurst. Commis in the Yorkshire Regt (Green Howards) served France then posted home sick. Trans to RFC Aug 1916 for pilot training. First flight 5.12.16 8 RS Netheravon on MFSH. To Egypt 21 RS Heliopolis Feb 1917, first solo 23.2.17. To 22 RS Sqn Aboukir 13.3.17, then 58 RS 7.4.17, 23 RS 25.4.17 then back to 58 RS as Instructor. Posted to 30 Sqn 11.8.17 remaining until Aug 1919 at least. Also flew with 63 Sqn post-war, Bushire South Persia and Kurdistan. Total time war flying 424 hours including 400 hours solo.

STEPHEN BURROWS HENSON
Born 25.9.1886. Educated Tonbridge School. Jnd 4(Res) East Kent Bn (The Buffs) as 2Lt 31.12.15. Seconded to RFC as obs 14.8.16. Flew with 59 Sqn France 13.2.17 until 30.8.17. To HE Sept 1917 Perivale Armament School. Asst instructor graded as Equipment Officer (3rd Class) 14.12.17. To India 3.1.18 then 30 Sqn arrived 28.2.18. Remained until 8.6.18 then transfer to 72 Sqn. Served until 6.3.19. To HE and demob 14.4.1919.

JUSTIN HOWARD HERRING
Born 2nd July 1889, Wargrave, Wokingham, Berks. Enlisted as a Sapper, Ceylon Engineers. Trans to RFC for pilot training 7.6.15. To Brooklands then Fort Grange Gosport 27.7.15. To 13 Sqn CFS 14.8.15 then to 8 Sqn France 23.9.15. WIA 14.1.16 and back to UK. 14 RS and 15 RS Feb-April 1916 then to 47 Sqn 29.4.16. To 30 Sqn Mespot 1.8.16 remaining until 2.1.17. Prom Lt 1.9.16, awarded DSO for work in Mespot 3.3.17. To Macedonia as CO 17 Sqn 4.2.17, to HE 5.4.18. OC 15 TDS 27.4.18 until 2.10.18 then to No.4 School Navigation & Bomb Dropping. Remained in RAF post-war. MC Gaz 3.6.16. CdeG Gaz 18.4.18. MID for both Mespot and Salonika Aug/Nov 1917.

LEONARD WILLIAM HODGES
Born 29.9.1891 in Portsmouth. Joined RNAS and learned to fly on Lake Windermere. Took his RAeC Cert 1667 at Hendon 29.8.15. Posted to Calshot then joined SqnCdr F.W. Bowhill's Sqn in Mesopotamia. Contracted cholera and died at Basra 31.5.16.

ALEXANDER FRANCIS ANDERSON HOOPER
Born 5.6.1885. Southbrook, Starcross South Devon. Educated Wellington. Commis in the Duke of Edinburgh's Own (Edinburgh

RGA Milita) 1905. 2Lt Gaz 16.1.1907. To Prince of Wales Own (North Staffs Regt) and saw service North West Frontier India. Took course of instruction Larkhill on a Bristol Boxkite 1913, RAeC Cert 149. Attended course at Upavon 1914. To France with BEF Sept 1914, WIA Nov 1914. Remustered RFC Equipment Officer. On 1st Sept 1915 as Capt formed Mesopotamia Aircraft Park at Farnborough. Left UK as a complete unit 16.9.15 arr 22.10.15. Left Mespot for India 1916, EO at Aircraft Park North West Frontier Aug 1916. To France June 1917. OC No.3 Air Park and later 6 AP Jan 1918. Prom Major 1918. MID 7.4.18. Granted Permt Commis in the RAF and Sqn Ldr by 1919.

JOHN DOUGLAS HUME
Only son of the Rev David Hume MA, Buckhaven, Fife Scotland. Born 30.11.1896. Trained as an engineer pre-war then joined the RNAS for pilot training. RAeC Cert 1643, 24.8.1915. Posted to SqnCdr Bowhill's unit and went to Mespot Feb 16. Flew Henri Farman 1540 during April and carried out ten food dropping flights to Kut-al-Amara. Dropped 2000lbs of stores into the town. Remained in Mespot until July 1916 then to UK. Reported died in the UK 14.12.16 (no details).

PERCY LLEWELLYN HUNTING
Born 6.3.1885, Hexham, Northumberland. Joined 4th(T) Bn Northumbld Fusiliers 1914. Remained until 1916, trans to RFC. Trained at The Curragh, Ireland and Aldershot as EO (Wireless) and posted to 30 Sqn. Arr 25.10.16 remained until 30.7.17, promoted Capt to 31 Wing HQ Baghdad. Left Mespot after April 1918 (no details).

NINIAN STEEL HYSLOP
Born Hastings, Hawkes Bay, New Zealand. Joined Wellington Mounted Rifles then transfer to RFC February 1917. Trained as a pilot (incl 26 RS Turnhouse) before being posted to 63 Sqn Cramlington 4.7.17. To Mespot. While flying SPAD A8809 on 30.10.17, lost control and crashed to his death.

HERBERT ILLINGWORTH
Born 19.1.1887, Bradford Yorkshire. Joined the RFC as a Kite Balloon observer, trained at Roehampton, Farnborough and Salisbury Plain. Posted to 51 KB Section Mespot. Invalided to India 9.2.18. Also served No.2 Balloon Base Alexandria Egypt. Posted HE 6.1.1919.

HENRY IZARD
Born 30.1.1892. Educated Lancing College, Capt Football, Rugby and School Capt. Commis East Africa Native Transport. Learnt to fly 12 TS 1.2.17 to 21.8.17 on BE2e MFSH and Martinsyde. Att 199 NTS Northern Home Defence Wing, then to 72 Sqn 'C' Flight 3.1.18. Remained with Sqn until 5.2.1919 then to HE this date.

HAROLD DREWETT JENSEN
Commis 9th Scots Fusiliers before transfer to RFC Kite Balloons. Served with No.9 and No.4 KB Sections France, 4.3.16 until 18.9.16. Posted 17 KBS (22nd Balloon Company) Salonika as CO from 21.10.16. Remained until 9.6.17 then to UK. Posted to Mespot as CO 23 Kite Balloon Company Nov 1917. Returned to UK 28.10.18.

HARRY ERNEST JONES
English born (no details) but living at Regina, Sask, Canada at the outbreak of war as a member of the North West Mounted Police. Joined CEF and WIA France June 1916. Joined RFC March 1917 for observer training. Posted from Wireless & Observers School Brooklands, to 63 Sqn Cramlington 27.4.17. Served in Mespot until 17.4.18 then to Egypt pilot training. Posted to UK 30.9.18, left RAF 6.12.18.

ALFRED LACY JORDON
Born June 1893, Palmers Green London. Educated Cranleigh School. Joined Army with his brother and both posted Seaforth Highlanders. Served France, later commis Machine Gun Corps. Joined RFC 1918, and posted to 72 Sqn 11.4.18. Prom Lt. 6.6.18 and went on loan to 63 Sqn 26.5.18. To UK pilot training 20.9.18. 14 TDS Jan 1919, demobbed 4.2.1919.

LAWRENCE HOPE KING-HARMAN
Born 1889 elder son of Sir Charles and Lady King-Harman. Grandson of Gen Sir Robert Biddulph GCB GCMG. Educated Bradfield College, and RMA Woolwich. Commis in the RFA July 1909 joined 74th Battery in India. Trans to 'M' Battery and saw action during Mohmand Expedition, North West Frontier, June 1915. MID. To Mespot June 1916, temp CO field artillery then to 30 Sqn as observer 12.9.16. Killed 26.10.16, with pilot Lt S. Haywood, when Voisin 8523 nose-dived to ground from 1200 feet. Died aged 27.

ALFRED GILMER LAMPLUGH
Born 19.10.1895. Educated King Edward VII School Birmingham. Commis North Staffs Regt then transfer to RFC pilot training 1915. No.1 School of Instruction Reading, then 5 RS Dec 1916. 28 RS 30.12.16 then Gunnery School. Posted Egypt 58 RS and 195 TS then to 72 Sqn 3.1.18. Remained until Aug 1918 continuous service except for two spells in hospital. Prom Capt left RAF 1919.

WALTER BROGDIN LAWSON
Born Barrie, Ontario Canada. Educated Malvern Collegiate and Upper Canada College Toronto, and Royal Military College Kingston, Ontario. Commis in the 48th Highlanders 1913, then enlisted in the 15th Bn CEF 1914. To UK and trans to RNAS for pilot trning. First flight Eastchurch 1.6.15, first solo 18.6.15 RAeC Cert 1459, 18.7.15. To Calshot then 2 Sqn RNAS 23.8.15.

Posted to Dardanelles/East Indies Station 13.9.15, then to Mespot 7.11.15. Remained until 22.5.16 then to UK due to sickness. At Great Yarmouth 14.7.16 then to Calshot same month. To Eastchurch Sept 16 as instructor. Instructed 89 pupils between 29.9.16 and 3.3.17 flying MFs Voisin and BE. To Eastchurch Gunnery School April 1917, then to Manston 15.10.17. Gunnery School Leysdown 5.11.17 then to Stonehenge for Inst on Handley Page Bombers. Posted 215 Sqn France 6.6.18 remaining until 3.11.18. DFC Gaz 3.6.1919 for raid on Mannheim Chemical Works 25.8.18 carried out at low level. Lawson recorded 4000 hours flying time during the war the fourth highest total of any RFC/RNAS/RAF officer.

EDGAR JAMES LEECH
Born 12.12.1895. Joined 15/ London Regt (TF) as a private 29.8.1914. Commis 2Lt 25.3.15 and transferred to the 9th (Service) Bn Lincoln Regt. To 5th Connaught Rangers 1915, then transfer to RFC pilot training 1916. 23 RS Egypt October 1916, but injured (in crash?) and remustered as EO3 (Stores). Lt RFC Gen list 1.7.17. Posted to 23(T) Sqn Aboukir Egypt June-November 1917 and HQ Aboukir 25.1.18. Posted 31 Wing HQ Mesopotamia 25.2.18. Remained until 1919. RAF Catering College Feb 1921, and 5 Sqn India 1922.

GEORGE MARTIN LEES
Born 16.4.1898. Educated St Andrews College Dublin then RMA. Commis Royal Artillery 1915, served France then to RFC as observer. To Reading for instruction 28.2.17 then Wireless & Obs school 2.3.17. Posted 6 Sqn 15.5.17 and commis 2Lt flying officer same date. Remained with 6 Sqn until 28.8.17, gaining an MC for his work. To HE and Reading 12.9.17 commis Lt. 12.12.17. Pilot training 31 TS Wyton, and 17 TS Yatesbury Oct 17, then to Egypt. Instructor 193 TS Nov 17, also 57 and 58 TS. Posted 31 Wing 27.1.18 joined 72 Sqn 23.2.18. Remained until 1.1.1919. DFC gaz this date for ground strafing work Kirkuk area 24 April-30 May 1918. Took up appt as civilian pilot in Mesopotamia post-war and Asst Political Officer Kurdistan 1920.

ALEXANDER NEVE LEESON
Born 1896 only son of Mr & Mrs E.A.Leeson of Mundesley, Norfolk. Educated Rugby School 1910-14. Joined school OTC then to RMA Woolwich. Commis in the RFA Feb 1915. Served Ireland then to the Dardanelles with the 13th Div. July 1915. Invalided to Mudros with scarlet fever Sept 1915 rejoined unit Jan 1916. To Mespot March 1916, transferred to 'S' Battery RHA Sept 1916. Transferred to RFC as observer, joined 30 Sqn 29.7.17. KIA 22.10.17 and buried at Sharaban on the Dialah River. Awarded DSO June 1917, MID Aug 1917.

HUMPHREY DE VERD LEIGH
Born 26.7.1897 Aldershot, his father being vicar of Holy Trinity church for 20 years and later Canon of Guildford Surrey. Educated

Cheltenham College then to Vickers Ltd to learn engineering. Joined RNAS for pilot training, and qualified at Graham White School Hendon, RAeC Cert 1321, 13.6.15. Commis 11.10.15 posted to Dunkirk to fly seaplanes. Transferred to Mespot with SqnCdr F.W. Bowhill's unit Feb 1916. Recce. bombing missions etc, including food drops into Kut. Posted Port Said Egypt. MID 20.7.17 awarded DFC 2.7.18, and by end of war was 2nd in command Dundee Seaplane Station.

JOSEPH NORMAN ELLIOTT LEWIS

Born Milton, Yorkshire 1.11.1892. After schooling joined Glass Houghton & Castleford Colleries for three years as a fitter. Joined RFC 17.3.15 as 2AM (No. 4172). Went to France 13.5.15 No.1 Aircraft Depot until 15.9.16. Return to UK and posted to 72 Sqn. To Mespot with unit. Prom Sgt 1.4.18, remained with Sqn until 1.3.1919 then return to UK. MSM for work in Mespot (Gaz 3.6.19). RAF service extended for four years from 4.4.19. To 'M' Depot Uxbridge 1920, then Aero Experimental Establishment Martlesham Heath 1922/23 as Sgt Fitter. Demobbed 3.4.1923.

KENNETH BUCHANAN LLOYD

Born 8.11.? in India, father a regular soldier stationed at Simla. Educated by a CofE Padre in India, won a scholarship to St. Bees, Cumberland. To Sandhurst and commis 2Lt Royal Welsh Fusiliers 15.9.15. To RFC as observer, 10 Sqn 22.9.15. Qual as obs 22.11.15. To UK pilot training, 3 RS Shoreham March 1916. 4 RS May 1916 and 9 TS June. Qual as a pilot RAeC Cert 2802, 27.4.16. Joined 30 Sqn 1.8.16 remaining until 6.4.17 when invalided to India. 198 NTS 5.11.17, 53 Wing 188 NTS March 1918, and 1 Sqn 86 Wing Feb 1919. Remained in RAF post-war retired as AVM 1949.

MAURICE LYON

Born 14.7.1887 at Railhill, St Helens, Merseyside. Attended Birkenhead School and joined RNVR as a Able Seaman 1915. Served HMS *Manica*, Dardanelles 1915, commis. As FSL 20.10.15. Trained as a Kite Balloon observer Roehampton, and joined 14 KBS RNAS in Mesopotamia. Prom FltLt 1.4.17 and MID August 1917 for his work in Mespot. Also served Malta February 1918, and Alexandria March 1918. Acting FltCdr 15.2.18, Temp Capt 1.4.18, temp Major 24.4.18. Posted to HE 16.3.1919.

SOMERLED DOUGLAS MACDONALD

Born 1899, Invernesshire, Scotland. Educated Edinburgh. Joined RFC August 1917 and posted 26 TS 8.8.17 for pilot trg. Flew MFSHs until 6.9.17 then to 54 TS. Left 6.11.17 with 36 hours solo on Avro, Pup and SPAD. Posted to 72 Sqn joining 7.2.18. First flight 16.2.18, flew mainly Bristol M.1C, SE5A and Sopwith Camel. In Mespot until 1920 flying with both 63 Sqn Kurdistan and 30 Sqn (Jan-July1920). DFC Gaz 10.7.1920 for work with 63 Sqn. Remained in RAF until 1955.

MORAY SUTHERLAND MACKAY

Born 6.2.1899, fourth son of the Rev George Mackay of the Free Church Manse, Doune, Perthshire. Educated Merchiston Castle School Edinburgh. RFC cadet 24.4.17, No.1 Officers Cadet Wing 14.5.17. To No.2 School of Aviation 15.6.17. To 7 TS Netheravon 20.7.17 flew MFLH and MFSH, first solo 3.9.17. Commis 2Lt RFC 19.7.17. To 79 TS Beaulieu with 16 hours flying time 6.9.17. With 79 Sqn until 28.11.17 flew Avro, Pup and SPAD total time 61hour 45min of which 43hr solo. Posted 72 Sqn Mesopotamia arrived 23.1.18. First flight 16.2.18. Remained in Mesopotamia until September 1919 at least. Post-war with 63 Sqn including operations in Kurdistan. DFC Gaz 15.7.1919 for actions at Baku Persia Sept 1918. Completed over 200 hours war flying.

JOHN DUNCAN GEORGE MACRAE

Scottish born? But resident of Otter Ferry, New Brunswick Canada when war declared. Cadet R.M.College, Commis 2Lt 17.2.15. Joined Seaforth Highlanders, (Rosshire Buffs the Duke of Albanys.) Transferred to RFC pilot training (no details) then to 63 Sqn as a instructor 28.8.16 one of the unit's first personnel. To Mespot with Sqn. On 5.10.17 with observer Lt J.W. Blake, MacRae force landed in enemy territory near Tabalham Rins in RE8 A4336 and became POW.

NORMAN DUCKWORTH KERR MACEWEN

Born 8.11.1881, Victoria Hong Kong. Educated Charterhouse and Sandhurst. Commis 2Lt Argyll and Sutherland Highlanders, 8.1.1901. Served South African war 1901/2. Prom Lt 13.12.1904, Capt 1.2.1913, Major 8.1.15. To Central Flying School 9.2.16 RAeC Cert 2896, 10.5.16. To Mespot arriving 1.8.16. Appointed Asst Director Aviation for the Indian Army with the rank of LtCol 16.8.16 (replacing Broke-Smith) Remained until 1.2.17 when post was abolished. To RFC HQ Middle East May 1917, and appoint Brig Gen Salmond's principal liason officer, and later Chief of Staff. Carried out various inspection tours for RFC ME Brig Wing HQ including Mesopotamia 31.8.17, India etc, To RAF HQ India Dec 1918 as officer commanding. Granted Permanent Commis in the RAF post-war.

SEATON DUNHAM MASSY

Born 5.4.1882 London. Commis in the 29th Punjabis Indian Army 8th Jan 1901. Learnt to fly with the Air Battalion, RAeC Cert 84 on Bristol Boxkite at Salisbury Plain 9.5.11. On 1.2.13 became commandant Indian Flying School Sitapur and seconded RFC. On 4.11.1914 sailed from Avonmouth to Egypt as CO RFC Egypt Detatchment remaining until Nov 1915 when posted to

30 Sqn as CO. Remained CO until 30.5.16, left Mespot 27.6.16. Awarded DSO. (Other service details not known).

FRANCIS PYM MANNOCK
Served with the 1/7Royal Welsh Fusiliers then transferred to RFC as a Kite Balloon equipment officer. Landed in France 28.2.18, to No.1 Kite Balloon Wing 1.3.18 posted No.4 KB Company. To HE 12.3.18 then posted Mesopotamia arriving 19.5.18. Remained until 12.4.1919 posted HE.

GERALD MERTON
Born 21.1.1893 London. Attnd Trinity College Cambridge, BA. In Nov 1914, still as a civilian, attended flying course at Beatty School of Flying Hendon, RAeC Cert 1059, 27.1.15. Enlisted in the RFC 2.3.15 and commis 2Lt 9.4.15. To Brooklands 2.3.15 then CFS Upavon 26.3.15. Posted 9 Sqn Swingate Downs near Dover 15.5.15. To France with Sqn flying BE2c, Bristol Scout and MFSH remaining until 1.2.16. Posted to UK, 10 days leave then 7 RS Netheravon until March 1916 when posted to 30 Sqn. Arrived 17.6.16 remaining until 17.2.18. Prom Capt and OC 'B' Flight. To India then Egypt. Prom Major and CO No.3 School Navigation & Bomb Dropping. To UK October 1918, demobbed 17.1.1919.

LESLIE ETHELBERT RUTHVEN MURRAY
Born 22.6.1896 Worcester. Educated Oundle School and London University. Degree in engineering. Joined RNAS for pilot training going to Grahame White School Hendon. RAeC Cert 1584, 12.8.15. To Calshot 17.8.15 until 17.11.15. To RNAS Chingford joined SqnCdr F.W. Bowhill's Sqn for Mesopotamia. First flight 10.3.16 on Short 8046. Remained in Mespot until 3.5.16 Recce, bombing and food dropping missions to Kut. Posted to India due to sickness then to UK 21.7.16. To RNAS Great Yarmouth 16.10.16, to Calshot 7.1.18, and RNAS Newlyn Cornwall Feb 1918.

SAMUEL BANKS NELSON
Born 1896 Philadelphia USA, father a Minister. Educated in the US then to Belfast. Graduated from Queen's University Belfast 1913, and entered Arts course. In 1913, to Queen's University Kingston, Ontario on exchange course. Commis in Canadian Infantry and sailed to the UK autumn 1916. Transferred to RFC as observer, joined 63 Sqn Cramlington from the Wireless & Observers School Brooklands 27.4.17. With the Sqn in Mespot but invalided out 2.9.17. To Egypt pilot trg at 193 TS Amria and 38 TS UK. Posted to 41 Sqn France 14.10.18, remained until end of the war.

BRIAN GEORGE MICHAEL FREDERICK NIXON
Born 5.6.1886. Educated at Tonbridge School and Commis 2Lt West Surrey Regt 23.5.1906. Prom Lt 23.8.1908. Transfer to 41st Dogras Indian Army 23.10.08. To Capt 23.5.15 and seconded as Asst Commandant Burma Military Police June 1914 to Sept 1915. Invalided to England then to Mespot April 1916 as company commander 41st Dogras and 2nd in command 37th Dogras Aug/Sept 1916. To 30 Sqn as observer from 13.9.16. To 31 Wing as Staff Capt Feb 1917. Appointed Wing Adj 22.10.17 to 31.3.18. To Egypt pilot training, including 18 TDS Ismailia, 10.7.18 to 26.12.18. At RAF Iraq HQ until 8.11.1919.

FRANK NUTTALL
Born 16 November 1887, New Brighton, Christchurch New Zealand. Joined RFC 6.4.16. Trained 40 and 41(T) Sqn May 1916, RAeC Cert 2803, 28.4.16. To 27(Res) Sqn CFS June 1916, then 16(Res) Sqn and 3(Res) Sqn as Asst Instructor Dec 1916. Posted to Egypt 22(Res) Sqn Aboukir, then to 30 Sqn 5.4.17. Prom Capt and FltCdr 7.10.17 and MC Gaz 26.3.18. Remained with 30 Sqn until 25.3.1919 then to 63 Sqn this date. To Egypt Sept 1919 then to UK same month. Back to Mespot Jan 1920, 63 Sqn. Assumed command 'B' 30 Sqn Kasvin Persia 29.2.1920. DFC July 1919, AFC Oct 1919. Killed while flying RE8 D4698 18.9.1920.

WALTER GERARD PALMER
Born 8.10.1883, Totnes Devon. Educated Tonbridge School and Sandhurst. Joined Connaught Rangers March 1903. Graduated Staff College Quetta, India as Capt 21.1.1912. In India with 113th Infantry IA until April 1915 as Quartermaster and Adjt of Regt. To Mesopotamia att 7th Rajputs until June 1915 then seconded to 30 Sqn as Special Staff Officer observer 21.6.15. Trained as pilot in Mespot, RAeC Cert 25.9.15. KIA while acting as observer to 2Lt R.H. Peck when down at Es Sinn near Kut-al-Amara 5.3.1916.

PERCIVAL PHILLIPS
Born at St.Austell, Cornwall in 1893. Joined Duke of Cornwall's Light Infantry and sailed to India with Regt. In August 1915 volunteered for the RFC and transferred to Basra as an Air Mechanic att 30 Sqn. Remained with the Sqn until June 1917 reaching the rank of FltSgt. To Egypt for pilot training including 194 TS Dec 17. Returned to 30 Sqn as 2Lt Flying Officer 16.4.18. Prom Capt, remained with 30 Sqn until 12.2.1919. Also served with 63 Sqn Kurdistan. DFC Gaz 10.7.1920.

JOHN REGINALD PHILPOTT
Born 12.7.1893, Stoke Albany, Northants, only son of the Rev J.N. and Mrs M.F. Philpott of Coleorton Rectory, Leicestershire. Joined 10th Suffolk Regt in 1914 then transferred to RFC for pilot training. RAeC Cert 1536, 5.8.15. Posted to 12 Sqn France and gained MC for his work with the Sqn. Prom Capt, to 63 Sqn Cramlington as OC 'A' Flight. To Mespot with unit. On 25.9.17 with his observer Cpl O.W. Grant, force landed in enemy territory and became POW. Died of dysentery at Afion Internment Camp 15.1.1918.

HERMAN WALTER VON POELLNITZ
Born 21.1.1891. Educ Repton and Sandhurst. Joined 2nd Bn Lincs Regt, WIA, hospitalized in UK then to RFC for pilot trg. RAeC Cert 1953. Castle Bromwich B'ham 26.10.15 graduated FO 20.1.16. To 33 Sqn Patchway (HD?) 28.1.16 then to 32 Sqn Netheravon 10.2.16. Prom Capt (Army title) 24.4.16 then to France with Sqn 31.5.16. First patrol with 32 Sqn 7.6.16, prom FltCdr. Temp Capt RFC 17.10.16. To 24 Sqn as 'B' FltCdr 18.10.16 remaining until 14.4.17. To UK, instructor Joyce Green then Upavon 2.7.17. Prom Major to form 72 Sqn for Mesopotamia this date. Sailed 2.1.18 via France, Italy Egypt and Bombay, arr 14.2.18. On 10.5.18 involved in car crash while returning from Baghdad aerodrome, and suffered a fractured skull resulting in his death.

RALPH PATRICK PHILLIP POPE
Born 24.4.1899, Kingston-upon-Thames Surrey. Father regular officer 1/East Surrey Regt. Educ Sacred Heart Coll Wimbledon. Helping mobilisation of reserves, made out his own enlistment papers adding three years to his age. Enlisted 2nd Bn East Surrey Regt 2.9.14 aged 15. To France as LCpl machine gunner seeing action Second Battle of Ypres and Loos, Commis in the field aged 16. On 25.12.15 Regt moved to Salonika Struma Valley. Trans to RFC Summer 1917, posted to Egypt for pilot trg. No.3 SMA Sept/Oct 17, then to 21 TS MFSH total flying time 10hr 33min with 5hr solo. To 22 TS for advanced instruction Avros and Bristols, then School of Aerial Gunnery. Graduated 13.12.17 and posted with 55hr 48min flying time to 72 Sqn en-route to Mespot. With Sqn until 11.4.1919. DFC Gaz 15.7.1919 for work at Baku Persia with 'Dunsterforce' Sept 1918. Also flew with 63 Sqn Kurdistan post-war and MID 10.7.1920. Reccomended for bar to DFC but not awarded.

HAROLD WARNICA PRICE
Born Toronto, Canada 1896. Educated University of Toronto, in first year of medicine when accepted by RFC. Sailed to UK 14.1.16 and enrolled in Course No.20 class 16 SMA Reading 22.11.16. To 41 RS Doncaster 15.2.17 then 15 RSalso at Doncaster flying MFSH before gaining his wings 25.5.17. To 63 Sqn Cramlington with 33hr 33min solo flying time. To Mespot, first flight 4.9.17. With 63 until 27.9.1919 seeing continuous action (including Persia).

JOHN CHARLES QUINNELL
Commis 2Lt RFA before transfer to RFC Feb 1915. Trained as a pilot at Shoreham March/April 1915, RAeC Cert 1175 23.3.15. To 10 Sqn France July 1915, FltCdr by Dec 1915 then to 1.1.16 as Capt. On 11.7.16 wounded (not seriously) when landing BE2d 5754. A bomb fell off the aircraft while landing and exploded wounding him in the legs and left arm. To UK, Prom Major, Formed 83 Sqn 1.12.16. To 63 Sqn as CO 27.4.17 taking the unit to Mespot. To HE 21.10.17 and OC Training Sqn in Canada (No details). To 104 Sqn on formation as CO. To France with Sqn until the end of the war.

HUGH LAMBERT REILLY
Born 18.10.1886 New Zealand. Educated Bedford School and RMC Sandhurst. Commis 82nd Punjabis IA 1906. Learnt to fly at Hendon, RAeC Cert 252, 24.7.1912. In 1913 posted to the newly formed Indian Flying School Sitapur. To RFC then to Egypt 2.11.14 as part of the RFC Egypt Detatchment. Remained until April 1915 then to 30 Sqn as CO. On 20.11.15 shot down by ground fire at Ctesiphon and became a POW.

FREDERICK OSWALD ROSE
Born 9.9.1892, Leytonstone, London. Ran away to sea 1907, apprenticed in the British India Line 1910-1914. Joined London Scottish (14th London Regt) then 7th Essex Regt and Camel Corps 1915. To RFC Gaz 2Lt 17.11.16. Pilot training, posted 30 Sqn 3.1.17. Remained until 13.1.1919 seeing continues action except for spells in hospital May 1917 and Aug/Oct 1918.

CAMPBELL THOMAS SANCTUARY
Born 31.7.1889. Educated Sherbourne School, prefect, and represented the school at Rugby. To Caius College Cambridge 1907, 2nd class hons degree in Agriculture. Joined CUOTC, commis Lt 3rd Wessex Brigade 1st Dorset Battery RFA. Went to India then Mespot with unit. Joined 30 Sqn as an observer Jan to Sept 1916 then to UK pilot trg. Reading Nov 1916, 4 RS Northolt Jan 1917 and 19 RS March 17. Remained in the UK until end of the war, test and ferry pilot Coventry No.1 AAP. Left RAF 21.12.18.

ALFRED ERNEST LIONEL SKINNER
Born 1897. Commis 2Lt 1/1 King's Own Royal Regt (Norfolk Yeo Territorials) in early 1915. Did not sail with Regt to Gallipoli but posted to Egypt 1916 and transferred to RFC pilot training. 21 RS Heliopolis, MFSH 2hr 30min dual inst before going solo. To 22 RS Aboukir and 23 RS graduated as 2Lt RFC 9.11.16 with 24hr 30min solo. To 30 Sqn arr Basra Dec 1916, remained until 11.4.18. Prom Capt, to India then Egypt with 454 hours flying time. To 57 TS Abu Sueir 18.5.18 then to London arr 3.7.18. In August 1918 to No.1 School of Special Flying Gosport, then 45 TDS Rendcombe Glos, as Instructor. On 4.11.18 posted back to Egypt 19 TDS El Rimal. Remained in Egypt until May 1919.

RONALD DAVIDSON SIMPSON
Commis 6th Dragoon Guards before transfer to the RFC as Obs. In 9 Sqn France Feb 1916 and later in the same Sqn as pilot 21.5.16 to 2.11.16. Posted to UK 31 RS and then 83 Sqn Spittlegate. Posted to 63 Sqn Cramlington 10.5.17. Prom Capt, appointed OC 'A' Flight, remained with Sqn 14.4.1919. DFC and bar Gaz. 1.1.1919.

HAROLD ST. CLAIR SMALLWOOD

Born 6.11.1883 Hornsea. Educated Eastbourne College. Joined Imperial Yeomanry Jan 1901, served Boer War, aged 17, awarded Queen's Medal with five clasps. Remained in South Africa, joined Transvaal Horse, then to Burma as Forestry Asst. Joined Burma Mounted Rifles 1907-1909 then Mounted Volunteers until 1914. Commis. 2Lt 15th Bengal Lancers Indian Army Dec 14, Lt April 1915. Joined RFC as observer July 1916 and posted to 30 Sqn 6.9.16. Remained until Jan 1917, then to UK pilot trg. Reading School of Instruction April 17, 75 (HD) Sqn 18.7.17. Injured in crash 31.8.17, then re-mustered as Staff Officer Class 2. HQ Eastern Training Brigade Jan 1918, 57 TS and later Air Ministry Directorate of Training. 30 TDS Feb 1919, demobbed April 1919. Post-war travelled extensively in China and Mongolia 1919-1929.

FREDERICK HIBBERD SONGHURST

Born 18.12.1894, in Sussex. Educ Colliers School Horsham, became a mechanical engineer. Enlisted in the Sussex Yeomanry 1914, and commis in the RFC as Asst Equipment Officer (2nd Class) Nov 1915. Posted to Aircraft Park Mespot arrived 29.8.16. Remained until 25.1.17 then posted to 16 Wing Aircraft Park Salonika. To UK 29.3.18, temp Major 7.4.18. Awarded MBE 3.6.18. In the UK at Aircraft Park York until end of war.

GERALD LOMAX STEDMAN
Born Timaru, New Zealand 27.10.1891. Educated Lincoln College Canterbury NZ, and enlisted 2.9.14 in the Canterbury Mounted Rifles. Prom Sgt. Unit sailed 16.10.14 arrived Suez 3.12.14. Served Gallipoli and Palestine. Commis 2Lt 21.10.15 and transferred to RFC pilot training Jan 1917. Trained Egypt (no details) then to UK and joined 63 Sqn 23.4.17. To Mespot. Still on RAF list Oct 1919.

HENRY SPURRIER

Born 16.6.1898. Educated Repton School. Apprentice motor engineer with Leyland Motors. Joined RFC for pilot training 1916. Oxford Nov 16, then 41 RS Doncaster. 36 RS and 15 RS May 17, commis 2Lt RFC 10.5.17. Posted to 63 Sqn 24.5.17 remained until 9.1.18 when invalided to India. Discharge hospital 13.2.18 then leave until posted HQ Training Brigade, 32(T) Wing Egypt 20.8.18. 23 TS Nov 1918 and Instructors School Jan 1919. To UK 18th March 1919.

GEORGE W. SUTCLIFFE

Born 13.6.1895, Bayswater, London. Joined RNAS 16.8.14 as leading mechanic, his civilian trade motor body builder. Posted to East Africa (Cdr Cull) 10.1.15, then to Mesopotamia as part of SqnCdr R. Gordon's Detachment sailing 21.8.15. Arr 6.10.15 remaining until 21.5.16 then to UK. Arr Calshot 9.8.16, then to France 3AD 17.3.17. To 4ASD 26.4.18. Back to 3AD at a later date, remaining until 21.11.18, then hospital with 'flu. To 214 Sqn, demobbed 20.2.1919.

ROBERT CHARLES TALBOT
Served with RFA and RHA before transfer to the RFC. Arrived No.1 Kite Balloon Wing 28.1.17. KB Officer 24.4.17. Qualified as KB observer 13.5.17. Balloon CO 25.5.17. Acting KB Company Commander No.1 KB Company (8 & 20 KB Sections) from 10.7.17. Prom Capt, posted HE 8.10.17. Posted Mespot arrived 20.12.17, CO 52 KB Section. Return to UK 28.10.18.

ROBERT F M. TAUNTON
English born, living in Canada at outbreak of war. Joined 11th Canadian Reserve Bn then transfer to RFC as observer. Came from Wireless & Observers School Brooklands to 63 Sqn Cramlington 27.4.17. To Mespot with Sqn remaining until 28.5.18. Posted to UK pilot training.

JOHN EDWARD TENNANT

Born 12.10.1890. Educated Repton School 1901-03, then to Osborne Royal Naval College Sept 1903. Left Navy Feb 1910 due to sickness and commis in the Scots Guards 21.3.1910. Learnt to fly at Brooklands, RAeC Cert 811 on a Vickers machine 9.6.14. Saw service with 6 Sqn and 4 Sqn (March 1916). Awarded MC 9.6.16. Prom Major and posted Mespot as CO 30 Sqn 7.8.16. On 11.1.17 assumed command of the newly formed 31 Wing Mespot with rank of Lt.Col. While flying a DH4 on 25.3.18, Tennant was shot down and made POW. Rescued by British Armoured Cars three days later. Posted to India May 1918 as Director of Aviation. Resigned commis 10.7.1919.

WILLIAM MILES WEBSTER THOMAS
Born 2.3.1897 North Wales. Educated King Edward VIth School Bromsgrove. Joined ASCMT (Motor Machine Gun Corps) 1914. Served East Africa then transferred to RFC pilot training. 2Lt Gen List 29.9.17. Posted 72 Sqn 3.1.18, remaining until 13.1.1919. To HE this date, 30 TDS March 1919. Demob 14.4.1919.

H.D.B. TURNER
Born 1879 India. Joined the Army aged 13 years as a trumpeter. Became Sgt Major Instructor West Riding RHA at Wentworth Barnsley. Posted to France 1914, and later commis in the field. Saw action Mons and Loos before transfer to RFC as observer. Posted to 30 Sqn 2.3.16 remaining until 21.4.16 including food dropping flights during siege of Kut. Contracted fever, invalided to UK, died last week of August 1917 (exact date not known).

HAROLD WILLIAM UNDERHILL

Born 12.5.1898, Upper Warlingham, Surrey the third of six children. Educated Upper Warlingham Infants School, Prep School Elmhurst, South Croydon 1907, then to Whitgift School Croydon. Joined OTC 1912, then to RMA.10.11.15 aged seventeen years. Commis 2Lt 10.5.16, joined 119th Siege Battery. To France 2.7.16 remaining until transfer to the RFC as an observer. Trained Wireless & Observers School Brooklands then to 63 Sqn Cramlington 20.4.17. To Mespot with Sqn remaining until 18.7.18 then to HE pilot training. Total war flying as an observer 139hr 35 min.

DOUGLAS ROY VEREY
Joined RNVR as FSL 5.7.15. Transferred to RNAS Kite Balloons as observer. Trained Roehampton, posted 14 KBS RNAS. To Mespot remaining until August 1917. Posted UK 15.8.17, to No.1 Balloon Training Depot on formation as acting Major. In charge of winch production and testing. Acting Major August 1918 No.1 Balloon Depot Workshops DSC.19.7.1919.

EDWIN GEORGE WALKER
Born 21.1.1880 London. Joined RNAS as air mechanic and trained at Roehampton 20.12.15 to 28.4.16 before joining 14 KBS RNAS. Served with this section including Mespot duty from 28.4.16 to 11.10.17. Prom 1AM 1.9.17. Returned Roehampton until July 1918 then commis 2Lt 16.5.18. To No.2 Balloon Base Depot Alexandria Egypt 17.8.18, to RAF Base Depot 13.2.1919.

FRANCIS MAPLETON IREMONGER WATTS
Born 1st July 1895, Newton Abbott Devon, sixth of seven children of Francis Watts a local Solicitor. Educated Newton College. Joined 1/5 Worcester Regt and went to France. Wounded in the ankle and invalided to UK. Joined the RFC as Equipment Officer (3rd Class) posted to Norwich. Learnt to fly and gained RAeC No.1742, 13.9.15. Posted to 17 Sqn 18.10.15 then 24 Sqn same month. With 24 Sqn until 3.6.16 then to HE. 21st Wing HQ 11.12.16 until 23.1.18. To Middle East Air Park this date. Posted 31st Wing AP as Equipment Officer 1st class 4.3.18. Prom Capt, remained in Mespot until August 1919. MBE 3.6.1919.

THOMAS RALPH WELLS
Born Cuckfield, Sussex 11.3.1887. Entered Sandhurst 1905. Commis 2Lt I.A. 1906, posted 1st Bn Royal Sussex Regt India. Transferred to 33rd Punjabis 1907, Lt. 1908, Signals Instructor 1910 and Quartermaster and Adjt of Regt. Learnt to fly at Hendon, gained RAeC cert 851 21.7.1914. Posted to Egypt with Regt then to RFC 29.3.15. to UK, then 30 Sqn arr 27.5.15. Trapped in Kut-al-Amara during the siege, became POW when the garrison surrendered 29.4.16, and was repatriated 11.11.1918. Returned to RAF duty in the UK 8.12.18, remained until 15.10.1919.

JOHN STEPHEN WINDSOR
Born 1894, Barry, Glamorgan, South Wales. Attended Barry Elementary School, apprenticed as locomotive engineer, Barry Dock Railway. Went to Sandhurst on scholarship, and commis in the South Wales Borderers 1915. Trans to RFC pilot training and posted 1 RAS Farnborough. First flight 2.12.15. Flew MFSH first solo 26.1.16, RAeC Cert 2407 same date. To CFS Upavon 1.2.16, BE, RE7 and RE5 until last flight 21.4.16. Total time 57hr 40min.

To 30 Sqn arr Sheikh Saad 17.6.16. First flight 22.7.16. Ops until 3.6.17, total time in Mespot 311hr 5min. To CFS UK 20.9.17 until 18.3.18, then 1 Sqn France 13.4.18. WIA ground strafing (no date). CFS Upavon Nov 1918 until 10.4.1919. To Belgium with 92 Sqn and 80 Sqn RAF. To Egypt with 80 Sqn July 1919-January 1920.

STEPHEN CHRISTOPHER WINFIELD-SMITH
Born 8.3.1892, Kandy District of Ceylon. Father a planter with the Central Rothschild Estate. To UK educated Brighton. Commis in East Surrey Regt, and learnt to fly at Brooklands in 1911 on a course run by the Bristol Aircraft Company. RAeC Cert 187, 27.2.1912. Attended course CFS Upavon 1912, then to Royal Aircraft Factory as (test?) pilot, on strength July 1914. To France on outbreak of war, Wireless Flight attached 4 Sqn and 9 Sqn. In 1915 posted 30 Sqn arr. 20.11.15. Trapped in Kut-al-Amara with four other officers of 30 Sqn and became POW when town surrendered.

EDWIN REGINALD WILLIAMS
born in Dublin, but resident at St James Winnipeg, Canada on the outbreak of war. Joined 11th Canadian Reserve Bn, later transferring to the RFC as observer. Joined 63 Sqn from the Wireless & Observers School Brooklands 27.4.17. To Mespot with unit remaining until 16.2.18 when posted Egypt pilot training. No other details known.

HORACE NELSON WITTING
Born 21.10.1897. Educated Dulwich Prep School and Dulwich College. Commis 2Lt 3 Queen's Royal West Kent Regt. To RFC Kite Balloons as an Observer. Posted Salonika, 26 KB Section, 22 KB Company 1.2.17. To 27 KB Company 4.2.18 then to Mespot 5.8.18. Became CO of 51 KB Section 23 KB Company.

FRANCIS OGILVIE WOODMAN
Born Winnipeg, Manitoba, Canada. Joined the CEF September 1914 and gained a commission. In the 2/17th London Regt, and won the MC (Gaz 25.11.16) in France. Trans to RFC autumn 1917, trained as a pilot including 3 SMA November 17 and 193(T) Sqn Egypt Dec 1917. Joined 63 Sqn 7.8.18. Posted to UK 13.1.1919.

POW Survivors up to the Fall of Kut-al-Amara
See Squadron Nominal Rolls for further details of Officers

Lt W.H. Treloar.

Lt E.J. Fulton.

Capt T.H. White.

Capt F.C.C. Yeats-Brown.

			Missing	Repatriated
TRELOAR Capt William Harold		AFC	16 SEP 15,	- NOV 18
ATKINS Capt Basil Sidney		11/Rajputs att RFC	16 SEP 15,	7 DEC 18
WHITE Capt Thomas		AFC	13 NOV 15,	- DEC 18
YEATS-BROWN Capt Francis Charles Claypon		Ind Army att AFC	13 NOV 15,	6 DEC 18
REILLY Maj Hugh Lambert.		82/Punjabis att RFC	20 NOV 15	16 DEC 18
FULTON Capt Edmund James		1/Lancers att RFC	22 NOV 15	- NOV 18
GASSON Flt Lt Cecil Bell		RNAS	26 APR 16	?
SLOSS FSgt James McKenzie		AFC	29 APR 16	5 NOV 18
HUDSON Sgt Keith Liston		AFC	29 APR 16	6 SEP 19
MORRIS Cpl H.L.		RFC	29 APR 16	?
HAYNES 2/AM W.		RFC	29 APR 16	?

Officers, NCOs and Air Mechanics of 30 Sqn & Australian Half-Flight made POW, Kut-al-Amara 1916

CORBETT R.D. de la Cour	Capt (O) RFC 47th Pioneers IA	Reported died while POW 25-7-17
COURTHOPE-MUNRO C.H.	2Lt (O) 33rd Cavalry IA	Survived captivity
MUNDY S.C.B.	Capt (O) Ox & Bucks LI	Survived captivity
WELLS T.R.	Capt (P) 34th Punjabis IA.	Survived. Repatriated 13-11-18
WINFIELD-SMITH S.C.	Capt (O) 3/East Surrey Regt	Survived captivity
ALLSTON Frank	PTE ASC att RFC.	Reported died 10-July-1918
ADAMS Francis Luke	AM AFC	Died while POW Aug – Nov 1916
BRAUND W	2/AM Devonshire Rgt att RFC	Died while POW
BULLEN Harold	2/AM RFC	Left in Kut Hospital, died later
BUTLER Sidney George	2/AM RFC	Died in captivity 10-Aug-1916
BLIGHT Reginald Sampson	2/AM RFC	Died 4-Sept-1917
CAMPBELL H	Flt/Sgt RFC	Died in captivity
CANDY William Henry Minter	1/AM RFC	Died in captivity 30-June-1916
CLARKE A	2/AM Middlesex Regt att RFC	Died while POW
CLARIDGE Lionel Victor	1/AM RFC	Died 31-5-1916
CARPENTER Reginald William	2/AM East Surrey Regt att RFC	Died while POW 31-12-1916
CURREN David	AM AFC	Reported died 16-June-1917
CROCKER Percy	2/AM RFC	Died 11-June-1917
DAGGER Victor	2/AM RFC	Died 29-April-1916
DEAN William Charles	PTE 1/4 Dorset Rgt att RFC	Died 22-October-1916
DODD Harry	2/AM RFC	Died 7-August 1916
DRAPER Victor George	1/AM RFC	Died 8 – May-1916
EAVES Joseph Richard	1/AM RFC	Died 7-May-1916
FAIRHEAD JohnWilliam	1/AM RFC	Died 15-October-1916
GEORGE Robert Edgar	2/AM RFC	Died 29-April- 1916
GILL W.T.C.	2/AM Middx Regt att RFC	Died in captivity
GUTHRIE Richard Casper	1/AM RFC	Died 5-December-1917
HARE Alfred James	2/AM RFC	Died 25-August-1916
HOGG J.	1/AM RFC	Fate not known
HUDSON K. L.	A/M AFC	Survived captivity
KEEFE William	2/AM RFC	Died 7-May-1916
LORD William Henry	AM AFC	Died 13-July-1916
MUNRO James	AM AFC	Died 13-October-1916
Manning George William	1/AM RFC	Died 17-October-1917
NICKOLLS Richard George	2/AM RFC	26-May-1918
NIXON F.E.	2/AM East Surrey Rgt att RFC	Died while POW
NUNCY F.	2/AM Middx Rgt att RFC	Died while a POW
PALGRAVE George Walter	L/Cpl 2/Norfolk Regt att RFC	Died 3-May-1916 at Kut
PALMER Thomas Newton	Sgt RFC	Died 13-March-1916
PASS W.G.	2/AM RFC	Died 26-1-1917
PONTING Daniel	2/AM RFC	Died 1-June-1916
RAYMENT William Charles	AM AFC	Died 11-November-1916
READ F.	Sgt RFC	Thought to have survived captivity
REID Alfred	Cpl RFC	Died 5-May-1916
ROOTES C.	2/AM 2/E Surrey Rgt Att RFC	Died in Captivity
ST.JOHN S.	2/AM Hants Regt Att RFC	Died while POW
SLOSS James McKenzie	Cpl AFC	Survived captivity
SMITH William	1/AM RFC	Died 19-July-1916
SNELL F.	2/AM RFC	Died in captivity
SOLEY Thomas M.	Cpl AFC	Died while a POW (June or July 1916)
TAYLOR Alfred	Sgt RFC	Died 22-July-1916
TREE George Robert	1/AM RFC	Died 15-July-1917
VINCENT Thomas William	1/AM RFC	Died 29-April-1916
WEBB Arthur	Flt/Sgt RFC	Died 11-June-1916
WELSH Sidney Basil	1/AM RFC	Died 26-January-1917
WELLS Samuel John	2/AM RFC	Died 20-Sept-1916
WILLIAMS Leo T.	AM AFC	Died 13-July-1916

ORIGINAL AUSTRALIAN HALF-FLIGHT OTHER RANKS

#	Name	Embarked/Arrived	Remarks
1	SHORLAND, SGT MAJ Alexander Edward	SS *Morea*, 20 Apr 15	To Egypt, 1916
2	HEATH, Staff SGT Cyril Victor	SS *Morea*, 20 Apr 15	DCM To No 2 Sqn, 25 Nov 16, RTA 10 Oct 18
3	GARLING, Sqn QMS Septimus Wm.	SS *Ulysses*, 8 May 15	To No 2 Sqn, 25 Nov 16, RTA 21 Jul 18
4	NEENAN, Farrier SGT John Francis Patrick	SS *Morea*, 20 Apr 15	RTA 12 May 16
6	WARDELL, CPL Charles Eric	SS *Morea*, 20 Apr 15	MID To No 2 Sqn, 25 Nov 16
7	DIXON, PTE Henry Secreton	SS *Morea*, 20 Apr 15	Disch 5 Sep 16
8	COWPER, SGT Gordon Henry	SS *Morea*, 20 Apr 15	To No 2 Sqn, 25 Nov 16, RTA 9 May 19
9	HEAD, SGT Edward John	SS *Morea*, 20 Apr 15	To Egypt To No 2 Sqn, 15 Oct 16, Disch to RFC 27 Feb 17, Commiss.
10	† SOLEY, CPL Thomas Montague	SS *Morea*, 20 Apr 15	Died as POW Jun or Jul 16
11	SLOSS, SGT James McKenzie	SS *Morea*, 20 Apr 15	MSM, POW, Survived RTA 5 Nov 18
12	HUDSON, SGT Keith Liston	SS *Morea*, 20 Apr 15	MSM, POW, Survived RTA 6 Sep 19
13	BISSETT, CPL Herbert J.	SS *Morea*, 20 Apr 15	To No 2 Sqn, 25 Nov 16, RTA 2 Mar 19
14	ABDY, SSGT Charles Ernest	SS *Morea*, 20 Apr 15	To No 2 Sqn, 25 Nov 16
15	YARROW, AM Frederick Thomas	SS *Morea*, 20 Apr 15	RTA 11 Nov 15
16	† WILLIAMS, AM Leo Thomas	SS *Morea*, 20 Apr 15	Died as POW 13 Jul 16
17	CLAYTON, SGT Sidney George	SS *Morea*, 20 Apr 15	To No 2 Sqn, 25 Nov 16, RTA 6 Mar 19
18	LORD, CPL Hector Fred	SS *Morea*, 20 Apr 15	RTA 4 Mar 19
19	PETERS, 1/AM George	SS *Morea*, 20 Apr 15	To Egypt
20	LONSDALE, SGT Richard	SS *Morea*, 20 Apr 15	To No 2 Sqn, 25 Nov 16, RTA 6 May 19
21	PASSMORE, DVR Reginald	SS *Morea*, 20 Apr 15	To AMDT RTA 5 Feb 19
22	JONES, DVR George Sidney	SS *Morea*, 20 Apr 15	2nd Sig Sqn, AMD Disch 17 Sep 19
23	† LORD, AM William Henry	SS *Morea*, 20 Apr 15	Died as POW 13 Jul 16
24	EASTLAKE, PTE Albert Sherwood	SS *Morea*, 20 Apr 15	RTA 5 Jul 16
25	DAVIS, PTE Stanley William	SS *Morea*, 20 Apr 15	
26	ROBINSON, CPL Stanley Gordon	SS *Morea*, 20 Apr 15	RTA 11 Jan 16, Disch 16 Mar 17, Later Commissioned
27	MENZIES, AM Kenneth Ricketson	SS *Morea*, 20 Apr 15	To Egypt, Later Commissioned, RTA 10 Jun 19
28	GARLING, SGT Arthur Blenheim	SS *Morea*, 20 Apr 15	RTA 2 Jan 19
29	MURRAY, Farrier SGT Alexander	SS *Morea*, 20 Apr 15	To AMTD
30	EDWARDS, PTE Henry John	SS *Morea*, 20 Apr 15	RTA 20 Nov 16
31	NISKANEN. 1/AM PTE Frederick	SS *Morea*, 20 Apr 15	Disch 28 Mar 19
32	CURTIN, CPL David Daniel	SS *Morea*, 20 Apr 15	RTA 4 Oct 16
33	MUNDY, DVR William Stewart	SS *Morea*, 20 Apr 15	RTA 19 Oct 17
34	GOWER, CPL John	SS *Morea*, 20 Apr 15	To AASC, RTA 9 Jul 19
35	BROWN, PTE John	SS *Morea*, 20 Apr 15	RTA 23 Aug 16
36	BELL, DVR Alfred Leslie	SS *Morea*, 20 Apr 15	To AMDT, RTA 15 Jan 19
37	BASS, PTE Robert James	SS *Morea*, 20 Apr 15	RTA 25 Sep 16
38	TREWEEK, PTE Leslie	SS *Morea*, 20 Apr 15	Disch Aug 16
39	FRASER, DVR Kenneth	SS *Morea*, 20 Apr 15	RTA 8 Mar 17
40	CARVELL, DVR Henry	SS *Morea*, 20 Apr 15	To No 2 Sqn, 25 Nov 16, RTA 26 Jan 19
41	LEWIS, 2/AM Oscar	SS *Morea*, 20 Apr 15	To No 2 Sqn, 25 Nov 16, To 7 TS, Disch 19 May 19
42	CHAPPLE, CPL Ernest	SS *Morea*, 20 Apr 15	To 6th MT Coy, RTA 1 May 19

First 10 Reinforcements

#	Name	Embarked/Arrived	Remarks
43	MACKINOLTY, FSGT George John William	RMS *Persia*, 10 Aug 15	To No 2 Sqn, 25 Nov 16 Later Commissioned
44	† ADAMS, AM Francis Luke	RMS *Persia*, 10 Aug 15	Died as POW 1 Aug 16 – Nov 16
45	† CURRAN, AM David	RMS *Persia*, 10 Aug 15	Died as POW 16 Jun 17
46A	DOBNEY, A/SGT William Edwin	RMS *Persia*, 10 Aug 15	To No 2 Sqn, 25 Nov 16 RTA 6 May 19
47	† MUNRO, AM James	RMS *Persia*, 10 Aug 15	Died as POW 13 Oct 16
48	PLAYER, SGT Sidney	RMS *Persia*, 10 Aug 15	Arrived Egypt 27 Dec 16
49	† RAYMENT, AM William Charles	RMS *Persia*, 10 Aug 15	Died as POW 11 Nov 16
50	SOLNICK, 1/AM Alexander Isador	RMS *Persia*, 10 Aug 15	RTA 10 Jul 16
51	STUBBS, SGT John	RMS *Persia*, 10 Aug 15	Arr Egypt 27 Dec 16 To 1 Sqn RTA 15 Nov 19
52	WHEELER, Chief Mech William Edwin	RMS *Persia*, 10 Aug 15	Arr Egypt 27 Dec 16 To UK 29 Jan 17 RTA 6 Oct 19

Last Reinforcements – 6 Drivers & Wheeler

#	Name	Embarked/Arrived	Remarks
436	SUTHERLAND, LCPL Charles	SS *Morea*, 30 May 16	Wheelwright To 1 Sqn RTA 15 Jan 18
437	SUTHERLAND, DVR Colin Sherson	SS *Morea*, 30 May 16	Driver RTA 4 Mar 19
438	CAMPBELL, DVR William Annesley	SS *Morea*, 30 May 16	Driver To 1 Sqn RTA 4 Mar 19
439	ANLEZARK, DVR John Alexander	SS *Morea*, 30 May 16	Driver To No 2 Sqn, 25 Nov 16 RTA 6 May 19
440	COLES, A/CPL Arthur Aplin	SS *Morea*, 30 May 16	Driver
441	LONG, DVR Albert Charles	SS *Morea*, 30 May 16	Driver – to 7 Div RTA 16 Mar 19
442	COLLINS, DVR William George	SS *Morea*, 30 May 16	Driver - to AMDT Disch 6 Oct 19

No 5 Samuel Hendy did not join the Half-Flight.   † died   (Source: The 13 to 68 Sqn – No 2 Sqn RO No 1. – 25 Nov 16 and AWM 22 31/4/2004 of 10 May 17.)

Known RFC/RAF Officers Mesopotamia 1915-1919
RFC DETACHMENT EGYPT – Later 'C' Flight 30 Squadron, RFC

Lt E.A. Floyer.

Sgt C.E. Foggin.

Sgt R.J. Lillywhite.

Cpl W.B. Power.

Name/Rank	Joined	Left	Remarks
BAXTER Fred Oscar 2Lt (O)	19.1.15	30.1.15	To French Seaplane Sqn Later MC Reported KIA 4/17
CLOGSTOUN Herbert Prinsep Somers Lt (P)	14.8.15	9.12.15	Arriv Mespot 27.12.15. RFC(SR)
COCKERELL Samuel Pepys 2Lt (P)	2.11.14	20.3.15	Died of smallpox this date. b Ismailia War Cemetery, grave A.117.
CONRAN Owen Mostyn Capt (P)	?-4.15	23.11.15	To 14 Sqn. Royal Lancs Regt
DAVIDSON Donald Alistair Leslie 2Lt (P)		09.12.15	Arriv Mespot 27.12.15
EXMOUTH Edward Addington Hargreaves Pellew, Visc (P)	?-6.15	?.9.15	To hospital. 7/Royal Berks Regt
FLOYER Ernest Ayscoghe Lt (O)	15.10.15	23.11.15	To 14 Sqn Trnd as pilot 6/16/. IA Cavalry
FOGGIN Cyril Edgar Sgt (P)	24.12.14	?	
GETHIN Percy Edward Lovell 2Lt (O)	20.1.15	23.1.15	To French Seaplane Sqn Port Said Trnd as pilot. 27th Punjabis IA
HILLAS H.G. Lt (O)	18.1.15	28.1.15	To French Seaplane Sqn. Egyptian Ministry of Finance
LEDGER Horace Martin Capon 2Lt (O)	20.1.15	30.1.15	To French Seaplane Sqn MIA 22.12.15. 27th Punjabis IA
LEONARDI B (P)	26.12.14	?	Italian pilot
LILLYWHITE Robert John Sgt(P)	24.12.14		Later Capt KIFA 11/16
MacKINTOSH Charles Alexander Gordon Lt (O)	18.1.15	?-10.15	Royal Irish Regt
MASSY Seaton Dunham Capt (P)	2.11.14	20.11.15	Sqn CO To 30 Sqn Mespot. 29th Punjabis IA
McCRINDLE John Robert Lt (P)	30.8.15	9.12.15	To Mespot arriv 27.12.15 Later CO 113 Sqn. 7/Gordon Highlanders
MURRAY Eric Mackay Lt (P)	?	9.12.15	To Mespot Arr 27.12.15. Royal Highlanders & Corps of Guides IA
O'FARRELL Ernest Harward Mayhew Capt (P)	25.8.15	23.11.15	To 14 Sqn Royal Irish Fusiliers
PARR Sydney Charles Lt	21.12.14	20.5.15	EO2 30 Sqn. RFC(SR)
PARTRIDGE B.G.N. 2Lt (O)	20.1.15	23.1.15	To French Seaplane Sqn 2/Rajputs IA
PAUL Sir Robert Joshua 2Lt (O)	2.1.15	28.1.15	To French Seaplane Sqn MIA & POW 9.10.15 Egyptian Irrigation Dept
POWER William Boyle Cpl(P)	24.12.14	?	KIFA Farnborough 17.7.16 RFC(SR)
REILLY Hugh Lambert Capt (P)	2.11.14	?-3.15	To Mespot as CO 30 Sqn 82nd Punjabis IA
RICKARDS Gilbert Braithwaite Capt/Maj (P)	23.12.14	9.12.15	To 30 Sqn 27.12.15 –20.5.16. R Munster Fusiliers/RFC
ROSS Arthur Justin Capt (P)	9.12.14	23.11.15	To 14 Sqn RE
ROYLE Leopold Victor Arnold Lt (O)	27.11.14	23.11.15	To 14 Sqn. Egyptian Coast Guard Admin
STIRLING Walter Francis 2Lt (O)	30.11.14	21.12.14	To French Seaplane Sqn 1/Royal Dublin Fusiliers
THOMSON-GLOVER John William Capt (O)	14.10.15	9.12.15	To Mespot arr 27.12.15 Royal Irish Regt & 35th Sikhs IA
TWEEDIE Douglas Royle Lt (O)	24.12.14	23.11.15	To 14 Sqn Egyptian Coast Guard Admin
WALMSLEY John Banks 2Lt (P)	?11.15	9.12.15	To Mespot 17 Sqn Salonika 1918 IA CBE DFC
WANLESS-O'GOWAN Lynedoch Lt (P)	?	9.12.15	To Mespot 2/Scottish Rifles
WILLIAMS Kenneth Lawson 2Lt (O)	20.1.15	30.1.15	2/Rajputs IA

Lt J.R. McCrindle.

Lt E.A. H. Pellew, Viscount Exmouth.

Capt G.B. Rickards.

Lt J.B. Walmsley.

30 SQUADRON RFC

Name/Rank	Joined	Left	Remarks
ADAMS Allen Percy Lt/Capt (P)	6.8.17	6.3.19	Ex 47 Sqn. KIA this date near Bushire, Persia. DFC Gaz 1.1.19, MID. RFC(GL). b Tehran War Cemetery, Iran, grave II.B.10.
ADELEY Gerald Graham Capt (P)	6.7.16	10.8.16	1/Royal Irish Rifles
AINSCOW James Arthur Lt (P)	17.10.16	26.5.17	9/Royal Warwicks Regt
ALLISON John Oliver Lt (P)	17.8.17	15.5.18	KIA this date. MC & bar. 162nd Bn Canadian Inf. Basra Memorial panel 43.
ANSON Henry Adelbert Lt (P)	15.7.17	13.2.19	MC. Still in Mespot 6/20. South Wales Borderers
ATHERTON Francis Wright Lt (O)	1.2.18	15.5.18	KIA this date. MC. Obs to J. O. Allison. RFA. Basra Memorial panels 43 & 64.
ATKINS Basil Sydney Capt (O)	3.7.15	16.9.15	POW This date. Obs to Treloar. 11th Rajputs IA
BACON John Leslie Walker Lt (P)	?-?-18	?	From 63 Sqn DFC 12/18 Still in Mespot 1/19. 1/7Cheshire Regt
BAGNALL Howard H Capt (O)/(P)	5.1.16	17.9.16	Instr 57(T) Sqn Egypt 1/18 Later 17 Sqn Salonika. 10/Middlesex Regt
BALBERNIE Arthur George 2Lt	29.3.16	30.4.16	MC. 2/Royal West Kent Regt
BALDWIN Claude Lorraine Lt (P)	2.12.16	17.8.18	Prom Capt/Instr. KIA Egypt 1918. RFC(SR)
BARNES Stuart Lt (P)	22.11.17	20.9.18	To Egypt pilot training. 1/Wessex Brig RFA
BARR Eric Noel Douglas 2Lt (O)	17.5.16	4.12.16	MC Gaz 6.10.16. To UK pilot training. 60th Howitzer Bn RFA
BAXTER Eric Gordon Capt (P)	17.7.17	4.12.17	108th Infantry IA
BAYLY Leonard Joseph StGeorge Capt (P)	3.2.17	7.10.17	C de G. Ex 17 Sqn Salonika Pilot 5/16, MID 14.8.17 OC 'A' Flt. To Egypt CO SMA 2/18. RFA
BEAN William Stuart 2Lt (P)	1.5.17	21.1.18	KIA this date. b Baghdad (North Gate) War Cemetery, grave III.D.6. East Riding RE(TF).
BECKETT Reinzi Stephen Barry 2Lt (O)	27.11.16	14.8.17	To UK 1/8 Ghurkas IA
BEEVOR-POTTS Lionel Lt (O)	18.8.16	4.4.17	1/4 South Wales Borderers
BENTLEY A 2Lt (O)	15.6.18	18.12.18	To Egypt. MGC
BERESFORD Rodney Lt (P)	12.8.18	22.2.19	Ex 63 Sqn and test pilot Basra AP Invalided to UK. 3/Staffs Regt
BERRINGTON Bernard Eddowes Lt (P)	2.10.16	28.3.18	To 47 Sqn Salonika as FltCdr from 5/18. 9/E Kent Regt
BOISSIER G V De Lt (P)	6.4.18	26.3.19	
BRADLEY Robert Anstruther Capt/Maj/LtCol (P)	5.11.15	2.3.16	To 58 RS as CO 2.17. 63 Sqn 5.11.17–8.4.18. OC 31 Wing 8.4.18–6.1.19. 1/North Staffs Regt.
BREARS Charles 2Lt (O)	2.6.18	22.2.19	Commis 13.5.18 To HE. 1/10 Middlesex Regt
BRODIE Philip Wyndham Capt(O)	9.1.17	26.5.17	Died of pneumonia in Italy 18.11.18. 1/Seaforth Highlanders
BROWNING Lancelot Harold 2Lt/Capt (O)	17.5.16	10.1.17	To pilot training. Returned Sqn 7.12.17 to 3.7.18 To Egypt 111 Sqn & SNBD. To 63 Sqn post-war DFC 10.7.20. RFA
BUIST Claude Napier Lt (O)	?	?	12/15
BULL Sydney Lt (P)	9.11.18	3.4.19	DFC Gaz 31.3.19 Still in Mespot 6/19 with 63 Sqn. RFC(GL)
BUNSTER Sydney Garfield 2Lt	28.11.18	24.3.19	EO3 (Wireless)
BURN William Wallace Allison Lt (O)	14.5.15	30.7.15	KIA this date. MiD. NZ Staff Corps att RFC. Aust Half-Flight. NKG. Basra Memorial.
BURNS James Rattray Lt (P)	2.7.16	1.1.18	MC. To Egypt as Instr 193(T) Sqn. KIFA 10.6.18. 6/Scot Rifles
BUSHE Charles Grattan 2Lt (O)	2.1.18	26.10.18	To Egypt training British West Indies Regt
BUXTON Vincent Capt (O)	14.2.17	14.10.17	To 31 Wing HQ 2/Leicester Regt
CAMPBELL Alan La Grand Lt (P)	18.2.18	?	To 63 Sqn post-war. 2/Highland Light Inf
CARRALL Eric Lawens Capt (O)	10.11.18	?-?-19	Asst Rec Officer. IARO
CARRYER Frederick William Lt (P)	17.4.18	?	Commis 1.12.17 Still in Mespot 1/19. ASC
CARTER Rodney Thomas Lt (O)	15.9.18	25.12.18	To Egypt
CASE J B Lt (O)	23.2.18	4.11.18	To HE pilot training. Indian Cavalry
CATLING Arthur Donald Skene Lt (P)	16.4.18	?	In Mespot 6/19 with 63 Sqn. Devon Regt
CHABOT Charles James Lt (P)	11.6.16	14.1.17	To UK. RFC(SR)
CHACKSFIELD John 2Lt (O)	5.8.18	25.4.19	Loan from 72 Sqn
CHARIG Arnold 2Lt (P)	17.4.16	21.9.16	RFC(SR)
CLOGSTOUN Herbert Prinsep Somers Lt/Capt	27.12.15	20.4.16	From Egypt with C Flt Returned to Egypt Act Adj 58 TS & HQ 40 Wing as Adj. RFC(SR)
COCHRANE Richard Pelham Inglis Lt (O)	13.6.16	9.10.16	To UK pilot training. 17th Cavalry IA
COLLEY Reginald Thomas 2Lt (P)	19.10.16	17.11.17	Invalided India 23.5.17
CORBETT Reginald de la Cour Capt (O)	15.11.15	29.4.16	POW Siege of Kut .Reported died while a POW 25.12.17. 47th Pioneers IA
CORY-WRIGHT Geoffrey Capt (P)	5.2.18	17.11.18	Ex 63 Sqn. Sqn F/Cdr To HE. 3/East Kent Regt
COURTHOPE-MUNRO Caryl Henry 2Lt	15.10.15	29.4.16	POW at KUT. 33rd Indian Cavalry
COWPER Gerald Audry Cadogan Capt (P)	21.5.16	30.6.16	To 31 Sqn India. 8/AIF
COX Charles 2Lt (P)	6.7.17	13.1.18	Invalided to India. To Training Brig Palestine 28.3.18. RFC(SR)
CRAIG Hedley William 2Lt (O)	28.1.17	15.4.17	KIA this date Obs to Capt Pickering. RE. b Baghdad (North Gate) War Cemetery, grave XIV.K.14.
CRAIK David Lt (O)	8.11.17	17.6.18	To HE pilot training. IARO
CREERY William Foster Lt (O)	25.10.17	28.5.18	To HE pilot training. Connaught Rangers
CROSS James Adam Lt (O)	?	?	11/17 RGA
CUFF Robin Ernest Lt (P)	20.11.15	22.5.16	3/Loyal North Lancs Regt
CULLEN Arthur Armstrong Lt (P)	21.3.18	12.4.18	On loan from 72 Sqn. Royal Dublin Fusiliers

Lt E.N.D. Barr.

Capt L.J.StG. Bayly.

Lt B.E. Berrington.

Lt W.W.A. Burn.

Capt H.J. Edgar.

2Lt R. B. Fricker.

2Lt H.R. Gardner.

Capt H.F.A. Gordon.

Name	Dates		Notes
DALE Charles Brodrick Mitcalfe Lt (P)	17.8.17	9.1.18	Invalided to India then Egypt as Instr. Northumberland Fusiliers
D'ARCY Morgan Rostron Lt (O)	3.11.16	1.1.18	To Egypt pilot training. 8th Cavalry IA
DAVIDSON Donald Alistair Leslie 2Lt (P)	27.12.15	6.5.16	MC, MiD. From Egypt with C Flight RFC(SR). KIA 30.4.17 with 19 Sqn. Arras Flying Services Memorial.
DE HAVILLAND Hereward Major (P)	1.8.16	30.4.18	DSO Sqn CO 11.1.17 to 21.4.18 To HE. RFC(SR)
DENNYS Cecil Hector Massy Capt	4.1.17	27.1.18	Sqn Rec Officer To India. Connaught Rangers
DEVONSHIRE Feray Vulliamy Capt (P)	28.8.18	2.11.18	From 63 Sqn Flt Cdr. To 31 Sqn India. 7/Hussars
DICKINSON Francis Gilbert Cunyngham Lt (O)	27.4.17	23.1.18	To Egypt. 3/Gloucs Regt
DICKINSON Thomas Malcolm 2Lt (O)	22.12.15	31.8.16	16th Cavalry IA
DINNAGEN Harry Alexander Lt	?.3.18	6.7.18	EO3 (Wireless) Sick leave then 52 Wing India 18.11.18
DUNSTON Ambrose Ellis Aspinwall 2Lt (O)	30.11.16	21.11.17	Re-joined Army unit. 1/4Dorset Regt
ECCLES Roger Joe 2Lt (P)	26.7.17	21.1.18	RFA
EDGAR Herbert James Capt (P)	11.6.16	28.8.16	4/Cheshire Regt
EDWARDS Arthur Strother Capt (P)	12.1.18	2.5.18	MIA & POW this date Died in captivity 13.5.18 Ex Instr 57 RS Egypt. 11/17 Kings Liverpool Regt & MGC
ELLIOT-SMITH Charles Henry Capt (P)	2.10.16	14.7.17	Invalided to India. To Egypt. CO 193 TS 3/18. Bedfordshire Regt
EVERIDGE James Major (P)	25.4.18	2.5.19	Sqn CO Came from 63 Sqn. Surrey Yeomanry
FIELDEN Geoffrey Lt (P)	29.8.18	2.4.19	Ex 63 Sqn. 7th Hussars
FLETCHER Eric Noel 2Lt (P)	25.9.18	?	Still in Mespot 6/19 with 63 Sqn
FORSYTH William Allan Lt (O)	19.6.16	10.1.18	RA
FRICKER Reginald Bertram 2Lt (P)	28.1.17	23.5.17	With Sqn prev (as obs?) to 12.11.16 To 22 RS Egypt, pilot training or instr. 9/DCLI
FULTON Edmund James Lt (O)	7.8.15	22.11.15	MIA & POW this date. Repatriated 11/18. DYO Lancers
GARDNER Harold Rolfe 2Lt (P)	17.7.17	9.11.17	To Training Brig Egypt 15.2.18. Bedfordshire Regt
GIBSON John Alexander Lt	17.2.16	15.11.17	EO3 (Stores) To Basra Air Park. RFC(SR)
GILES John Howard Robert Lt (O)	21.3.16	17.7.16	3/Hants Bn Wessex Brig RFA
GORDON Harry Francis Adam Capt (P)	18.10.16	4.4.17	Yorks & Lancs Regt
GORDON Jeffrey William Campbell Lincoln Lt (P)	14.9.18	?	Arr. Mespot 7.8.18 Still in Mespot 6/19 with 63 Sqn
GORST E J Capt (O)	29.4.18	?	Ex 113 Sqn Palestine. RHA
GRAVES Arnold Capt (P)	5.11.15	2.12.16	To Egypt Instr 21(T) Sqn 1/17. Dorset RE(TF)
GRESWELL Eric Walker Lt (O)	29.7.16	6.3.17	Trnd as pilot 111 Sqn Jan/June 1918. 8/Cheshire Regt
HAIGHT Walter Lockwood Capt (P)	17.8.17	4.3.18	MIA & POW this date. 162nd Bn Canadian Inf. Repatriated 16.12.18.
HANCOCK Harold Lindsey Watkins Lt (O)	1.8.17	4.3.18	MIA & POW this date Obs to Capt Haight. RFA. Repatriated 16.12.18.
HANNAY William Andrew Capt	16.9.16	4.1.17	Sqn RO Trnd as obs. 2/Kings(Liverpool) Regt
HAWKER Trevor McDonnel 2Lt (P)	6.7.16	17.5.17	FltCdr. From Australia To UK. 4/Royal Irish Fusiliers
HAWKINS Arthur William Lt (P)	11.8.17	?	To 63 Sqn post-war Still in Mespot 8/19. 3/Yorks Regt
HAWORTH-BOOTH Osbert Moore 2Lt (O)	1.8.17	10.10.17	RFA
HAYWOOD Sydney Lt (P)	17.7.16	26.10.16	KIFA this date. 11/East Lancs Regt
HEAD Edward John 2Lt (P)	17.7.17	17.8.17	Commis 28.2.17 from Aust Flying. Corps Invalided to India. With 47 Sqn South Russia 1919
HENSON Stephen Burrows 2Lt	28.2.18	8.6.18	EO3 (Gunnery) Commis 12/17. To 72 Sqn. 4(Res) E Kent Regt
HERON R A Lt (O)	4.12.16	19.4.17	RFA
HERRING Justin Howard Lt/Capt (P)	1.8.16	2.1.17	DSO To 17 Sqn Salonika as CO Ceylon Engineers
HERRING Robert Browning Lt	31.8.17	20.5.18	EO3 (Photo) Back in Mespot 10/18. RFC(SR)
HOLLAND Charles Henry Haymann Lt (O)	10.10.18	18.3.19	Invalided to India. 7/Glos Regt
HOLSTIUS Edward Nils 2Lt (P)	6.7.16	5.10.16	Durham Light Inf
HOPKINSON Harry Cunliffe 2Lt (P)	2.7.16	23.12.16	To UK. Shropshire Light Inf
HUDSON Frederick Walter Capt(O)	19.8.16	27.11.16	To pilot training 145 Sqn Palestine & 47 Sqn Salonika. 8/18 Norfolk Regt
HUGHES Edward Douglas Gwynn 2Lt (P)	8.3.18	?	
HUNTING Percy Llewellyn Lt	25.10.16	30.7.17	EO3 (Wireless) To 31st Wing HQ. 4/Northumberland Fusiliers
JENOURE Eric Maynard 2Lt (P)	17.8.17	?-?-18	5/British West Indies Regt
JOLLY Evelyn Hugh Parker Lt (P)	9.11.18	3.4.19	IA Cavalry
KING-HARMAN Lawrence Hope Capt (O)	12.9.16	26.10.16	KIFA this date. Obs to Lt Haywood. MiD, RHA.
KINGSLEY Douglas Lt (O)	25.11.16	14.8.17	1/Seaforth Highlanders
KINGHORN Ernest Carr 2Lt (O)	29.1.18	4.11.18	WIA 10.3.18. 4/Border Regt & Ox & Bucks LI
KIRBY T H 2Lt	8.12.16	7.1.17	Invalided to Egypt
KIRK Franklin Christopher de Lamplugh Lt (P)	5.3.18	1.1.19	Still in Iraq 6/19 as Political Officer. 2/Norfolk Regt
KIRWAN Laird Lt (O)	1.8.18	20.8.18	KIFA this date. 1/5 Lancs Regt. b Baghdad (North Gate) War Cemetery, grave IV.J.4.
LAMB William George Lt	4.1.18	25.3.19	EO3 (Stores). 3/East Yorks Regt
LANDER Thomas Eaton Lt (P)	6.7.16	6.5.17	WIA, FTL, POW this date. MC 6.10.16. 3/Highland Light Inf. Repatriated 27.11.118
LAWRENSON Cyril Arthur Lt (O)	19.11.18	14.12.18	3/Royal Irish Regt Att 8/R Welsh Fusiliers
LEESON Alexander Neve Lt (O)	29.7.17	22.10.17	KIA this date DSO. RHA. b Baghdad (North Gate) War Cemetery, grave IV.C.4.
LELEU Lionel Louis Lt (P)	13.3.18	28.10.18	Ex 72 Sqn. Invalided this date. DCLI
LEWIS William Reginald Lt	16.6.16	18.11.17	EO3 (Wireless) From South Africa. S/A Ambulance Corps
LINDOP Adrian Haratius Erskine Lt (O)	30.11.17	28.5.18	MC & Bar Gaz 7.6.18 To HE Pilot training. 37th Dogras IA

Name	Dates	Notes
LINES George Frederick 2Lt (O)	26.10.16 8.1.17	To Egypt as Instr 21 RS. RFC (GL)
LLOYD Kenneth Buchanan 2Lt (P)	1.8.16 ?-5.17	WIA 28.4.17 invalided to India. Royal Welsh Fusiliers
MacFARLANE Ruthven Montgomerie Chase Lt (O)	19.9.16 4.4.17	RFA
McKICHAN Kenneth William Lt (P)	7.4.17 4.12.17	RFA
MAGUIRE Matthew Laurence 2Lt (P)	2.10.16 28.4.17	MIA & POW this date DOW in captivity. NKG. Basra Memorial. MC Gaz 25.5.17. 1st Connaught Rangers.
MASSY Seaton Dunham Major (P)	20.11.15 27.6.16	Sqn CO – 22.11.15 to 30.5.16 DSO. 29th Punjabis IA. Prev RFC Egypt Detach
MAXWELL Francis Severn Lt (P)	7.3.18 ?	From 72 Sqn Still in Mespot 5/19 with 63 Sqn. From South Africa RFC(SR)
McCRINDLE John Robert Capt (P)	27.12.15 24.12.16	DSO. Came with 'C' Flight from Egypt To 57 RS Egypt as Flt Cdr. 7/Gordon Highlanders
McINTOSH Robert Henry Lt (P)	6.5.18 10.10.18	
McNAB Robert Johnston Lt (O)	5.3.18 23.11.18	To HE pilot training. 131 MG Corps
MELLOWS Arthur Holdich Capt (O)	21.5.18 21.6.18	To HE pilot training. 1/1 Hunts Cyclist Bn
MERTON Gerald Capt (P)	17.6.16 17.2.18	MC. To Egypt prom Major. CO 3SNBD 4/18. RFC(SR)
MERZ George Pinnock Lt (P)	15.6.15 30.7.15	KIA this date. NKG. Basra Memorial. Melbourne Univ Rifles & AFC. Aust Half-Flight.
MILLER L E 2Lt (P)	31.5.16 15.7.16	RFC(SR)
MILLS Algernon S Lt (O)	2.1.18 17.1.18	MIA & POW this date. Repatriated 16.12.18. 2/Lovat Scouts
MITCHELL J 2Lt (O)	29.2.16 28.9.16	28th Bn RFA
MORAN Denis Joseph 2Lt	16.7.18 ?	EO3 (Wireless) Still in Mespot with 63 Sqn 2/19. 1/2 Border Regt
MORDEN-WRIGHT Herbert Lt (O)	2.3.18 20.9.18	MC. To Egypt pilot training. RFA
MORGAN Albert Edward Lt/Capt (P)	6.8.17 4.11.18	South Wales Borderers
MORRIS Robert Kay Lt (P)	31.12.16 11.4.18	MC. To Egypt Capt & F/Com Instr 58 TS. DLI
MOXEY Edgar Reginald Lt/Capt	27.5.16 28.7.17	EO1 (Photo) To 31st Wing HQ. RFC(GL)
MUNDEY Stanley Cyril Beresford Capt (O)	? 29.4.16	POW at KUT. Ox & Bucks Light Inf
MURRAY Eric Mackay Capt (P)	20.11.15 15.8.16	DSO, MC. Sqn CO 31.5.16 to 7.8.16. Royal Highlanders & Corps of Guides
MURRAY W A Capt (P)	4.1.17 ?	
NEAME Eric Mowbray Lt (O)	5.4.18 17.4.18	Re-joined Army unit. Royal West Kent Regt
NIXON Brian George Michael Frederick Capt (O)	13.9.16 ?-2.17	To 31st Wing HQ. 41st(Dogra) Bengal Infantry IA
NORMAN C W B 2Lt (O)	24.6.16 7.10.16	To KB's as Met Officer
NUTTALL Frank Lt/Capt (P)	5.4.17 23.3.19	NZ. Ex instr 22 RS Egypt. MC. With 63 Sqn 6/19. KIFA 18.9.20 with 30 Sqn. RFC(SR). b Tehran War Cemetery, Iran, grave III.G.16.
O'CONNELL Maurice James 2Lt (O)	2.5.18 26.5.18	Re-joined Army unit. RFA
O'NEILL William Hickley Lovell Capt (O)	4.2.17 18.6.17	MC. To 31st Wing HQ as Wing Adjt. 51st Sikhs IA
ORTON John Overton Cone Capt (O)	15.12.16 31.8.16	Pilot training 4/17. 2/Norfolk Regt
PAGE Lancelot St Allard March Capt (O)	8.12.16 20.8.18	KIFA this date. 10/East Kent Yeomanry
PALMER Walter Gerard Capt (O)	21.6.15 5.3.16	KIA this date Obs to R.H. Peck. 113th Infantry IA att RFC. Basra Memorial.
PARR Sydney Charles Lt	30.5.15 17.3.16	Equip Off Came from 'C' Flight Egypt To Air Park as CO
PECK Roland Henry 2Lt (P)	?-6.15 5.3.16	KIA this date. Dorset Regt att RFC. Basra Memorial.
PETRE Henry Aloysius Capt/Maj (P)	14.5.15 23.5.16	Aust Half-Flight. DSO, MC, MID*. Invalided to India. To UK. Commonwealth Mil. Forces
PHILLIPS Percival 2Lt/Capt (P)	16.4.18 12.2.19	Served with Sqn as Air Mech 1915/16 To 63 Sqn post-war DFC Gaz 10.7.20 MSM. DCLI
PICKERING Charles Leigh Capt (P)	31.12.16 15.4.17	KIA this date. 6/Cheshire Regt. b Baghdad (North Gate) War Cemetery. Recorded as Lieut by CWGC.
PRATT Edwin Lambert Lt (P)	2.3.18 16.6.18	Loan from 72 Sqn. Scottish Rifles
RATTRAY Arthur Rullion Lt (O)	7.11.16 4.6.17	Royal Indian Marine & RFC(GL)
REILLY Hugh Lambert Capt/Maj (P)	30.3.15 21.11.15	Major from 29.10.15. Sqn CO. DSO & MID. MIA & POW this date. Repatriated 16.12.18. 82nd Punjabis
RETTIE James Elrick Lt (P)	2.7.16 7.9.16	Canadian
RICH Percival Augustus 2Lt	30.3.17 22.5.17	EO3 (Photo) To 31st Wing HQ. RFC(GL)
RICHARDSON Harold 2Lt (O)	20.8.16 26.3.17	Norfolk Regt
RICKARDS Gilbert Braithwaite Capt (P)	27.12.15 20.5.16	Ex 'C' Flt Egypt Returned Egypt as Major & CO 21 RS. Munster Fusiliers
RIDPATH Claude Herbert Ernest Lt	17.11.17 15.12.18	EO3 (Wireless) To Trg Brig Egypt. RFC(SR)
RODNEY Hon. James Henry Bertie Lt (P)	21.5.16 27.10.16	Ex 17 Sqn Egypt WIA. 5/Rifle Brigade
ROSE Frederick Oswald 2Lt (P)	3.1.17 13.1.19	To HE. 14/London Regt(London Scottish) & 7/Essex Regt
SANCTUARY Campbell Thomas Lt (O)	16.3.16 21.9.16	1/1 Dorset Bn RFA
SCHNEIDER Lionel Woodhams Capt	25.4.17 23.1.18	To Egypt RFC
SCOTLAND James William Humphreys Lt (P)	5.9.15 7.11.15	Invalided to India. NZ Forces
SCOTT	? ?	1915
SHARP William Flt/Sgt 2Lt	? 12.11.16	EO3 (Stores) To 'X' AD Egypt 12/16. RFC(SR)
SIEVIER Robert Brudenell Bruce Lt (O)	17.1.17 21.5.18	MC, MiD. To Egypt. RFA. Surname sometimes given as Siever.
SKINNER Alfred Ernest Lionel Lt (P)	8.12.16 11.4.18	MC. Prom Capt To Egypt Training Brigade as Flt Cdr. 1/1Kings Own Royal Regt (Norfolk Yeo)
SKINNER Reginald Onslow Lt (O)	29.3.16 31.5.16	MC. To 14 Sqn Palestine as pilot 3/17. RGA
SMITH E Capt (P)	2.10.16 ?	
SMALLWOOD Harold St Clair 2Lt (O)	6.9.16 10.1.17	To HE pilot training. 25th Bengal Lancers 12th Cav IA

2Lt T.M. Hawker.

Lt T.E. Lander.

Capt J.O.C. Orton.

2Lt R.H. Peck.

2Lt G.W. Swanson.

Capt I.D. Truman.

SMYTHE Geoffrey Meliss Capt		24.8.17	?-3.18	EO3 (Stores) Ex 57 RS Egypt. Returned Egypt. Ret Mespot 9/18. 31 Wing HQ. 6/North Lancs Regt
SOPER Vivian Lt (O)		4.6.18	10.1.19	1/4 Dorset Regt
SOUTHAN John Harold Price 2Lt (O)		2.6.18	12.12.18	3/Royal West Kent Regt
SPAIN Granville Alaric Richard Lt		15.11.15	29.7.16	103rd Mahrattas IA
STRANGER Edwin Robert 2Lt (O)		1.9.17	18.10.17	RFA
SWANSON George William 2Lt (P)		6.7.16	28.10.16	Invalided to India To Instr 3 SMA Egypt. 4/Hants Regt
TANNER Francis James Lt (P)		8.12.16	17.8.18	To Egypt as Capt/Instr. 1/1 Welsh Horse Yeo
TAYLOR Walter 2Lt (P)		1.5.17	17.1.18	MIA & POW this date Repatriated 12/18. 1/4 East Lancs Regt
TENNANT John Edward Major (P)		7.8.16	11.1.17	Sqn CO To Lt/Col and OC 31 Wing this date. Scots Guards
THOMSON-GLOVER John William Lt		27.12.15	21.9.16	Came from 'C' Flt Egypt. Royal Irish Regt & 35th Sikhs IA
THORPE Eric Tom 2Lt (P)		2.3.18	26.3.19	Ex 72 Sqn. 4/Royal Warwicks Regt
THOULESS Archibald Cecil 2Lt (O)		?	26.4.16	KIA this date. Pilot C.B. Gasson RNAS. 9th Bn Norfolk Regt. Basra Memorial panel 6 & 61
TINDLE Tom Alderton Lt (O)		11.6.18	25.12.18	4/Wiltshire Regt
TRELOAR William Harold Lt (P)		18.5.15	16.9.15	Aust Half-Flight. MIA & POW this date. Repatriated 11.11.18.
TRUMAN Ivor Dudley Capt (P)		20.11.15	29.6.16	ASC
TURNER H D B 2Lt (O)		2.3.16	21.4.16	20th Bn RFA
WALMSLEY John Banks 2Lt (P)		10.12.15	16.9.16	To India 3.10.16 To 20 (Res) Wing as Instr 11.1.17. IA
WANLESS-O'GOWAN Lynedoch Capt (P)		27.12.15	17.1.17	Came with 'C' Flt from Egypt. 2/Scottish Rifles
WELLS Thomas Ralph Capt (P)		27.5.15	29.4.16	POW at Kut. 34th Punjabis IAu
WELMAN John Barthroppe 2Lt (P)		2.5.17	31.10.17	WIA & POW this date Repatriated 7.12.18 RFA
WEST Percy Francis 2Lt (P)		6.7.17?	21.8.17	To Mespot on grad 12.4.17 Died in India 24.3.18. 1st Royal Australian Navy Bridging Train
WESTENDARP Oscar Alfred Major (P)		21.4.18	11.5.18	Ex CO 22 TS Egypt 11/17. To 72 Sqn as CO. Wiltshire Regt & 19/London Regt
WHITE Thomas Walter Capt (P)		18.5.15	13.11.15	Aust Half-Flight. MIA & POW this date. Repatriated 25.11.18. Commonwealth Forces. KBE, DFC, MiD
WILLIAMS Richard Clywd Lt (O)		1.11.17	20.6.18	MG Corps, awarded MC, & 13th LAMBs
WILLS Wilfred Ridout Capt		30.4.15	?	Equipment Officer. Trained as pilot 2/17. IARO
WILSON H R Lt (O)		?	2.7.15	Invalided malaria. 114th Mahrattas IA
WINDSOR John Stephen Lt (P)		17.6.16	3.6.17	MC Gaz 3.6.17. South Wales Borderers
WINFIELD-SMITH Stephen Christopher Capt (P)		20.11.15	29.4.16	POW at Kut. 3/East Surrey Regt
YEATES Sydney Percival John 2Lt (O)		15.6.18	18.12.18	5/P of W Bn(TF) Devonshire Regt
YEATS-BROWN Francis Charles Claypon Capt (O)		7.8.15	13.11.15	MIA & POW this date. Obs to T.W. White. Repatriated 6.12.18. DFC for activities as a POW. 17th Cavalry IA

30 Squadron RFC in November 1916.

Left to right – Back row: 2/Lt M.L. Maguire (P), Lt M.R. D'Arcy (P), 2Lt H.StC. Smallwood (O), Capt F.W. Hudson (O), Capt G. Merton (P), Lt W.A. Forsyth (O), Lt J.A. Gibson (EO3 Stores), 2Lt R.T. Colley (P), Lt A.R. Rattray (O).
Second row: Lt J.A. Ainscow, Lt J.R. Burns (P), Capt B.G.M.F. Nixon (P), 2Lt H.L. Browning (P), W.L. Haight? 2Lt H.C. Hopkinson (P), Lt L. Beevor-Potts (O), Lt C.J. Chabot (P), Capt W.A. Hannay (Sqn RO), Lt E.R. Moxey (EO1 Photo), Lt B.E. Berrington (P).
Front row seated: Capt L. Wanless O'Gowan (P), Lt J.R. McCrindle (P), Lt J.H. Herring (P), Maj J.E. Tennant (Sqn CO), Col N.D.K. MacEwen (Asst Dir Aviation, IA), Capt H. de Havilland (P), Capt C.H. Elliott-Smith (P).
Seated on ground: Lt R.M.C. MacFarlane (O), 2Lt K.B. Lloyd (P), Lt J.S. Windsor (P).

63 SQUADRON RFC

Name/Rank	Joined	Left	Remarks
AINSWORTH Percy Lt/Capt (P)	23.4.17	17.8.18	Ex Obs 1 AFC To 20 TDS Egypt as Inst. Manchester Regt
AMORY Lt (P)	?	?	Returned Egypt further training
AVERY George William Percy Lt (P)	19.2.18	26.4.18	On loan from 72 Sqn these dates. ASC
BACON John Leslie Walker 2Lt (P)	5.12.17	?	To 30 Sqn. 1/7 Cheshire Regt
BAILEY Ernest John 2Lt (P)	29.4.18	13.1.19	To UK. RFC(SR)
BAILLON Edward Noel Lt (O)	30.4.17	25.9.17	MIA & POW this date. Canadian
BEGG Malcolm Glassford Lt (P)	7.5.17	25.9.17	MC. MIA & POW this date. Rifle Brig
BELL Percy Harrison Lt (P)	17.9.18	12.12.18	To India then South Africa. RFC(SR)
BERESFORD Rodney 2Lt (P)	12.12.17	25.1.18	To Basra AP as test pilot. 3/North Staffs Regt
BESWICK Norman Sutcliffe Lt (P)	8.12.16	13.1.19	To HE. 4/West Riding Regt
BIRTWISTLE William Lt	1.12.16	20.3.18	EO3(Wireless) To 31st Wing HQ. RFC(SR)
BLAKE John Wallace Lt (O)	21.4.17	5.10.17	MIA & POW this date Obs to Lt MacRae. 6/KRRC
BLAKE Robert Anthony 2Lt (O)	2.7.18	31.12.18	RA
BLUCKE Robert Stewart 2Lt (O)	25.5.18	20.9.18	To HE pilot training. 3/Dorset Regt. Later AVM, CB CBE DSO
BODDAM-WHETHAM Arthur Courtney Major (P)	31.8.16	27.4.17	First Sqn CO. To 14 Sqn Egypt. Argyll & Suth Highlanders
BOYES Alfred 2Lt (O)	24.7.18	11.9.18	From 72 Sqn. Still in Mespot 11/18 att civilian police MGC
BRADLEY Robert Anstruther Major (P)	5.11.17	8.4.18	Sqn CO .To 31st Wing as Lt/Col & OC this date. North Staffs Regt
BULLOCK F H Lt (O)	19.12.17	15.2.18	RGA
BUTLER Frank Harold Lt (O)	26.7.18	18.12.18	Dragoon Guards/13th Hussars
CALDWELL John Hay 2Lt (P)	15.6.17	12.1.18	FTL this date. DOW 24.1.18. Body not recovered until 27.1.18. Cameron Highlanders. b Baghdad (North Gate) War Cemetery, grave I.A.9.
CLAYTON George Henry 2Lt (P)	18.10.18	?	Still in Mespot 3/19 Royal Highlanders
CONEY Charles Herbert Law Capt (O)	27.4.17	12.3.18	To Egypt pilot training. 3/North Staffs Regt
COOPER Phillip Alan Lt (O)	28.7.18	18.12.18	3/Sappers & Miners
CORY-WRIGHT Geoffrey Lt/Capt (P)	20.1.18	5.2.18	Ex 23 RS instr. To 30 Sqn as Flt Cdr. 3/East Kent Regt
CRICHTON Edward James 2Lt (P)	14.3.18	?	Still in Mespot 3/19. Royal Highlanders
CROWTHER Gordon Douglas 2Lt (P)	9.6.17	26.10.17	Invalided to India. Canadian Field Artillery
DEACON Henry Wynn Capt (O)	12.9.18	18.12.18	Later Brigadier CBE DFC Gaz 1.1.19. RFA
DEVONSHIRE Feray Vulliamy Lt (P)	17.12.17	29.8.18	Ex instr 22 TS Egypt 9/17 To 30 Sqn as F/Cdr
DICKINSON Cecil Stanley 2Lt (O)	3.8.18	18.12.18	Arriv Mespot 28.6.18 .Canadian RFC(SR)
EVANS Arthur Edward 2Lt (P)	19.2.18	4.1.21	DFC. With 63 Sqn 1919 To 30 Sqn 1920. 2/E Surrey Regt
EVANS Christopher James Moule Lt (P)	29.4.18	?	From 72 Sqn Still in Mespot 3/19. RFC(SR)
EVERIDGE James Capt/Maj (P)	2.6.17	25.4.18	To 30 Sqn as CO Later W/Cdr MC. Surrey Yeomanry
FFISKE Herbert Guy Capt/Maj (P)	18.8.17	26.4.18	To Egypt F/Cdr Instr 57 TS. RFA.
FIELDEN Geoffrey Lt (P)	27.8.18	29.8.18	Arriv Mespot 16.7.18 Ex 144 Sqn Palestine To 30 Sqn Later Lt/Col OBE. 7th Hussars
FRANCIS Thomas Archdale Capt (P)	18.8.18	?	Ex 72 Sqn Still in Mespot 7/19. Royal Irish Regt
FROGLEY Sidney Gilbert Lt/Capt (P)	26.3.18	20.9.18	F/Cdr To Egypt then 17 Sqn Salonika 11/18 R Berks Regt
GATTENS Charles Lt (P)	28.1.19	15.6.19	Ex 72 Sqn KIFA this date. South African RE
GRIFFITHS Harold John 2Lt (O)	14.11.17	16.8.18	WIA 17.12.17 To Egypt pilot training. South Wales Borderers
GUYER Albert Charles 2Lt (P)	1.12.17	31.12.18	Commis 2Lt 3.8.17. RFC(GL)
HALL Richard Stuart Lt (O)	18.5.18	23.11.18	To HE pilot training. 3/Dorset Regt
HITCHENS E W T 2Lt (O)	13.8.18	11.9.18	ASC(MT)
HODGSON D 2Lt (O)	10.9.18	18.12.18	To Egypt. IARO
HOGAN James 2Lt	30.3.18	31.12.18	EO3 (Wireless) Prev 31 Wing HQ
HUNT Percy Thompson Lt (P)	15.9.18	31.12.18	Arriv Mespot 16.8.18 1/3 London Yeomanry
HUSBAND Victor Radclyffe Lt (O)	7.7.18	23.11.18	To HE. RFA
HYSLOP Ninian Steele 2Lt (P)	4.7.17	30.10.17	KIFA this date. Wellington Mtd Rifles NZ. b Basra War Cemetery, grave V.Q.1.
JACKS Wilfred Gray Lt (P)	24.5.17	1.4.18	To India but returned to Sqn With 30 Sqn 6/20. 6/HLI
JAMIESON John Andrew Lt (P)	31.5.17	12.9.18	Invalided to India. 4/Loyal North Lancs Regt
JEFFERIES Leonard Stanton (O)	14.7.18	11.9.18	9/Royal Warwicks Regt
JONES Harry Ernest Lt (O)	27.4.17	17.4.18	Canadian GL & RFC
JORDON Alfred Lacey 2Lt (P)	26.5.18	20.9.18	On loan from 72 Sqn these dates
KEATING Thomas Joseph Capt (O)	13.5.18	14.6.18	KIA this date. RFA. b Baghdad (North Gate) War Cemetery, grave III.E.5.
KNUDSEN Harold Jaures Lt (O)	18.7.18	18.12.18	Kings Own Royal Lancs Regt
LACE A George 2Lt (P)	1.12.17	?	Still in Mespot 7/19. 3/Cheshire Regt
LAHAYE Noel Hilton 2Lt (P)	17.5.17	4.12.17	Invalided to India. RFC(GL)
McFARLANE Norman Arthur Capt	18.10.17	28.6.18	Rec Off Trnd as obs and returned Sqn 29.1.18. 3/E Lancs Regt
MacRAE John Duncan George Lt (P)	28.6.16	5.10.17	MIA & POW this date. 1/Seaforth Highlanders
MAIR Frederick Clark Lt (P)	26.4.18	?	Still in Mespot 2/19. RFA & HLI
MATTHEWS Stuart Leslie Lt (O)	31.1.18	18.7.18	Temp attach 72 Sqn To HE pilot training. 32nd Cav IA
McDONALD Cedric Yeats Capt (P)	?-4.17	?-7.17	To UK from South Africa en-route to Mespot. Seaforth Highlanders
McMENAN William Rigg 2Lt (O)	27.4.17	14.3.18	To Egypt pilot training. 10/Highland Light Inf
MITCHELL Robert Cleare 2Lt (O)	27.4.17	28.5.18	To Egypt pilot training. Royal Scots Fusiliers
MOLLER Christopher William Henry Lt (O)	11.10.17	18.7.18	To Egypt pilot training. Seaforth Highlanders

2Lt W.R. McMenan and Lt N.S. Beswick.

Lt P.H. Bell.

Maj A.C. Boddam-Whetham.

Lt H.G. Ffiske.

Lt W.G. Jacks.

Lt J.A. Jamieson.

2Lt A.G. Lace.

Name		Date 1	Date 2	Notes
NELSON Samuel Banks 2Lt (P)		27.4.17	2.9.17	Invalided to India. American 7/Canadian Res Bn
O'BRIEN Humphrey Donatus Stafford	Capt (P)	26.6.18	14.9.18	MC* KIA this date. 1/Northants Regt. b Baghdad (North Gate) War Cemetery, grave III.H.9.
OCKERBURY Edric Oswald Lt (P)		24.8.18	7.3.19	RFC(SR)
PARKER Charles Allen Capt (P)		?	19.2.18	MC, RFA. KIFA this date. b Basra War Cemetery, grave III.K.11.
PEARCE Lt		?	?	Invalided to India
PHILPOTT John Reginald Capt (P)		20.3.17	25.9.17	MIA & POW this date MC with 12 Sqn. 10/Suffolk Regt
PRICE Harold Warnica Lt (P)		1.6.17	27.9.19	Canadian Inf
PUCKLE George Hale Lt		23.4.17	20.5.18	Originally pilot but defective sight. Retained by Sqn as Rec Off from 19.5.17 To 31 Wing HQ as Wg Adj. 17 Cav IA
QUINNELL John Charles Maj (P)		27.4.17	21.10.17	Sqn CO To HE Prev 10 Sqn & later CO 104 Sqn IF Retired A/C CB DFC. RFA
RHODES John Walter 2Lt (O)		2.6.18	15.12.18	Commis 13.5.18 21st MG Sqn
ROBERTS George Gerald 2Lt		27.4.17	?	Invalided to India 1/South Staffs Regt
ROBINSON Francis Lubbock Major (P)		13.6.17	?	DSO, MC. Sqn CO from 8.4.18 With 63 Sqn 3/19 and 30 Sqn 6/20 To UK. 2/21 Royal Inniskilling Fusiliers
SHALLOW George Lt (O)		14.9.18	18.12.18	IARO
SHERLOCK Walter Nugent Lt (O)		1.11.17	28.6.18	1/Seaforth Highlanders
SIMPSON Ronald Davidson Capt (P)		10.5.17	11.4.19	F/Cdr DFC & Bar. 6/Dragoon Guards
SMITH Percival Arnold Capt (P)		3.9.17	13.4.18	Sqn Rec Off. To Egypt pilot training. Durham Light Inf
SPENCE Leonard Rolls Bowness Lt (O)		27.4.17	16.2.18	To Egypt pilot training. Qual 23.9.18. 20 King's (Liverpool) Regt
SPURRIER Henry 2Lt (P)		24.5.17	9.1.18	Invalided to India Returned duty Trg Brig 28.8.18. RFC(GL)
STEDMAN Gerald Lomax Lt (P)		23.4.17	?	Still in Mespot 2/19. Canterbury Mtd Rifles NZ
STEWART George Vernon Lt (P)		12.3.18	?	Still in Mespot 3/19. 3/Royal Highlanders
STYRAN Arthur John Graham Lt (P)		7.5.17	5.4.18	MC Invalided to India To Egypt 15.7.18 Returned Mespot 11/19. RFA
TAUNTON Robert E M Lt (O)		27.4.17	28.5.18	To HE pilot training. 11/Canadian Light Inf
TIGAR Anthony Augustine 2Lt (O)		15.6.17	18.12.18	To Sqn as EO. RAeC 4298 27.2.17 To Egypt for pilot trng again. RFC(GL)
TREGALE John William Walter Lt (O)		31.1.18	16.8.18	To Egypt pilot training. 1/5 Ghurkha Rifles
UNDERHILL Harold William 2Lt (O)		20.4.17	18.7.18	To HE pilot training. RGA
WALKER Alfred Charles Lt (O)		5.1.18	?	Still in Mespot 5/19. Bedfordshire Regt
WARWICK John Lacy 2Lt (P)		9.6.18	14.6.18	KIA this date. RFC(SR). b Baghdad (North Gate) War Cemetery, grave III.H.4.
WEST Theodore James 2Lt (P)		24.5.17	17.3.18	MC. To Egypt. RFC(GL)
WILLIAMS Edwin Reginald Capt (O)		30.4.17	16.2.18	To Egypt pilot training. 11/Canadian Res Inf
WILSON M F C Capt		19.9.18	?	Sqn Rec Off. Invalided to India. 2/20 London Regt
WINTON Arthur James Sim 2Lt (P)		15.9.18	?	NZ Ex Force
WOODMAN Francis Ogilvie Lt (P)		7.8.18	13.1.19	MC. To HE. Canadian. 2/17 London Regt
WORTLEY Hugh Eames 2Lt (P)		19.12.17	?	Still in Mespot 12/18. 3/Suffolk Regt
WRIGHT George Robert 2Lt (P)		6.10.18	?	Still in Mespot 5/19. 7/Hants Regt
WYCHERLEY Lawrence 2Lt (O)		2.6.18	15.12.18	King's Shropshire Light Inf

Officers and ground crew of 'A' Flight, 63 Squadron at Mosul, January 1919.
L-r: Lt E.D. Ockerby, Capt T.A. Francis (P), Lt J.W.L. Bacon (P), Capt R.D. Simpson (P), Flt Cdr, Lt H.W. Price (P), Lt P.T. Hunt (P), 2Lt A.J.S. Winton (P).

72 SQUADRON RFC

Name/Rank	Joined	Left	Remarks
AVERY George William Percy Lt (P)	3.1.18	26.4.18	To Training Brig Egypt as instr? ASC
BADDILEY Phillip John Taylor Lt (P)	23.2.18	30.9.20	With 63 Sqn 3/19 With 30 Sqn 6/20. RFC(SR)
BANHAM Wilfrid Johnson Lt	2.3.18	30.6.18	Sqn Rec Off. Inj in car crash with CO 10.5.18. Invalided to India. 8/Royal Fusiliers.
BEATTY James Stanley Capt (P)	27.7.17	7.11.18	DFC. Canadian DFC Gaz 15.7.19 To Egypt as Instr
BELLORD Cuthbert George Capt (P)	3.1.18	30.6.18	Invalided to India. King's Shropshire Light Inf
BOYD Owen Tudor Capt/Maj/LtCol (P)	7.7.18	6.1.19	OBE MC AFC .Sqn CO Ex 66 Sqn France. To 31st Wing as OC this date. 5th Cavalry IA
BOYES Alfred 2Lt (O)	4.4.18	24.8.18	
CANNELL Hugh Featherstone Cameron Lt (P)	3.1.18	31.10.18	Died of wounds this date. RE & Skinners Horse. Basra Memorial, panel 44.
CHACKSFIELD John Lt (O)	28.6.18	5.8.18	To 30 Sqn RAF
COLEMAN Francis Henry Capt (P)	?-8.17	2.4.19	F/Cdr Act CO 6.1.19–13.2.19 DSO. 15/Middlesex Regt
CULLEN Arthur Armstrong Lt (P)	3.1.18	31.8.18	MIA & POW this date Repatriated 30.12.18. 6/R Dublin Fusiliers
EDWARDS Arthur Strother Capt (P)	3.1.18	12.1.18	To 30 Sqn. Ex Instr 57 TS Egypt. King's Liverpool Regt. DOW while POW 14.5.18. b Baghdad (North Gate) War Cemetery, grave XVIII.E.14.
EVANS Arthur Edward Lt (P)	3.1.18	19.2.18	To 63 Sqn. 2/East Surrey Regt.
EVANS Christopher James Moule Lt (P)	10.1.18	29.4.18	To 63 Sqn Commis from Flt/Sgt 14 Sqn 1917. RFC(SR)
FANSHAWE Evelyn Dalrymple Lt (P)	7.12.17	2.9.18	Prom Capt 23.8.18 To Egypt Trg Brig as instructor Later Maj/Gen Sir Evelyn OBE CBE
FRANCIS Thomas Archdale Capt (P)	31.1.18	18.8.18	To 63 Sqn. Royal Irish Regt
FULLER Norman Berwick Lt/Capt (P)	7.12.17	11.4.19	Remained in Mespot as Asst to Political Officer MBE. Kings Royal Rifle Corps
GATTENS Charles Lt (P)	10.1.18	28.1.19	To 63 Sqn. South African, RE. KIFA 5.6.19. b Baghdad (North Gate) War Cemetery, grave XX.D.8.
HENRY Harry Andre Capt (P)	3.1.18	20.11.18	Ex Asst Instr 57 RS Egypt. 1/17 Ox & Bucks Light Inf
HENSON Stephen Burrows Lt	?-7.18	6.3.19	EO3 (Gunnery) From 30 Sqn. 4/Res East Kent Regt
HOLLINGSWORTH Samuel Gerald Lt (P)	10.10.18	?	With 63 Sqn 3/19 & 30 Sqn 6/20
IZARD Henry Lt (P)	3.1.18	5.2.19	To HE. East African Native Transport
JOHNSON George Harold Burgoyne Lt (P)	16.5.18	14.6.18	To Sqn as EO (Stores) Trnd as pilot 1916 Invalided to India. 8/Durham Light Inf
JORDAN Alfred Lacey 2Lt (O)	11.4.18	20.9.18	To HE pilot training. MGC
LAMPLUGH Alfred Gilmer Lt (P)	3.1.18	25.9.18	Instr 58 TS Egypt 5/17 Prom Capt. To Trg Brig Egypt. North Staffs Regt
LAPRAIK Douglas Fairlie Lt/Capt (P)	3.1.18	1.10.18	Ex Instr 22 TS & 58 TS Egypt. Capt 31.10.18 To 31st Wing HQ this date 63 Sqn 6/19 DFC Gaz 1.1.19. Middlx Rgt
LAWSON Vincent Wade 2Lt	7.12.17	12.11.18	EO (Gunnery) Invalided to India 6/18 but returned to Sqn. RFC(SR)
LEES George Martin Lt/Capt (P)	3.1.18	?	Ex Instr 193 TS & 57 TS Egypt F/Cdr 63 Sqn 6/19 Still in Mespot 1920 Asst Political Officer. RA
LELEU Lionel Louis Lt (P)	3.1.18	13.3.18	To 30 Sqn. Killed flying for Imperial Airways 1933. DCLI
MacDONALD Somerled Douglas Lt/Capt (P)	7.2.18	?	With 63 and 30 Sqn until 6/20 at least DFC 10.7.20
MacKAY Moray Sutherland Lt (P)	23.1.18	?	Still in Mespot 9/19 with 63 Sqn
MAXWELL Francis Severn Lt (P)	3.1.18	11.4.19	To 30 Sqn Commis 2Lt 30.10.17. From South Africa

Lt H.F.C. Cannell.

Capt N.B. Fuller.

Lt S.G. Hollingsworth.

Capt D.F. Lapraik.

Breakfast at Hilla on the Euphrates, 1918. L-r: Lt G.M. Lees, Lt A.W. Hawkins (30 Sqn), Lt L.H. Paddle, Lt D.F. Lapraik.

Lt C. Gattens.

Lt G.H.B. Johnson.

Lt K.M. Pennington.

McKEE George Sears Lt (P)	19.11.18	15.2.19	To UK. RFC(SR)
PADDLE Leslie Harold Lt (P)	23.2.18	6.1.19	Invalided to India. RFC(SR)
PENNINGTON Kenneth Misson Lt (P)	7.12.17	7.3.19	AFC Gaz 4.7.18. South African RFC(SR)
PITT Thomas Alfred Lt (P)	3.1.18	11.4.19	To UK. Returned as Stores Officer Basra from 16.12.19 With 30 Sqn 6/20
POPE Ralph Patrick Phillip Lt (P)	10.1.18	11.4.19	DFC Gaz 15.7.19 With 63 Sqn to 8/19. E Surrey Regt
PRATT Edwin Lambert Lt (P)	10.1.18	16.6.18	Ex Instr 22 TS Egypt 11/17 Invalided to India Returned Egypt 30.10.18 on special duty. Cameronians att Scottish Rifles
SCALES Edgar Athole Lt	?	14.3.18	To KBs as recording officer With 63 Sqn 8/19
SPURR Percy William Lt (P)	7.12.17	11.9.18	Prom Capt 3.8.18 To Trg Brig Egypt as Instr. 3/R Berks Regt
TAYLOR D'Arcy Edward Derrick Lt (P)	10.1.18	22.5.18	MC Gaz 25.9.16 To India. Royal Fusiliers
THOMAS William Miles Webster Lt (P)	3.1.18	13.1.19	DFC. Ex Instr 22 TS & Aerial Fighting School Egypt 11/17. Later Sir Miles Thomas, MD of Morris Motors, Chairman of BOAC. ASC(MT)
THORPE Eric Tom Lt (P)	31.1.18	2.3.18	To 30 Sqn. 4/Royal Warwicks Regt
VON POELLNITZ Herman Walter Major (P)	2.7.17	10.5.18	Sqn CO. In car crash this date, DOI 11.518. Prev with 32 Sqn France. 2/Lincolnshire Regt. b Baghad (North Gate) War Cemetery, grave X.F.8.
WALL Gerald Robin Philip Lt (P)	7.8.18	?	Still in Mespot 7/19 with 63 Sqn. 3/Lincolnshire Regt
WARD Frederick 2Lt	3.7.17	8.3.18	EO3 To HE
WESTENDARP Oscar Alfred Major (P)	11.5.18	7.7.18	Sqn CO. Ex Instr & CO 22 TS Egypt 11/17 To HE 17.8.18. Wilts Regt & 19/London Regt
WILLIAMS Trevor Lewis Lt (P)	3.1.18	1.1.19	KIFA this date. RFC(SR). b Baghdad (North Gate) War Cemetery, grave X.C.2.

Maj O.A. Westendarp.

Lt G.R.P. Wall.

Lt E.L. Pratt.

RFC personnel in Mesopotamia, summer 1918.
L-r: Lt A.W. Hawkins, 30 Sqn, Lt D.F. Lapraik, 72 Sqn, Lt G.M. Lees, 72 Sqn, Lt J. Durward EO2 (Photo) 31 Wing, Lt L.H. Paddle, 72 Sqn. The three 72 Sqn pilots flew Bristol M.1Cs with 'C' Flight.

31 WING HQ and AIRCRAFT PARK 1915-20

Name	Joined	Left	Remarks
ARNOLD Kenneth Lt	23.3.18	29.6.18	EO2 (Photo) To Training Brigade Egypt. RFC(SR)
BIRTWISTLE William Lt	20.2.18	7.3.19	EO3 (Wireless) Ex 63 Sqn To HE this date. RFC(SR)
BOURN Dudley George Lt	2.10.18	?	EO (Tech Armament) Still in Mespot June 1920. MGC
BOYD Owen Tudor Capt (P)	25.11.17	7.7.18	SO2 31st Wing HQ To 72 Sqn as CO this date Prom Lt Col To OC 31 Wing from 6.1.1919 OBE 10.10.19 Still in Mespot June 1920. 5th Cavalry IA
BOWEN Trevor lifyd Lt	30.1.18	?	EO3 (Engines) Air Park. Yorkshire Regt
BRADLEY Robert Anstruther Major (P)	8.4.18	6.1.19	Prom Lt/Col To OC 31st Wing this dates Ex 30 Sqn and 63 Sqn. North Staffs Regt
BROKE-SMITH Philip William Lilian LtCol	9.4.15	16.8.16	Deputy then Asst Director Aviation Mesopotamia for the Indian Army DSO 3.6.16. RE
BUNSTER Sydney Garfield 2Lt	6.6.18	28.11.18	EO2 (Wireless) To 30 Sqn and later 63 Sqn post-war
BUXTON Vincent Capt	14.10.17	?	Prom Major SO3 31st Wing HQ Ex 30 Sqn Still in Mesopotamia June 1920. 2/Leics Regt
CLEMENT Donald Holt Lt	2.6.18	?	EO3 (Stores) Air Park Basra
COXON Atwell John Lt	5.9.18	2.10.18	EO3 (Stores) To 23 Kite Balloon Company
DARNELL Hubert 2Lt	22.5.17	?	EO3 (Stores) RFC(SR)
DENLY Arthur Henry Lt	14.9.18	29.11.18	EO (Tech Wireless) To 63 Sqn To HE 27.1.1919
DINNAGE Harry Alexander Lt	16.2.18	?-3.18	EO3 (Wireless) To 30 Sqn
DURWARD James Lt	22.1.18	?	EO2 (Photo) Still in Mespot 8/1919 with 63 Sqn. RE
GIBSON John Alexander Lt	15.11.17	?	EO3 Air Park Ex 30 Sqn Still in Mespot June 1919
GRINLINTON John Lieching Major	?	?	Staff Off 31st Wing HQ till 9/18 at least. RGA
HEATHER Leonard Edward Lt	20.12.17	?	EO3 (Engines). East Yorkshire Regt
HIRTZEL Eric Francis Capt	18.10.16	?	EO3 (Stores) MT & Port duties Basra until 1918 at least. 3/Welsh Regt
HOGAN J 2Lt	19.3.18	?	EO3 (Wireless)
HOOPER Alexander Francis Anderson Capt	1.9.15	?.3.16	CO Aircraft Park To India as CO Air Park. N Staffs Regt
HUNTING Percy Llewellyn Capt	30.7.17	?-?-18	EO3 (Wireless) From 30 Sqn To 31 Wing HQ. 4/Northumberland Fusiliers
LAMB William George 2Lt	20.12.17	4.1.18	EO3 (Stores) Air Park To 30 Sqn. 3/East Yorks Regt
LEACH Frederick Edward Lt	25.6.17	12.5.18	EO3 (Stores) Air Park To India reported died of heatstroke. 1/8 Manchester Regt
LEECH Edgar James Lt	25.2.18	?-?-19	EO3 (Stores) Ex 23 RS Palestine. 5/Connaught Rangers & 9/Lincs Regt
LEVER Graham George Capt	28.10.18	?	EO (Tech Wireless) 31 Wing HQ
LILLEY Leonard Moore Capt	10.4.17	?-8.18	EO2 From 'X' Aircraft Park P Egypt to replace Capt Tullis Prom Major 18.6.18 Returned Palestine Brig CO 'X' Air Park 8/18
MacEWEN Norman Duckworth Kerr Lt/Col	16.8.16	1.2.17	Asst Director Aviation IA. Replaced Broke-Smith. Post abolished this date. To Palestine Brig. 1/Argyll & Sutherland Highlanders
MAIR Charles William Clanan Lt	?	?	CO Aust and NZ Wireless Sqn Mespot and Persia
MOXEY Edgar Reginald Capt	28.7.17	17.2.18	EO1 (Photo) Royal Engs Prev 30 Sqn 27/5/16 Asst EO
NIXON Brian George Michael Frederick Lt/Capt	?-2.17	26.5.18	From 30 Sqn Capt & Wing Adj from 22.10.17 to 31.3.18 To Egypt pilot training 10.7.18. 41st Dogras IA
O'NEILL William Hickley Lovell Capt	18.6.17	?	From 30 Sqn became Wing Adj. 51st Sikhs IA
PARKER Charles Allen Capt (P)	16.2.18	19.2.18	KIFA this date Basra Air Park. From Tasmania RFA

Lt K. Arnold.

Capt W.L. Broke-Smith.

Lt D.G. Bourn.

Capt E.F. Hirtzel.

Capt B.G.M.F. Nixon.

Left: 2Lt G.F. Wilson, with camera; Lt J. Durward, with friend.

2Lt N. Pellew.

Lt R.M. Weaver.

Name	From	To	Notes
PARR Sydney Charles Capt	17.3.16	29.8.16	Ex 30 Sqn To CO Basra Air Park. RFC(SR)
PELLEW Norman 2Lt	1.9.15	?-6.16	Asst EO aircraft park. Invalided this date. RFC(SR)
PRICE Trevor Llewellyn 2Lt	16.7.18	?	Asst Recording Officer 31 Wing HQ
PUCKLE George Hale Lt	20.5.18	?	From 63 Sqn to 31 Wing as Adj. IARO
RICH Percival Augustus 2Lt	22.5.17	21.6.17	EO3 (Photo) Invalided to India To Palestine 197(T) Sqn 10/17
SCOTT (P or F?) D Lt	23.2.18	8.10.18	EO (Gunnery) Re-joined Army unit. LAMBs
SHARP A Sgt/2Lt	12.10.16	12.11.16	Commis 2Lt EO AP Basra To India
SMYTH Geoffrey Meliss Lt	7.9.18	2.4.19	SO3 From Egypt ex 30 Sqn. 6/Loyal North Lancs Regt
SOMERS-CLARK Geoffrey 2Lt/Capt	1.9.15	?	Asst EO Formed AP for Mespot in the UK Arrived Basra 22.10.15 Prom Capt To 31 Wing HQ 30.1.17 To AP as CO 28.4.17 OBE 2.6.1919. RFC(GL)
SONGHURST Frederick Hibberd Capt	29.8.16	25.1.17	EO2 Air Park To Salonika AP as CO
SPIERS Alexander Donaldson Capt	11.9.17	?	EO1 Air Park TO HQ MF Brig by 1/18 SO (inspector of compasses). RFC(SR)
TENNANT John Edward Major (P)	11.1.17	17.4.18	Prom Lt/Col First OC 31 Wing ex 30 Sqn Shot down and POW 25.3.18 but rescued 28.3.18 To India as OC 52 Wing. Scots Guards
TULLIS Walter Wood Capt	29.8.16	3.5.17	EO1 CO Aircraft Park Basra To OC Air Park India
TWEDDELL William Henry 2Lt	14.4.18	?	EO3 Air Park Still in Mespot April 1920 Traffic Officer Basra Port. 9/Durham Light Inf
WATSON Richard Thomas Humphries Capt	14.9.18	?	Admin Officer 31 Wing HQ. East Kent Regt
WATTS Francis Mapleton Ironmonger Capt (P)	4.3.18	?-8.19	EO1 Air Park Baghdad MBE 3.6.1919 Trnd as pilot March 1915. Worcestershire Regt
WEAVER Robert Martin Lt	21.5.18	?	EO3 (Aircraft Repair Section) Basra Air Park. RFC(SR)
WILSON George Frederick 2Lt	3.10.16	24.3.19	EO3 (Stores) Prom Capt Basra AP and advanced A/P Amarah 9/17. RFC(SR)
WING Henry 2Lt	3.10.16	2.8.17	EO3 (Stores) Ex 5 Wing HQ Pal Prom Capt CO advanced Air Park Amarah Returned Palestine 40 Wing HQ on formation 10/17
YOUNG Arthur Evelyn 2Lt	10.2.17	23.2.19	EO3 (Engines) Ex Palestine Invalided to India. RGA

31 Wing RAF: personnel at the Maude Hotel, Baghdad, 4 February 1919.

Back row l-r: Lt E.A. Scales, Lt P.T. Hunt, 2Lt J.L.W. Bacon, 2Lt G.F. Wilson, Lt J.A. Gibson, Lt G.L. Stedman, Lt C. Gattens, Lt E.J. Leech, Lt J.W.C.L. Gordon, Capt E.F. Carrall, Lt F.C. Mair, 2Lt E.J. Crichton.
Standing l-r: Capt J.H. Herring, Lt G.V. de Boissiere, Lt A.E. Morgan, Lt D.H. Clement, Lt T.A. Pitt, Lt P.J.T. Baddiley, 2Lt W.G. Lamb, Lt G.M. Lees, Capt E.F. Hirtzel, Capt T.A. Francis, Lt G.R.P. Wall, Lt E.T. Thorpe, Lt J. Durward.
Seated l-r: 2Lt G.R. Wright, Lt D.G. Bourne, Lt D.F. Lapraik, Capt F. Nuttall, Clarke, Lt Col O.T. Boyd, Maj F.L. Robinson, Capt V. Buxton, Capt F.M.I. Watts, Capt R.T.H. Watson, 2Lt G.M. Smyth.
On floor l-r: Lt C.J.M. Evans, Lt M.S. Mackay, Capt F.H. Coleman, Lt H.W. Price, Lt S.D. MacDonald, 2Lt E.N. Fletcher, 2Lt D.J. Moran, 2Lt S.G. Bunster, 2Lt G.P. Wilson.

RNAS DETACHMENT

Name/Rank	Joined	Left	Remarks
ARNOLD Harwood James FSLt (P)	28.2.16	15.5.16	Canadian Came from East Africa DSO
BARTLETT Robert Dudley FltLt (P)	8.2.16	17.7.16	To UK
BISHOP Alan George FltLt (O)	5.9.15	3.7.16	From East Africa To UK this date
BLACKBURN Vivian Gaskell FltLt (P)	5.9.15	3.7.16	DSO Gaz 21.1.16 For work during advance of KUT Ex East Africa
BOWHILL Frederick William SqnCdr (P)	8.2.16	20.6.16	Later Air Chief Marshal Sir F.W. Bowhill, GBE, KCB, CMG, DSO*, MiD From East Africa
DUNN William Henry FSL (P)	28.11.15?	8.7.16	Invalided to India .To East Africa Oct 1916
ELLIOTT William Henry FltLt	24.3.16	11.9.16	To UK
GASSON Cecil Bell FSL (P)	8.2.16	26.4.16	South African. WIA & POW this date dropping food into Kut-al-Amara
GOODWIN James Alfred FSL	29.5.16	17.6.17	Invalided to UK
GORDON Robert SqnCdr (P)	5.9.15	11.7.16	From East Africa To Wg Cdr OC Combined RFC/RNAS unit
HODGES Leonard William FSL (P)	?	31.5.16	Died of Cholera this date. b Baghdad War Cemetery, grave III.M.7.
HUME John Douglas FSL (P)	8.2.16	1.6.16	To Egypt
LAWSON Walter Brogdin FSL (P)	7.11.15	22.5.16	Canadian To UK. 4000 hrs war flying, the 4th highest total of any RFC/RNAS/RAF officer
LEIGH Humphrey de Verd FSL (P)	8.2.16	1.6.16	To Egypt
MORGAN John Emil	?	30.3.17	KIA this date. b Baghdad (North Gate) War Cemetery, grave XXI.E.3.
MURRAY Leslie Ethelbert Ruthven FSL (P)	?-12.15	3.5.16	Invalided to India
NELSON Gilbert Dirk Lt	5.9.15	1.6.16	From East Africa Civilian Mechanic with Short Bros, Commis Lt
ROBERTSON Alan Knighton FltLt	7.11.15	14.2.16	To UK
SHIRE Reginald George FltLt	8.2.16	7.8.16	To UK
TURNER Edward Fisher FltS/Lt	8.2.16	7.8.16	EO (Wireless) To UK

FltLt J.E. Morgan.

FSL H. de V. Leigh.

FSL L.E.R. Murray.

Lt G.D. Nelson.

FltLt W.H. Elliott.

Officers of the RNAS Detachment in Mesopotamia, March 1916.

Standing, l-r:
Lt A.G. Bishop,
Lt R.G. Shire,
FSL J.D. Hume,
FSL H.deV. Leigh.
Seated l-r:
Lt G.D. Nelson,
Sqn Cdr F.W. Bowhill,
Wg Cdr R. Gordon,
FSL W.H. Dunn.

RNAS/RFC KITE BALLOON PERSONNEL 1915-18

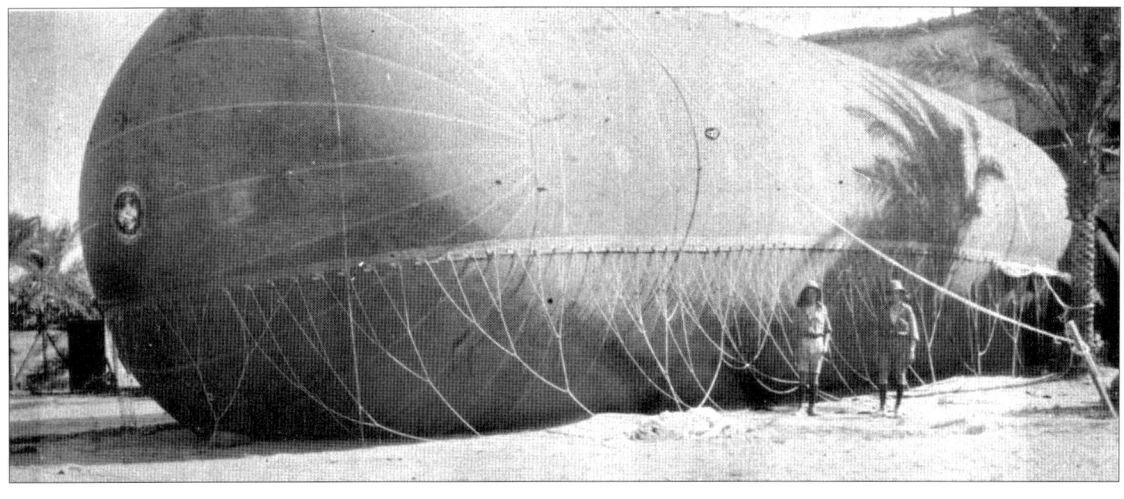

14 Kite Balloon Section RNAS inflating and testing their kite balloon in the shade of a wind-blown palm tree at Basra after arriving in Mesopotamia on 28 June 1916.

Name	Joined	Left	Remarks
ANDERSON Alan John 2Lt	?	28.10.18	51 Kite Balloon Section RFC Nov 1917 RFC(SR)
BATEMAN Philip George Capt	?	28.10.18	51 KBS Nov 1917 CO from 17.8.17 18/London Regt (London Irish Rifles)
BOMPAS Hugh Steele FSL	24.4.16	9.4.17	14 KB Section RNAS
BOULGER Valentine Trevor 2Lt	?	28.10.18	51 KBS 11/17 TO UK
BROWNE Guy Francis FSL	24.4.16	?-9.17	14 KBS RNAS
CASSY Alexander William FltLt	?-?-16	?-8.17	14 KBS In Mespot Aug 16 to 2.17 AFC Gaz 3.6.19 OBE Gaz 17.7.19
CLEVERLY Edwin George FltLt	?	?	14 KBS RNAS. DSC Gaz 17.7.19
COXON Atwell John Lt	2.10.18	28.10.18	23 Kite Balloon Company EO3(Stores) Ex 31st Wing HQ
CURRIE Ulric Algernon FltLt	15.12.17	28.10.18	52 KBS To UK. 8/Lanark Bn (TF) HLI
FLECK Reginald Augustus 2Lt	?	28.10.18	52 KBS. RFC(SR)
GILL Maxwell Gordon	24.4.16	?	14 KBS
GREEN Owen Peter Scott-Waring 2Lt (O)	?	28.10.18	52 KBS 11/17 MC To UK. Middlesex Regt
HARDING William Oliver Fielding FltLt	27.11.16	?-9.17	14 KBS
HARRISON Frank Charles 2Lt	?	14.5.18	51 KBS Invalided to India. RFC(SR)
HAYWARD Henry Stanley 2Lt	?	28.10.18	52 KBS 11/17. RFC(SR)
HUGHES Kenneth Stanley 2Lt	?-11.17	?-2.18	EO3 from 20.3.17 23 KB Company. RFC(SR)
ILLINGWORTH Herbert 2Lt	?	9.2.18	51 KBS Invalided to India. RFC(SR)
JENSEN Harold Drewett Major	?-11.17	28.10.18	CO 23 KB Company Ex Salonika KBs. 9/Royal Scots Fusiliers
LANE Rex Willington FltLt	16.4.17	?-9.17	14 KBS
LE-LORRAINE William 2Lt	?	?-?-18	EO3 51 KBS To Egypt. RFC(SR)
LYON Maurice FSL	?	?	14 KBS served Mespot AFC Gaz 3.6.1919
MacFIE Douglas Arthur FSL	?	?	14 KBS 9/17
MANNOCK Francis Pym Lt	19.5.18	12.4.19	EO3(Stores) Kite Balloons. 1/7 Royal Welsh Fusiliers
MALET-VEALE John Eades	4.5.18	28.10.18	23 K B Company Obs. 3 Res Brigade RFA
SANCTUARY James Thompson FltLt	6.11.16	?-9.17	14 KBS
SCALES Edgar Athole Lt	14.3.18		Rec Off 23 KB Company From 72 Sqn To 63 Sqn p/war
SCOTT Alexander Walkinshaw 2Lt	?	?	52 KBS 11/17. RFC(SR)
SHAND Francis Byam Berkeley	?-9.17	23.8.18	23 K B Company Rec Officer
STANTON Claude Herbert Oscar 2Lt	?	28.10.18	52 KBS EO3 11/17. RFC(SR)
STRIBLING William Clarkson 2Lt	6.3.18	28.10.18	52 KBS EO3 RFC(SR) To UK
STRICKLAND Walter Claude Lt	7.2.18	28.10.18	51 KBS Obs. Worcestershire Regt
TALBOT Robert Charles Capt	20.12.17	28.10.18	CO 52 KBS. 7/Country of London Bn & RFA(TF)
VEREY Douglas Roy FSL	?	?	14 KBS In Mespot 8/16 to 2/17 DSC Gaz 19.7.19
WITTING Horace Nelson Capt	5.8.18	28.10.18	CO 51 KBS Ex Salonika KBs. 3/Queens Royal West Surrey Regt
WOODROW Thomas William Lt	4.5.18	28.10.18	23 Kite Balloon Company. RFA
WROTTESLEY Francis Robert FltLt/Capt	?-6.15	?-4.17	CO 14 KBS. Formerly CO Egypt KB Section RNAS. DSO 17.7.1919

Two distinguished members of 14 Kite Balloon Section.

Left: FltLt A.W. Cassy, AFC, OBE, taking a casual approach to life.

Right: FSL M. Lyon, AFC, in a more formal pose.

Other Ranks and their Work

Unfortunately, due to the paucity of records, the authors have been unable to compile a list of other ranks.

Posting dates are a complete nightmare! In general we have noted the dates 'JOINED' and date 'LEFT' as those when an officer joined the squadron/Wing HQ etc and was recorded as such. 5 Wing/Palestine Brigade, and Wing HQs in the UK would record an officers posting date, but that officer in the UK or Egypt would take a considerable time to reach his allocated unit. We also know from some records, that an officer once noted as leaving a squadron on a certain date, could remain in that country i.e. Mesopotamia for some time after. An officer's log book or RFC record card may list yet another date, and we must make an assumption that recording officers or office clerks entered dates correctly!

63 Sqn Air Mechanics on 31 August 1916. Second left in the second row from the back is AM (later Sgt) Herbert W. Partridge, who served with 63 Sqn right through the 'Mespot' campaign. The names of his comrades are not recorded.

NCOs of 31 Wing HQ Summer 1918. Standing l-r: Cpl S. Staniforth, Cpl T.R.H. Chassuck(?), Cpl C. Smith, Cpl J.W. Symons. Seated l-r: Sgt Clerk G. Downs MSM, Sgt Clerk T.H. Tollfree MSM, Sgt Clerk S.B. Ayling MSM, Sgt G?R. Bowler.

Below: RFC Wireless Section personnel.
Front: Capt P.L. Hunting EO2 Wireless; Cpl Allen;
Back: (left) Cpl Samuel Hall, awarded the DCM for repeatedly repairing his aerial under fire at Ramadi, 11 July 1917, to maintain contact with supporting aircraft. (right) Unidentified AM.

Below centre right: FltSgt T.A. Rhaney MSM, responsible for the RE8s of 'B' Flt, 63 Sqn.

Below outer right:
Cpl Germain (left) and AM Carter, who maintained the RE8 flown by Capt J. Everidge, OC 'B' Flt, 63 Sqn, 1917-19.

Flt Sgt P. Phillips (left) and another 30 Sqn ground crew man at Sheikh Saad. Phillips became a pilot in 1918.

Flt Sgts P.W. Evans (left) and W.T. James, 30 Sqn, who both received the MSM for service in Mesopotamia.

Flight Sgt and Air Mechanics from 'A' Flight, 72 Squadron, on Baghdad aerodrome, December 1918.

Negotiating a hairpin bend on the Takguia Pass road while recovering a BE2c after Lt P. Phillips of 30 Squadron force-landed in the Persian mountains.

The wreck of Short Seaplane 822 at Ora on 14 February 1916.

Short Type 827, Serial 825, overturned on landing. Pilot, Lt H.P.S. Clogstoun, Observer Capt W.G. Palmer.

Above: 'All steel' Henry Farman 1573. It was struck off 30 Sqn charge and returned to X AD, Egypt, on 4 May 1917.
Left: Removing the remains of BE2c 4421 from a palm grove at Basra. The pilot, Capt J. Everidge, escaped injury.

The work of Other Ranks involved a lot of time spent picking up the pieces, but here things are more positive: RE8 B7704 of 30 Sqn, usually flown by Lt A.W. Hawkins, has a new engine installed.
It carries the white fuselage band marking adopted by the unit.

The Importance of Water Transport

Bellum 1043 of the Inland Water Transport, with two Fly Class gunboats, the cruiser HMS Proserpine, and other ocean-going steamers on the Shatt-al-Arab.

From the beginning of the campaign, logistics in Mesopotamia were primarily water-based, but the difficulties and inadequacies of the system contributed largely to the failure of Townshend's advance on Baghdad, and ultimately to the disaster of Kut.

A total reorganisation was therefore undertaken, the scope and detail of which is suggested by the registering and numbering of even small local craft for management purposes by the new Directorate of Inland Water Transport, as seen in the photograph above.

New and used: BEs ready for shipment up-river by barge (below), and damaged machines sent back to Basra for repair or salvage.

Both the vessels and the crews of the IWT were assembled by international effort. LtCol J.E. Tennant later wrote of this vital service:

Of these seamen who had volunteered for the Tigris, some came from river boats on the Yukon, some from the Irawaddy or Brahmaputra, others from blue water. It seemed incongruous to meet the ex-captain of an 8,000-ton tramp navigating a shallow-draught paddle-boat in the uniform of a Second Lieutenant RE.

Some scenes of life and work on the rivers follow.

A large pre-war paddle-steamer with cabins on the upper deck and an open lower cargo deck, and barge in side-tow.

The main RNAS supply and workshop barge on the Tigris. It was known as the Iron Duke.

SS Bahmashir *at Sheikh Saad in July 1916 with 30 Sqn 'A' Flt barges RFC1 and RFC3, HMS* Mantis *and a mahaila behind.*

The fuselage of a Short Seaplane shares space with a horse-drawn wagon on board the Iron Duke.

This view of SS Bahmashir *and the RFC barges at Sheikh Saad reveals the difference between low and high water levels on the Tigris, the former adding a muddy foreshore to the difficulties of loading and unloading.*
Because of the nature of the soft, easily scoured river bed, low water did not necessarily indicate reduced navigable depth.

Changing the engine of a BE on board Iron Duke *at Basra.*

Moving aircraft crates at the Basra Aircraft Park.

A gun barge with 4.7in naval gun. Barges like this were towed into action by tugs, to bombard the enemy from the river.

RFC motor transport and other supplies loaded onto a barge for transport to the advanced base at Amara.

Fore and aft views of the workshop barge Vulcan, *with crew, equipment, and the object of their attentions.*

Below and right: Overhauling a Sunbeam engine at Basra.

Short Seaplane 822 in landplane configuration after colliding with a telegraph wire at Ali Gharbi on 1 February 1916. It was repaired at Basra Aircraft Park on 6/7 February.

A Henry Farman at Ora, well picketed down by the front axle, tail skid and wingtips against the fierce desert winds.

Henry Farman F27 'all steel', 1573, originally intended for the RNAS but used by 30 Squadron.

At Ali Gharbi, BE2c 4135 is ready to take-off on a photographic mission. The importance of aerial photography to the army on the ground in this vast and essentially unmapped theatre of war can hardly be overestimated.

RFC/RNAS AIRCRAFT SERIALS 1915-1919

SERIAL	TYPE	REMARKS
IFC1	Maurice Farman Shorthorn	MF1 From India Arr 4.15. Crashed at Ali Gharbi 11.9.15
IFC2	Maurice Farman Longhorn	MF2 From India Arr 4.15. Destroyed near Baghdad 13.11.15 Lt T.W. White & Capt F.C.C. Yeats-Brown POW
IFC10	Maurice Farman Shorthorn	MF10 Arr 20.5.15. 30 Sqn Del from Egypt without engine ex-RNAS.
IFC7	Maurice Farman Shorthorn	MF7 Arr 20.5.15 From Egypt without engine. Converted to seaplane 8.15
IFC3	Caudron G.III	C1 Arr 14.5.15. Lt Treloar & Capt Atkins force landed and POWs 16.9.15
IFC4	Caudron G.III	C2 Arr 14.5.15. Lt Merz & Lt Burn force landed and killed by Arabs 30.7.15
822	Short Seaplane	RNAS Arr 5.9.15. (Sqn Cdr Gordon) Later converted to land machine. Wrecked 14.2.16 W.H. Dunn RNAS
825	Short Seaplane	RNAS Arr 5.9.15 Converted to land plane 13.10.15
827	Short Seaplane	RNAS Arr 5.9.15 Converted to land plane 22.10.15
920	Sopwith Seaplane	RNAS Came from East Africa
1265	Bristol Scout 'C'	30 Sqn
1540	Henry Farman F27	RNAS Arr 8.2.16 Food drops siege of Kut-al-Amara. Struck off 23.1.17
1541	Henry Farman F27	30 Sqn Arr 8.2.16 Lt R.H. Peck & Capt W.G. Palmer KIA 5.3.16
1542	Henry Farman F27	RNAS Written off Feb 1916
1568	Henry Farman F27	30 Sqn To Egypt 25.1.17 Struck off charge 'X' AD 4.5.17
1569	Henry Farman F27	30 Sqn To Egypt 25.1.17 Struck off charge 'X' AD
1572	Henry Farman F27	30 Sqn To Egypt Struck off charge 'X' AD 25.1.17
1573	Henry Farman F27	30 Sqn To Egypt & Struck off charge 'X' AD 25.1.17
2672	BE2c	30 Sqn Sept 1916
2690	BE2c	30 Sqn Struck off charge 25.11.16
2702	BE2c	30 Sqn Struck off charge 8.11.17
4135	BE2c	30 Sqn Apr 1916
4141	BE2c	30 Sqn Aug 1916 still on charge 21.7.17
4182	BE2c	30 Sqn Dec 1916
4183	BE2c	30 Sqn Dec 1916
4185	BE2c	30 Sqn Feb 1917
4186	BE2c	30 Sqn Arr 20.3.16
4191	BE2c	30 Sqn 11/16 Capt L.S.A.M. Page force landed, machine burnt to prevent capture 2.9.17
4194	BE2c	30 Sqn 11/16 LIA 15.4.17, Capt Pickering/2Lt Craig shot down by Halberstadt Scout – Hptm Schüz
4243	Martinsyde S1	30 Sqn MH5 IFC5 Arr 27.8.15 Destroyed at Ali Gharbi 13.9.15
4244	Martinsyde S1	30 Sqn MH6 IFC6 Arr 27.8.15 Major H.L. Reilly shot down and POW 21.11.15
4250	Martinsyde S1	30 Sqn MH8 IFC8 Arr 27.8.15 Came from Egypt Shot down 22.11.15 Lt E.J. Fulton POW
?	Martinsyde S1	30 Sqn MH9 IFC9 Arr 27.8.15 Abandoned at Kut-al-Amara 29.4.16
4302	BE2c	30 Sqn Pres a/c 'MAHARAJAH OF REWA-BANDHAVA' Oct/15
4303	BE2c	30 Sqn 13.9.1915
4322	BE2c	30 Sqn erected 30.4.16 Pres a/c 'GWALIOR' Struck off charge 19.9.16
4323	BE2c	30 Sqn Food drops siege of Kut April 1916 Struck off charge 1.5.16
4324	BE2c	30 Sqn
4327	BE2c	30 Sqn Oct 1916 Struck off charge 5.12.16
4328	BE2c	30 Sqn Struck off charge 1.5.16
4347	BE2c	30 Sqn Jan 17 Struck off charge 6.8.17
4348	BE2c	30 Sqn March 1917 Struck off charge 6.8.17
4350	BE2c	30 Sqn Erected 30.10.15
4352	BE2c	30 Sqn 1916
4361	BE2c	30 Sqn April 1916 Struck off charge 6.9.17
4362	BE2c	30 Sqn Food drops siege of Kut 4/16 Last BE on charge To Basra Air Park 25.2.18
4363	BE2c	30 Sqn 'B' Flt 1917
4364	BE2c	30 Sqn 7/16 Struck off charge 25.11.16
4373	BE2c	30 Sqn 11/16 Struck off charge 15.12.16
4379	BE2c	30 Sqn From UK Arr 27.6.16
4394	BE2c	30 Sqn Feb 1917
4395	BE2c	30 Sqn
4398	BE2c	30 Sqn From UK Arr 27.6.16
4405	BE2c	30 Sqn
4411	BE2c	30 Sqn Struck off charge 1.5.16
4412	BE2c	30 Sqn Arr 2/16 Struck off charge Basra AP Feb 1918
4414	BE2c	30 Sqn 8/16 Force landed by Capt L.S.A.M. Page and burnt to prevent capture 12.9.17
4421	BE2c	30 Sqn arr 2/16 Engine failed and machine hit palm tree 16.8.17 when flown by Capt J. Everidge 63 Sqn Struck off charge

BE2c 2702 of 30 Squadron, with the observer's cockpit covered and the sides of the pilot's cockpit raised.

Above and below: Two views of BE2c 4362, used by 30 Squadron for food drops in April 1916 during the siege of Kut.

4423	BE2c	30 Sqn To Basra Air Park 11.2.18
4431	BE2c	30 Sqn Presentation a/c 'MANIPUR'
4437	BE2c	30 Sqn Feb 1917
4438	BE2c	30 Sqn July 1916 In Egypt by 10/16
4443	BE2c	30 Sqn Feb 17 – July 17 at least
4449	BE2c	30 Sqn Arr 27.6.16 Struck off charge ME Wing 18.1.17
4458	BE2c	30 Sqn Erected 30.4.16 Struck off charge 25.11.16
4459	BE2c	30 Sqn Arr 2/16 Struck off charge 11.10.16
4461	BE2c	30 Sqn Mar 16 – Feb 1917 at least
4473	BE2c	30 Sqn Dec 1916
4486	BE2c	30 Sqn Arr 7/16 On charge until October 1917
4487	BE2c	30 Sqn Arr 7/16
4491	BE2c	30 Sqn Arr 26.7.16
4500	BE2c	30 Sqn Escaped from Kut 7.12.15 Food drops during siege Still on charge June 1917.
4510	BE2c	30 Sqn Struck off charge 13.10.16
4512	BE2c	30 Sqn Wrecked 8.7.16 after engine failure Lt Rettie
4513	BE2c	30 Sqn December 1916
4537	BE2c	30 Sqn Engine failed and crashed 28.9.16 Lt J.S. Windsor Rebuilt. Totally wrecked 19.1.17 Lt A.E.L. Skinner and Capt Brodie Arab Village Crew OK
4558	BE2c	30 Sqn Arr 15.7.16 Struck off charge 16.8.17
4562	BE2c	30 Sqn Food drops siege of Kut To Basra AP Jan 1918
4564	BE2c	30 Sqn Dec 1916
4573	BE2c	30 Sqn Arr July 1916 Struck off charge ME Wing 23.1.17
4584	BE2c	30 Sqn
4585	BE2c	30 Sqn Pres a/c 'MAHARAJAH OF REWA–BANDHAVA' Lt Page & Lt Rattray collided with Oblt Schüz 3.4.17 Struck off charge 12.4.17
4594	BE2c	30 Sqn Arr 12.12.16
5427	BE2c	30 Sqn Struck off charge 8.11.17
5901	Maurice Farman	30 Sqn
5907	Maurice Farman	30 Sqn 1916. Struck off charge 'X' AD Egypt 25.11.17
5908	Maurice Farman	30 Sqn Destroyed by hangar fire 14.10.16
5909	Maurice Farman	30 Sqn arr Basra 26.4.16 Wrecked in storm 2.5.16 Struck off charge 'X' AD Egypt 25.11.17
6324	BE2c	30 Sqn August 1917
6804	BE2d	30 Sqn Force landed by Lt A.P. Adams and burnt to prevent capture 31.10.17
6805	BE2d	30 Sqn Struck off charge 7.10.17
7033	Bristol Scout 'D'	30 Sqn
7034	Bristol Scout 'D'	30 Sqn 2Lt M.L. Maguire MIA & POW 28.4.17
7047	Bristol Scout 'D'	30 Sqn
7308	Maurice Farman	30 Sqn Wrecked in storm Ora 2.5.16
7346	Maurice Farman	30 Sqn Wrecked in storm 2.5.16
7347	Maurice Farman	30 Sqn October 1917
7348	Maurice Farman	30 Sqn
7369	Maurice Farman	30 Sqn To Egypt 17.11.16
7370	Maurice Farman	30 Sqn To Egypt 17.11.16
7459	Martinsyde G.100	30 Sqn Jan 17 Later 72 Sqn Destroyed by Lt R P P Pope at Baku Persia 15.9.18
7460	Martinsyde G.100	30 Sqn Destroyed by hangar fire 11.3.17
7461	Martinsyde G100	30 Sqn Capt A.P. Adams KIA by ground fire Khun Bushire South Persia 6.3.19
7466	Martinsyde G.100	30 Sqn Lt T.E. Lander MIA & POW 6.5.17
7467	Martinsyde G.100	30 Sqn 11/16 To 72 Sqn Lt T.L. Williams force landed in Persia 6.10.18 and burnt to prevent capture
7468	Martinsyde G.100	30 Sqn 1/17 Later 63 Sqn Written off 18.7.19
7493	Martinsyde G.100	30 Sqn Later 72 Sqn Destroyed at Baku Persia 15.9.18 Lt M.S. Mackay
7494	Martinsyde G.100	30 Sqn Force landed and burnt to prevent capture 16.10.17 Lt A.E.L. Skinner
8043	Short Seaplane	RNAS Arr Feb 1916 Sqn Cdr Bowhill Sqn
8044	Short Seaplane	RNAS Feb 16 2Lt C.B. Gasson RNAS & 2Lt A.C. Thouless RFC shot down dropping food into Kut-al-Amara 26.4.16
8046	Short Seaplane	RNAS Regularly flown by FSL L.E.R. Murray
8047	Short Seaplane	RNAS Feb 1916
8088	Short Seaplane	RNAS Arr May 1916
8505	Voisin	RNAS Arr 17.1.16 Wrecked by Lt H.P.S. Clogstoun 30 Sqn at Basra Air Park 31.1.16
8506	Voisin	RNAS Arr 17.1.16 Flown by FSL W.H. Dunn for food drops siege of Kut Struck off charge 11.10.16
8518	Voisin	30 Sqn Arr June 1916 Struck off charge 25.11.16
8523	Voisin	30 Sqn Lt S. Haywood & Lt L.H. King-Harman Killed in crash 26.10.16
A1327	BE2d	30 Sqn

A later view of 4362, now completely re-covered and khaki doped. It was the last BE2c to remain on 30 Squadron charge, being finally struck off on 25 February 1918.

Two BE2cs of 30 Squadron ready for take-off. 4322 was a presentation aircraft. 'Gwalior No 2'. In the background is 4352.

BE2c 4537 crashed at Sheikh Saad, 1916. It was rebuilt, as replacements took so long to arrive, and finally wrecked in January 1917.

A1385	BE2d	30 Sqn
A1584	Martinsyde G.102 Elephant	30 Sqn Arr 23.5.17
A1594	Martinsyde G.102 Elephant	30 Sqn Also 63 Sqn Jan 1918 and then to 72 Sqn
A1595	Martinsyde G.102 Elephant	30 Sqn Pres a/c 'AUSTRALIA No.4 NEW SOUTH WALES No 3' Struck off at 'X' AD Egypt 25.11.17
A1596	Martinsyde G.102 Elephant	30 Sqn then 72 Sqn Struck off charge 5.7.18
A1599	Martinsyde G102 Elephant	30 Sqn
A1763	Bristol Scout 'D'	30 Sqn Arr 29.5.17
A1765	Bristol Scout 'D'	30 Sqn Still on charge Jan 1918
A1768	Bristol Scout 'D'	30 Sqn then 63 Sqn At Baghdad 12.17
A3068	BE2e	30 Sqn and 63 Sqn 7.18 To 6 Sqn RAF post-war. Presentation a/c 'Gold Coast'
A3069	BE2e	30 Sqn and 6 Sqn RAF post-war Struck off charge 11.11.1919 Presentation a/c 'SHANGHAI RACE CLUB No.3'
A3078	BE2e	30 Sqn Arr 25.8.17 Presentation a/c 'BHARATPUR'
A3079	BE2e	30 Sqn Arr 18.8.17 Presentation a/c 'RAJPUTANA No.2' Struck off charge 28.8.19
A3080	BE2e	30 Sqn Arr 21.8.17
A3086	BE2e	30 Sqn Arr 13.10.17 Presentation a/c 'PUNJAB No.35 HARIANA'
A3087	BE2e	30 Sqn and 72 Sqn Presentation a/c 'RIVER PLATE' Struck off charge 10.2.1919
A3088	BE2e	30 Sqn Arr 25.8.17 Presentation a/c 'THE SEVEN SEAS' Machine crashed and burnt taking off 22.10.17 2Lt Gardner & 2Lt Leeson
A3089	BE2e	30 Sqn Arr 13.10.17 Presentation a/c 'QUEENSTOWN CAPE' Still on charge 1/19
A3940	Martinsyde G.102 Elephant	30 Sqn Lt C. Cox hit by AA fire 31.10.17 Machine force landed and burnt to prevent capture
A3943	Martinsyde G.102 Elephant	30 Sqn on charge 9.5.17
A3972	Martinsyde G.102 Elephant	30 Sqn Arr 16.8.17 To 72 Sqn Lt A.A. Cullen MIA & POW 31.8.18 Force landed Persia
A3973	Martinsyde G.102 Elephant	30 Sqn then 72 Sqn Lt K.M. Pennington Force landed in Persia 11.10.18
A3974	Martinsyde G.102 Elephant	30 Sqn Arr 30.7.17 To Basra Air Park 10.2.18
A3975	Martinsyde G.102 Elephant	30 Sqn Arr 30.7.17
A4334	RE8	63 Sqn Arr Basra 11.8.17 Capt J.R. Philpott & Lt M.G. Begg POW 25.9.17
A4335	RE8	63 Sqn Arr 11.8.17 Lt N. Baillon & Cpl Grant POW 25.9.17
A4336	RE8	63 Sqn Lt J.D.G. MacRae & Lt J.W. Blake MIA and POWs 5.10.17
A4337	RE8	63 Sqn Arr 11.8.17 Written off 3.10.18
A4338	RE8	63 Sqn Arr 11.8.17
A4339	RE8	63 Sqn Later 30 Sqn
A4340	RE8	63 Sqn Arr 11.8.17
A4341	RE8	63 Sqn Later to 30 Sqn
A4342	RE8	63 Sqn Struck off charge 20.11.17
A4343	RE8	63 Sqn Struck off charge 3.9.18
A4344	RE8	63 Sqn Written off 12.2.1919
A4345	RE8	63 Sqn Arr 11.8.17
A4346	RE8	31 Wg Arr 11.8.17 63 Sqn by 9.1918 (Lt Cooper) deleted on unit 9.6.19
A4347	RE8	63 Sqn Written off 23.4.1919
A4348	RE8	31 Wg AP 11.8.17 to 63 Sqn, deleted on unit 24.1.19
A4349	RE8	63 Sqn Later to 30 Sqn
A4350	RE8	63 Sqn Arr Baghdad 18.10.17
A4351	RE8	63 Sqn Also 30 Sqn Written off 24.1.19
A4352	RE8	63 Sqn Burnt after force landing (damaged by enemy fire) 24.10.18 Capt R.D. Simpson & Lt A.A. Tigar Also 30 Sqn 1/18
A4353	RE8	63 Sqn Arr Baghdad 18.10.17
A4354	RE8	63 Sqn Arr 11.8.17 Written off 27.9.1919
A4355	RE8	63 Sqn Written off 20.12.18
A4356	RE8	63 Sqn Also 30 Sqn Nov 1918 Hamadan Persia Written off 22.2.1919
A4357	RE8	63 Sqn Also 30 Sqn Persia 11/18 Back to 63 Sqn Written off 5.1.1920
A4413	RE8	31 Wg Arr 9.11.17 wrecked 9.12.17, Capt O.T. Boyd IIFA lost flying speed, first flight in type
A4415	RE8	63 Sqn Written off 29.9.1919
A4416	RE8	31 Wg arr 9.11.17, 30 Sqn late 1917
A4460	RE8	Arr Baghdad 9.11.17
A4461	RE8	Arr Baghdad 9.11.17
A4462	RE8	Arr Baghdad 9.11.17
A4658	RE8	30 Sqn Arr Baghdad 9.11.17 Written off 24.1.1919
A4659	RE8	30 Sqn February 1918
A4660	RE8	30 Sqn Feb 1918 Written off 28.8.1919
A4661	RE8	30 Sqn Feb 1918 Lt J.L. Warwick & Lt T.J. Keating KIFA 14.6.18 Machine spun in from 800 feet and caught fire
A4662	RE8	30 Sqn March 1918

Voisin 8506, with which FSL Dunn delivered stores to Kut.

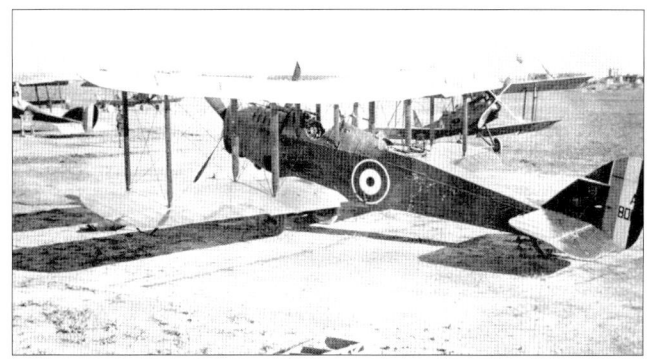

DH4 A80-- and RE8 A4355 at Baghdad, summer 1918.

Martinsyde Elephant A1595.

Left: Bristol Scout D A1768 on Baghdad airfield in December 1917. It served with 30 and 63 Squadron.

Below: Martinsyde Elephant A3974, flown by both 30 and 72 Sqn. Photgrophed at Baghdad in December 1918.

A4699	RE8	63 Sqn May 1919
A7561	DH4	30 Sqn
A7591	DH4	30 Sqn Lt Bean & Sgt Castor shot down by AA fire 2.1.18
A7601	DH4	Arr Baghdad 9.11.17
A7604	DH4	Arr Baghdad 9.11.17
A7621	DH4	30 Sqn Capt F. Nuttall force landed machine after it caught fire 26.1.18
A7623	DH4	30 Sqn Feb 1918
A7695	DH4	72 Sqn Struck off charge 20.8.18
A7756	DH4	72 Sqn Struck off charge 19.6.18
A7757	DH4	Written off 31 Wing Aircraft Park 10.6.19
A7803	DH4	To 31 Wing AP 28.9.18
A7806	DH4	To 31 Wing AP 28.9.18 written off 30.5.1919
A7944	DH4	Written off 28.9.1919
A7949	DH4	Written off 28.9.1919
A8003	DH4	To 31 Wing AP 17.2.1919
A8004	DH4	63 Sqn Written off 4.4.1919
A8005	DH4	63 Sqn Written off 23.7.1919
A8007	DH4	Written off 31 Wing AP 10.6.1919
A8008	DH4	63 Sqn To 31 Wing AP 17.2.1919 Written off 3.12.1919
A8009	DH4	To 31 Wing AP 17.2.1919 Written off 3.12.1919
A8036	DH4	To 31 Wing Air Park 17.2.1919
A8806	SPAD S.VII	30 Sqn and 72 Sqn Struck off charge 28.1.1919
A8807	SPAD S.VII	30 Sqn Written off 28.8.1919
A8808	SPAD S.VII	30 Sqn and 72 Sqn Struck off charge 28.1.1919
A8809	SPAD S.VII	30 Sqn then 63 Sqn Lt N.S. Hyslop killed in crash 31.10.17
A8810	SPAD S.VII	30 Sqn and 72 Sqn Struck off charge 22.7.18
A8811	SPAD S.VII	30 Sqn Arr 12.9.17 To 63 Sqn Lt J.H. Caldwell KIA 12.1.18
A8812	SPAD S.VII	30 Sqn Arr Baghdad 18.8.17 Lt A.E.L. Skinner claimed EA 31.1.18
A8813	SPAD S.VII	72 Sqn Struck off charge 28.1.1919
A8824	SPAD S.VII	72 Sqn Lt T.L. Williams KIFA 25.12.18
A8838	SPAD S.VII	Written off 28.8.1919
A8839	SPAD S.VII	72 Sqn Written off 28.8.1919
A8840	SPAD S.VII	72 Sqn Written off 28.8.1919
A8853	SPAD S.VII	Written off 28.8.1919
A8869	SPAD S.VII	Written off 28.8.1919
A8870	SPAD S.VII	Written off 28.8.1919
A8871	SPADS.VII	Written off 28.8.1919
A8893	SPAD S.VII	Written off 28.8.1919
A9147	SPAD S.VII	Written off 28.8.1919
A9148	SPAD S.VII	Written off 28.8.1919
B106	SE5a	To 31 Wing Aircraft Park 6.11.18
B107	SE5a	To 31 Wing AP 6.11.18
B685	SE5a	72 Sqn March 18 'A' Flt May 18 Written off 13.11.18
B686	SE5a	72 Sqn Arr March 1918 Written off 28.8.1919
B687	SE5a	72 Sqn March 1918
B1214	RE8	To 31 Wing AP from France 17.9.1919
B3445	RE8	63 Sqn 'B' flt Samarra Later 30 Sqn and Written off 1919
B3446	RE8	63 Sqn Written off 14.7.1919
B3447	RE8	30 Sqn Written off 21.3.1919
B3448	RE8	30 Sqn
B3449	RE8	30 Sqn Lt A.E. Morgan & Lt J. Chacksfield force landed in Persia trying to rescue Lt K.M. Pennington 72 Sqn 11.10.18
B3450	RE8	30 Sqn Arr 16.11.17 Lt W.L. Haight & Lt Hancock MIA & POW 4.3.18 Machine burnt to prevent capture
B3459	RE8	30 Sqn Feb 18
B5869	RE8	30 Sqn April 18
B5870	RE8	63 Sqn Destroyed in storm at Samarra 1.4.18
B5871	RE8	63 Sqn Also 30 Sqn Feb 18 63 Sqn June 1919
B5872	RE8	63 Sqn Struck off charge 31.5.18
B5873	RE8	63 Sqn then 30 Sqn 'A' flight Kasvin Persia Sept 1918
B5875	RE8	Capt C.A. Parker & AM Nielson KIFA Crash Basra AP 19.2.18
B5876	RE8	30 Sqn Lt J.O. Allison & Lt M.C. Atherton shot down and KIA 15.5.18
B5877	RE8	30 Sqn Written off charge 28.8.1919
B5878	RE8	63 Sqn Written off 25.10.18
B5879	RE8	63 Sqn Written off 28.8.1919

RE8 A4340. One of the essentials of aircraft maintenance, a stepladder, is ready to hand on a little cart with aircraft wheels.

Spad A8813 at Mirjana, April 1918. Pilot Lt Charles Gattens.

RE8 B5877 of 'A' Flt 30 Sqn, overturned by Lt A.L.G. Campbell at Kifri, September 1918.

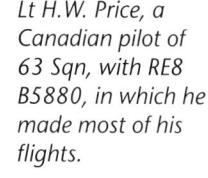

Lt H.W. Price, a Canadian pilot of 63 Sqn, with RE8 B5880, in which he made most of his flights.

Below: RE8s of 'A' Flt 63 Squadron at Samarra, A4343 nearest to camera.

B5880	RE8	63 Sqn Damaged in storm at Samarra 1.4.18
B5881	RE8	63 Sqn 'B' Flight Sept 18 Written off 23.4.1919
B5882	RE8	63 Sqn Written off 12.5.1919
B5883	RE8	30 Sqn 'A' Flt Persia Oct 18 then to 63 Sqn Written off 6.4.1919
B5884	RE8	63 Sqn Written off 7.7.1919
B5892	RE8	63 Sqn June 1919
B6468	RE8	63 Sqn Written off 19.1.1920
B6469	RE8	63 Sqn Oct 1918 Written off 1919
B6470	RE8	30 Sqn March 1918
B6585	RE8	30 Sqn Fitted with Davis gun Nov 18 Also 72Sqn and 63 Sqn Written off 22.11.1919
B6586	RE8	63 Sqn Written off 14.8.1919
B6587	RE8	63 Sqn Written off 23.4.1919
B6588	RE8	30 Sqn Oct 1918
B6589	RE8	63 Sqn Sept 1918 to June 1919 at least
B6590	RE8	63 Sqn Written off 3.5.1919
B6591	RE8	30 Sqn then 63 Sqn Lt C. Gattens KIFA 15.6.1919
B6592	RE8	30 Sqn with 63 Sqn July 1919
B6596	RE8	63 Sqn June 1919
B6611	RE8	30 Sqn Capt L.S.A.M. Page & Lt L. Kirwan KIFA. Spun in from 600 feet mg practice Baqubah 20.8.18
B6612	RE8	30 Sqn Still on charge with 63 Sqn Aug 1919
B6613	RE8	30 Sqn then 63 Sqn May 1919
B6614	RE8	63 Sqn Written off 23.7.1919
B7645	DH9	To 31 Wing AP from Egypt (ex 142 Sqn) 24.3.1919
B7704	RE8	30 Sqn and 63 Sqn Written off 14.6.1919
B7705	RE8	63 Sqn Written off 15.11.18
B7706	RE8	To 31 Wing AP 17.2.1919
C4914	Bristol M.1C Monoplane	72 Sqn January 1918
C4915	Bristol M.1C Monoplane	72 Sqn Jan 1918
C4917	Bristol M.1C Monoplane	72 Sqn Jan/October 1918
C4918	Bristol M.1C Monoplane	72 Sqn 'C' Flt Oct 1918
C4919	Bristol M.1C Monoplane	72 Sqn until Jan 1919
C4920	Bristol M.1C Monoplane	72 Sqn May 1918
C4921	Bristol M.1C Monoplane	72 Sqn October 1918
C4923	Bristol M.1C Monoplane	72 Sqn Nov 1918
C4924	Bristol M.1C Monoplane	72 Sqn 'C' Flt April 1918
C4925	Bristol M.1C Monoplane	72 Sqn Lt C. Gattens force landed and burnt this machine to prevent capture 20.5.18
C4934	Bristol M.1C Monoplane	72 Sqn Lt S.D. MacDonald force landed and burnt this aircraft to prevent capture 25.10.18
C4936	Bristol M.1C Monoplane	72 Sqn
C4937	Bristol M.1C Monoplane	72 Sqn written off Sqn charge 2.10.18
C6295	DH9	Flown to 31 Wing from Egypt (ex 142 Sqn) 14.3.1919
C9502	SE5a	72 Sqn and 63 Sqn Engine failed, crashed and Written off 19.3.19 Lt H.A. Anson
C9503	SE5a	72 Sqn 1918
C9504	SE5a	72 Sqn 'A' Flt 1918
C9564	SE5a	72 Sqn 'A' Flt Capt J.S. Beatty 1918
D2933	DH9	Flown direct to 31 Wing AP from Egypt (142 Sqn) 14.3.1919
D3522	SE5a	To 31 Wing Aircraft Park 9.9.18
D3523	SE5a	To 31 Wing Aircraft Park 9.9.18
D3524	SE5a	To 31 Wing Aircraft Park 9.9.18
D3574	SE5a	To 31 Wing Aircraft Park 9.9.18
D3575	SE5a	To 31 Wing AP 9.9.18
D4697	RE8	30 Sqn 1919
D4698	RE8	30 Sqn Capt F. Nuttall KIA 18.9.1920
D4699	RE8	To 31 Wing Air Park 11.8.18
D4700	RE8	63 Sqn Written off 12.5.1919
D4701	RE8	30 Sqn Aleppo then 63 Sqn Written off 13.9.1919
D4702	RE8	63 Sqn written off 1.11.1919
D4703	RE8	To 31 Wing AP 11.8.18
D4704	RE8	6 Sqn RAF post-war Written off 23.10.1919
D4708	RE8	30 Sqn Sept 1919
D5951	SE5a	To 31 AP 22.9.18
D6441	Sopwith Camel	72 Sqn Arr 28.8.18
D6443	Sopwith Camel	72 Sqn Arr 27.6.18 Written off 2.9.1919
D6445	Sopwith Camel	72 Sqn Arr 27.6.18
D6447	Sopwith Camel	72 Sqn Arr 27.6.18

Above: Lt A.P. Adams of 30 Sqn in one of the unit's long-serving BE2c machines at Baquba, November 1917. This particular BE was armed with two Lewis guns.

Upper left: Not wanted on the Western Front. Bristol M.1C, C4914, was one of 13 included in the mixture of types that found their place in Mesopotamia. It was assigned to 'C' Flight and is seen here at Tuz Khurmatli on the Diyala Front in November 1918.

Sopwith Camel D6447 'Susan'.

D6449	Sopwith Camel	72 Sqn ' '
D6451	Sopwith Camel	72 Sqn ' '
D6555	Sopwith Camel	72 Sqn ' '
D6557	Sopwith Camel	72 Sqn ' '
D6559	Sopwith Camel	72 Sqn ' '
D6561	Sopwith Camel	72 Sqn ' '
D6563	Sopwith Camel	72 Sqn ' '
D6565	Sopwith Camel	72 Sqn ' '
D6708	RE8	63 Sqn written off 11.2.1920
D6709	RE8	30 Sqn 'C' Flt Bushire South Persia March 1919
D6710	RE8	To 31 Air Park 22.9.18
D6711	RE8	30 Sqn Persia Jan – March 1920
E1214	RE8	30 Sqn and 63 Sqn 1920
H754	Sopwith Camel	To 31 Wing Air Park 28.11.18
H755	Sopwith Camel	To 31 Wing Air Park 28.11.18
H756	Sopwith Camel	To 31 Wing Air Park 28.11.18
H757	Sopwith Camel	To 31 Wing Air Park 28.11.18
H758	Sopwith Camel	To 31 Wing Air Park 28.11.18
H759	Sopwith Camel	31 Wing Aircraft Park Arr 28.11.18

Sopwith Camel D6443 overturned while landing. The pilot's seat cushion lies on the undersurface of the top wing, with the fire extinguisher nearby, just as they fell out of the cockpit.

A souvenir of Mesopotamia. This DH4 flown by the RFC is embellished with the photographs of five officers. The signatures are identified as follows: Major G. Somers-Clarke, OC Aircraft Park; Lt J.A. Gibson, EO3, AP; 2Lt A.E. Young, EO3(Engines); 2Lt W.G. Lamb, EO3 (Engines); Lt M.R. D'Arcy, Observer, 30 Sqn. In the DH4 cockpit is Lt J.R. Burns, 30 Sqn pilot, who also signed the original picture.

BIBLIOGRAPHY

The National Archives (UK)
Air 1/674/21/6/87 – The Campaign in Mesopotamia 1914-18.
Air 1/408/15/237/1 – The History of No. 72 Squadron from its Formation until the Cessation of Hostilities and its Concentration at Baghdad.
Air 1/408/15/238/1 – History of No. 63 Squadron RAF Mesopotamian Expeditionary Force.
Air 1 505 – Personnel and Seaplanes, RNAS Stations in Mesopotamia – Proposed withdrawal of, May 1916.

Air Historical Branch Records
Air 1/408 *The Campaign in Mesopotamia*.
No. 63 Squadron Short History.
No. 72 Squadron Short History.
The Campaign in Mesopotamia, Operations Section, Air Historical Branch, June 1922.
The Royal Air Force in the Great War, Air Historical Branch, HMSO, London.

RAF Museum Records
AC 73/23/53 – Mesopotamia Diary of Operations 1914-1918.
AC1997/127/9 – The Diary of Three Officers in the Hands of the Turks from the Date of their Internment to the Arrival at Place of Internment.
Nixon Photographic Collection.
Windsor Photographic Collection.

Australian Archives
CRS 2023 Item No A38/8/188 – First and Second Half Flights.
CRS 2023 Item No A38/8/202 – Petre Reports.

Australian War Memorial
AWM 44 Item No 8/1/Part 13 – Notes by T. White.
AWM 224, MSS 511.
AWM 224, MSS 513.
PR84/244 – Treloar Letters.
Report Upon the Department of Defence; From the First of July, 1914, until the Thirtieth of June, 1917, Part 1, Government Printers, Melbourne.

RAAF Museum
Wheeler, Cpl W., *Formation of First Half-Flight*, Unpublished manuscript.

Secondary Sources
Barker, A.K., *The Neglected War: Mesopotamia 1914-1918*, Faber and Faber, London, 1967.
Bean, C.E.W., 'The Australians in France During the Main German Offensive, 1918', *The Official History of Australia in the War of 1914-1918*, Angus and Robertson, Sydney, 1938.
Bruce, J.M., *British Aeroplanes 1914-18*, Putnam, London, 1957.
Bruce, J.M., *The Aeroplanes of the Royal Flying Corps (Military Wing)*, Putnam, London, 1982.
Burke, Keast, *With the Horse and Morse in Mesopotamia*, Arthur McQuitty & Co, Sydney, 1927.
Chandler, Edmund, *The Road to Baghdad*, Vols 1 & II Cassell & Company, London, 1919.
Cutlack, F.M., 'Australian Flying Corps', *Official History of Australia in the War of 1914-18*, Vol VIII, Angus & Robertson, Sydney, 1938.
Everidge, Major J., *History of No. 30 Squadron*, Royal Air Force.
Franks, Norman L.R., Bailey, Frank W., and Guest, Russell, *Above the Lines*, Grub St, London, 1993.
Franks, Norman L.R., Bailey, Frank W., and Duiven, Rick, *Casualties of the German Air Service 1914-1920*, Grub Street, London, 1999.
Hamlin, John F., *Flat Out, The Story of No. 30 Squadron Royal Air Force*, Air-Britain, Tunbridge Wells, 2002.
Henshaw, Trevor, *The Sky Their Battlefield*, Grub Street, London, 1995.
History of No. 30 Squadron – Egypt and Mesopotamia – 1914-1919, The Naval & Military Press, Uckfield, undated reprint.
Hobson, Chris, *Airmen Died in the Great War 1914-1918*, J.B. Hayward &Son, London, 1995.
James, Lawrence, *Raj: The Making and Unmaking of British India*, Little, Brown & Co, London, 1997.
Jefford, Wing Commander C.G., *RAF Squadrons*, Airlife, Shrewsbury, 1988.
Jones, H.A., *The War in the Air*, Vols V & VI, Clarendon Press, Oxford, 1935.
Keogh, Colonel E.G., *The River in the Desert*, Wilke & Co, Melbourne, 1955.
List of British Officers Taken Prisoner in the Various Theatres of War between August 1914 and November 1918. Cox & Co., London, 1919.
Martyn, Errol W., *For Your Tomorrow*, Vol 1, Volplane Press, Christchurch, 1998.
Millar, Ronald, *Kut: The Death of an Army*, Secker & Warburg, London, 1969.
Moberly, Brig-Gen F.J., *The Campaign in Mesopotamia*, Vols I - IV, HMSO, London, 1924-25.
Moyes, Philip, *Bomber Squadrons of the RAF*, Macdonald, London, 1964.
Neumann, Major Georg Paul, *The German Air Service in the Great War*, Hodder & Stoughton, London, 1920.
Nikolajsen, Ole, and Yilmazer, Bülent, *Ottoman Aviation 1909-1919*, Self-Published, Andorra.
Robertson, Bruce, *British Military Aircraft Serials 1912-1966*, Ian Allan, London 1967.
Tennant, Lt.Col. John E., *In the Clouds Above Baghdad*, The Battery Press, Nashville, 1992 (reprint).
The Army in India and its Evolution, Government Printer, Calcutta, 1924.
Williams, Richard, *These Are Facts*, AWM, Canberra, 1971.

Magazine Articles
Barton, Len, 'The Mesopotamian Half Flight, Australian Flying Corps', *Wings*, Winter 2000.
Flanagan, Dr Brian P., 'Part 4 – Last Days of the Ottoman Air Force: The Reports of Major Serno', *Cross & Cockade US Journal*, Vol 11, 1970.
Flanagan, Dr Brian P., 'The Indian Flying Corps and the Australian Half-Flight', *Cross & Cockade US Journal*, Vol 17, No 2, 1976.
'Iraq – The First Time Around', *Pathfinder*, Air Power Development Centre, Issue 1, June 2004.
Lax, Mark, 'The Skies over Mesopotamia Part 1 – 4', *The '14-'18 Journal*, 2005; 2007; 2011 & 2013 Vol 2.
Lax, Mark, 'The Mesopotamia Aircraft Park: A Brief History 1915-18', *The '14 –'18 Journal*, 2014 Vol 1.
Rogers, Don and Flanagan, Brian, 'Under the Iron Cross and Turkish Crescent: The Wartime Career of August Quoos', *Cross & Cockade US Journal*, Vol 7, No 2, Summer 1966.
'The Mesopotamian Half Flight, Australian Flying Corps', *The '14-'18 Journal*, 1987.
Thomas, Sir Miles, 'Mesopotamia: The Air War', *The History of the First World War*, Vol 7, No 5, Purnell, London.
Vann, Ray, 'Mesopotamia RFC/R.A.F. Operations 1915-1918', *Cross & Cockade UK Journal*, Vol 2 No 3, 1971.
Wright, Peter, 'Captain Gerald Merton, MC', *Cross & Cockade International Journal*, Vol 15, No 1, 1984.
Wright, Peter, 'Lieutenant A.E. Lionel Skinner, MC', *Cross & Cockade International Journal*, Vol 15, No 2, 1984.

Others
The London Gazette
Principal Events 1914-1918, HMSO, London, 1922.
www.cwgc.org
www.nationalarchives.gov.uk/records/raf-officers-ww1.htm
www.nationalarchives.gov.uk/pathways/firstworldwar/battles/mesopotamia.htm